T0336929

VOLUME ONE HUNDRED AND ONE

ADVANCES IN
COMPUTERS

VOLUME ONE HUNDRED AND ONE

Aᴅᴠᴀɴᴄᴇs ɪɴ
COMPUTERS

Edited by

ATIF MEMON
College Park, MD, USA

AMSTERDAM • BOSTON • HEIDELBERG • LONDON
NEW YORK • OXFORD • PARIS • SAN DIEGO
SAN FRANCISCO • SINGAPORE • SYDNEY • TOKYO
Academic Press is an imprint of Elsevier

Academic Press is an imprint of Elsevier
50 Hampshire Street, 5th Floor, Cambridge, MA 02139, USA
525 B Street, Suite 1800, San Diego, CA 92101-4495, USA
The Boulevard, Langford Lane, Kidlington, Oxford OX5 1GB, UK
125 London Wall, London, EC2Y 5AS, UK

First edition 2016

Notices
Knowledge and best practice in this field are constantly changing. As new research and experience broaden our understanding, changes in research methods, professional practices, or medical treatment may become necessary.

Practitioners and researchers must always rely on their own experience and knowledge in evaluating and using any information, methods, compounds, or experiments described herein. In using such information or methods they should be mindful of their own safety and the safety of others, including parties for whom they have a professional responsibility.

To the fullest extent of the law, neither the Publisher nor the authors, contributors, or editors, assume any liability for any injury and/or damage to persons or property as a matter of products liability, negligence or otherwise, or from any use or operation of any methods, products, instructions, or ideas contained in the material herein.

ISBN: 978-0-12-805158-0
ISSN: 0065-2458

For information on all Academic Press publications
visit our web site at http://store.elsevier.com/

Working together
to grow libraries in
developing countries

www.elsevier.com • www.bookaid.org

CONTENTS

PREFACE

This volume of *Advances in Computers* is the 101st in this series. This series, which has been continuously published since 1960, presents in each volume four to seven chapters describing new developments in software, hardware, or uses of computers.

This 101st volume is the second in a miniseries of volumes based on the theme "Advances in Software Testing." The need for such a thematic miniseries came up when I was teaching my graduate class "Fundamentals of Software Testing," in which students were asked to study and report on recent (years 2010–15) advances in various topics surrounding software testing. They failed to find up-to-date survey papers on almost all topics. In this miniseries, I have invited leaders in their respective fields of software testing to write about recent advances. In the first volume in the miniseries (Volume 99), we focused on combinatorial testing, constraint-based testing, automated fault localization, automatic black-box testing, and testing access control.

Volume 101 focuses on five important topics. In Chapter 1, entitled "Security Testing: A Survey," Felderer *et al.* provide an overview of recent security testing techniques. They first summarize the required background of testing and security engineering. Then, they discuss the basics and recent developments of security testing techniques applied during secure software development, ie, model-based security testing, code-based testing and static analysis, penetration testing and dynamic analysis, as well as security regression testing. They illustrate security testing techniques by adopting them for an example three-tiered web-based business application.

In Chapter 2, entitled "Recent Advances in Model-Based Testing," Utting *et al.* provide an overview of the field of model-based testing (MBT), particularly, the recent advances in the last decade. They give a summary of the MBT process, the modeling languages currently used by various communities who practice MBT, the technologies used to generate tests from models, and best practices, such as traceability between models and tests. They also briefly describe several findings from a recent survey of MBT users in industry, outline the increasingly popular use of MBT for security testing, and discuss future challenges for MBT.

In Chapter 3, "On Testing Embedded Software," Banerjee *et al.* describe the unique challenges associated with testing embedded software, which is specialized software intended to run on embedded devices. As embedded devices have expanded their reach into major aspects of human lives, from small handheld devices (such as smartphones) to advanced automotive systems (such as antilock braking systems), the complexity of embedded software has also grown, creating new challenges for testing. In particular, embedded software are required to satisfy several nonfunctional constraints, in addition to functionality-related constraints. Such nonfunctional constraints may include (but not limited to) timing/energy consumption-related constraints or reliability requirements. Additionally, embedded systems are often required to operate in interaction with the physical environment, obtaining their inputs from environmental factors (such as temperature or air pressure). The need to interact with a dynamic, often nondeterministic physical environment, further increases the challenges associated with testing embedded software. The authors discuss advances in software testing methodologies in the context of embedded software. They introduce key challenges in testing nonfunctional properties of software by means of realistic examples. They also present an easy-to-follow, classification of existing research work on this topic.

The importance of test automation in web engineering comes from the widespread use of web applications and the associated demand for code quality. Test automation is considered crucial for delivering the quality levels expected by users, since it can save a lot of time in testing and it helps developers to release web applications with fewer defects. The main advantage of test automation comes from fast, unattended execution of a set of tests after some changes have been made to a web application. Moreover, modern web applications adopt a multitier architecture where the implementation is scattered across different layers and run on different machines. For this reason, end-to-end testing techniques are required to test the overall behavior of web applications. In the last years, several approaches have been proposed for automated end-to-end web testing and the choice among them depends on a number of factors, including the tools used for web testing and the costs associated with their adoption. In Chapter 4, "Advances in Web Application Testing, 2010–14," Sampath and Sprenkle provide background on web applications and the challenges in testing these distributed, dynamic applications made up of heterogeneous components. They then focus on the recent advances in web application testing that were published between 2010 and 2014, including work on test-case generation, oracles, testing evaluation, and regression testing. Through this targeted survey, they identify trends in web application testing and open problems that still need to be addressed. In Chapter 5, entitled "Approaches and Tools for Automated End-to-End Web Testing," Leotta *et al.* provide a comprehensive overview of automated end-to-end web testing approaches and summarize the findings of a long-term research project aimed at empirically investigating their strengths and weaknesses.

I hope that you find these articles of interest. If you have any suggestions of topics for future chapters, or if you wish to be considered as an author for a chapter, I can be reached at atif@cs.umd.edu.

PROF. ATIF M. MEMON, PH.D.,
College Park, MD, USA

CHAPTER ONE

Security Testing: A Survey

**Michael Felderer*, Matthias Büchler[†], Martin Johns[‡],
Achim D. Brucker[‡], Ruth Breu*, Alexander Pretschner[†]**
*University of Innsbruck, Innsbruck, Austria
[†]Technische Universität München, Munich, Germany
[‡]SAP, Karlsruhe, Germany

Contents

Abstract

Identifying vulnerabilities and ensuring security functionality by security testing is a widely applied measure to evaluate and improve the security of software. Due to the openness of modern software-based systems, applying appropriate security testing techniques is of growing importance and essential to perform effective and efficient security testing. Therefore, an overview of actual security testing techniques is of high value both for researchers to evaluate and refine the techniques and for practitioners to apply and disseminate them. This chapter fulfills this need and provides an overview of recent security testing techniques. For this purpose, it first summarize the required

Advances in Computers, Volume 101
ISSN 0065-2458
http://dx.doi.org/10.1016/bs.adcom.2015.11.003

background of testing and security engineering. Then, basics and recent developments of security testing techniques applied during the secure software development life cycle, ie, model-based security testing, code-based testing and static analysis, penetration testing and dynamic analysis, as well as security regression testing are discussed. Finally, the security testing techniques are illustrated by adopting them for an example three-tiered web-based business application.

1. INTRODUCTION

Modern IT systems based on concepts like cloud computing, location-based services, or social networking are permanently connected to other systems and handle sensitive data. These interconnected systems are subject to security attacks that may result in security incidents with high severity affecting the technical infrastructure or its environment. Exploited security vulnerabilities can cause drastic costs, eg, due to downtimes or the modification of data. A high proportion of all software security incidents is caused by attackers who exploit known vulnerabilities [1]. An important, effective, and widely applied measure to improve the security of software are security testing techniques which identify vulnerabilities and ensure security functionality.

Software testing is concerned with evaluation of software products and related artifacts to determine that they satisfy specified requirements, to demonstrate that they are fit for purpose and to detect defects. Security testing verifies and validates software system requirements related to security properties like confidentiality, integrity, availability, authentication, authorization, and nonrepudiation. Sometimes security properties come as classical functional requirements, eg, "user accounts are disabled after three unsuccessful login attempts" which approximates one part of an authorization property and is aligned with the software quality standard ISO/IEC 9126 [2] defining security as functional quality characteristic. However, it seems desirable that security testing directly targets the above security properties, as opposed to taking the detour of functional tests of security mechanisms. This view is supported by the ISO/IEC 25010 [3] standard that revises ISO/IEC 9126 and introduces Security as a new quality characteristic which is not included in the characteristic functionality any more.

Web application security vulnerabilities such as Cross–Site Scripting or SQL Injection, which can adequately be addressed by security testing techniques, are acknowledged problems [4] with thousands of vulnerabilities reported each year [5]. Furthermore, surveys as published by the National Institute of Standards and Technology [6] show high cost of insecure software due to inadequate testing even on an economic level. Therefore, support for security testing, which is still often considered as a "black art," is essential to increase its effectiveness and efficiency in practice. This chapter intends to contribute to the growing need for information on security testing techniques by providing an overview of actual security testing techniques. This is of high value both for researchers to evaluate and refine existing techniques and practitioners to apply and disseminate them. In this chapter, security testing techniques are classified (and also the discussion thereof) according to their test basis within the secure software development life cycle into four different types: (1) *model-based security testing* is grounded on requirements and design models created during the analysis and design phase, (2) *code-based testing and static analysis* on source and byte code created during development, (3) *penetration testing and dynamic analysis* on running systems, either in a test or production environment, as well as (4) *security regression testing* performed during maintenance.

This chapter provides a comprehensive survey on security testing and is structured as follows. Section 2 provides an overview of the underlying concepts on software testing. Section 3 discusses the basic concepts of security engineering and the secure software development life cycle. Section 4 provides an overview of security testing and its integration in the secure software development life cycle. Section 5 discusses the security testing techniques model-based security testing, code-based testing and static analysis, penetration testing, and dynamic analysis as well as security regression testing in detail. Section 6 discusses the application of security testing techniques to three tiered business applications. Finally, Section 7 summarizes this chapter.

2. SOFTWARE TESTING

According to the classic definition in software engineering [7], *software testing* consists of the *dynamic* verification that a program provides expected behaviors on a *finite* set of test cases, a so called *test suite*, suitably *selected* from the usually infinite execution domain. This dynamic notion of testing, so called *dynamic testing*, evaluates software by observing its execution [8]. The executed system is called *system under test* (SUT). More general notions of testing [9] consist of all life cycle activities, both static and dynamic, concerned with evaluation of software products and related artifacts to determine that they satisfy specified requirements, to demonstrate that they are fit for purpose and to detect defects. This definition also takes *static testing* into account, which checks software development artifact (eg, requirements, design, or code) without execution of these artifacts. The most prominent static testing approaches are (manual) reviews and (automated) static analysis, which are often combined with dynamic testing, especially in the context of security. For security testing, the general notion of testing comprising static and dynamic testing is therefore frequently applied [10–12], and thus also in this chapter testing comprises static and dynamic testing.

After running a test case, the observed and intended behaviors of a SUT are compared with each other, which then results in a *verdict*. Verdicts can be either of *pass* (behaviors conform), *fail* (behaviors do not conform), and *inconclusive* (not known whether behaviors conform) [13]. A *test oracle* is a mechanism for determining the verdict. The observed behavior may be checked against user or customer needs (commonly referred to as testing for *validation*), against a specification (testing for *verification*), A *failure* is an undesired behavior. Failures are typically observed (by resulting in verdict fail) during the execution of the system being tested. A *fault* is the cause of the failure. It is a static defect in the software, usually caused by human error in the specification, design, or coding process. During testing, it is the execution of faults in the software that causes failures. Differing from active execution of test cases, passive testing only monitors running systems without interaction.

Testing can be classified utilizing the three dimensions objective, scope, and accessibility [14, 15] shown in Fig. 1.

Test objectives are reason or purpose for designing and executing a test. The reason is either to check the functional behavior of the system or its nonfunctional properties. *Functional testing* is concerned with assessing the functional behavior of an SUT, whereas *nonfunctional testing* aims at assessing nonfunctional requirements with regard to quality characteristics like security, safety, reliability or performance.

The *test scope* describes the granularity of the SUT and can be classified into component, integration, and system testing. It also determines the *test basis*, ie, the artifacts to derive test cases. *Component testing* (also referred to as *unit testing*) checks the smallest testable component (eg, a class in an object-oriented implementation or a single electronic control unit) in isolation. *Integration testing* combines components with each other and tests those as a subsystem, that is, not yet a complete system. *System testing* checks the complete system, including all subsystems. A specific type of system testing is *acceptance testing* where it is checked whether a solution works for the user of a system. *Regression testing* is a selective retesting to verify that

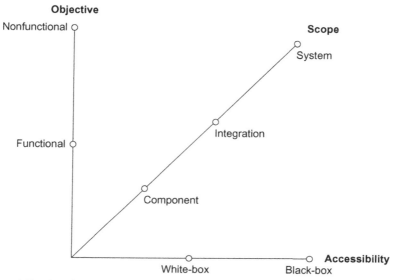

Figure 1 Testing dimensions objective, scope, and accessibility.

modifications have not caused side effects and that the SUT still complies with the specified requirements [16].

In terms of *accessibility* of test design artifacts, we can classifying testing methods into white- and black-box testing. In *white-box testing*, test cases are derived based on information about how the software has been designed or coded [7]. In *black-box testing*, test cases rely only on the input/output behavior of the software. This classification is especially relevant for security testing, as black-box testing, where no or only basic information about the system under test is provided, enables to mimic external attacks from hackers. In classical software testing, a related classification of test design techniques [17] distinguishes between *structure-based testing techniques* (ie, deriving test cases from internal descriptions like implementation code), *specification-based testing techniques* (ie, deriving test cases from external descriptions of software like specifications), and *experience-based testing techniques* (ie, deriving test cases based on knowledge, skills, and background of testers).

The process of testing comprises the core activities test planning, design, implementation, execution, and evaluation [9]. According to Refs. [18] and [9], *test planning* is the activity of establishing or updating a test plan. A test plan includes the test objectives, test scope, and test methods as well as the resources, and schedule of intended test activities. It identifies, amongst others, features to be tested and exit criteria defining conditions for when to stop testing. Coverage criteria aligned with the tested feature types and the applied test design techniques are typical exit criteria. Once the test plan has been established, test control begins. It is an ongoing activity in which the actual progress is compared against the plan which often results in concrete measures. During the *test design* phase the general testing objectives defined in the test plan are transformed into tangible test conditions and abstract test cases. For test derivation, specific test design techniques can be applied, which can according to ISO/IEC/IEEE 29119 [17] be classified into specification-based, structure-based, and experience-based techniques. *Test implementation* comprises tasks to make the abstract test cases executable. This includes tasks like preparing test harnesses and test data, providing logging support or writing test scripts which are necessary to enable the automated execution of test cases. In the *test execution* phase, the test cases are then executed and all relevant details of the execution are logged and monitored. In manual test execution, testing is guided by a human, and in automated testing by a specialized application. Finally, in the *test evaluation* phase the exit criteria are evaluated and the logged test results are summarized in a test report.

In *model-based testing* (MBT), manually selected algorithms automatically and systematically generate test cases from a set of models of the system under test or its environment [19]. Whereas test automation replaces manual test execution with automated test scripts, MBT replaces manual test designs with automated test designs and test generation.

3. SECURITY ENGINEERING

In this section, we cover basic concepts of security engineering as well as an overview of the secure software development life cycle.

3.1 Basic Concepts

Security testing validates software system requirements related to security properties of assets that include confidentiality, integrity, availability, authentication, authorization, and nonrepudiation. These security properties can be defined as follows [20]:

- *Confidentiality* is the assurance that information is not disclosed to unauthorized individuals, processes, or devices.
- *Integrity* is provided when data is unchanged from its source and has not been accidentally or maliciously modified, altered, or destroyed.

- *Availability* guarantees timely, reliable access to data and information services for authorized users.
- *Authentication* is a security measure designed to establish the validity of a transmission, message, or originator, or a means of verifying an individual's authorization to receive specific categories of information.
- *Authorization* provides access privileges granted to a user, program, or process.
- *Nonrepudiation* is the assurance that none of the partners taking part in a transaction can later deny of having participated.

Security requirements can be formulated as *positive requirements*, explicitly defining the expected security functionality of a security mechanism, or as *negative requirements*, specifying what the application should not do [10]. For instance, for the security property authorization as positive requirements could be "User accounts are disabled after three unsuccessful login attempts," whereas a negative requirement could be formulated as "The application should not be compromised or misused for unauthorized financial transactions by a malicious user." The positive, functional view on security requirements is aligned with the software quality standard ISO/IEC 9126 [2] defining security as functional quality characteristic. The negative, nonfunctional view is supported by the ISO/IEC 25010 [3] standard that revises ISO/IEC 9126 and introduces Security as a new quality characteristic which is not included in the characteristic Functionality any more.

An *asset* is a data item, or a system component that has to be protected. In the security context, such an asset has one or multiple security properties assigned that have to hold for that asset.

A *fault* is a textual representation of what goes wrong in a behavioral description. It is the incorrect part of a behavioral description that needs to be replaced to get a correct description. Since faults can occur in dead code—code that is never executed—and because faults can be masked by further faults, a fault does not necessarily lead to an error. At the other side, an error is always produced by a fault. A fault is not necessarily related to security properties but is the cause of errors and failures in general.

A *vulnerability* is a special type of fault. If the fault is related to security properties, it is called a vulnerability. A vulnerability is always related to one or more assets and their corresponding security properties. An exploitation of a vulnerability attacks an asset by violating the associated security property. Since vulnerabilities are always associated with the protection of an asset, the security relevant fault is usually correlated with a mechanism that protects the asset. A vulnerability either means that (1) the responsible security mechanism is completely missing, or (2) the security mechanism is in place but is implemented in a faulty way.

An *exploit* is a concrete malicious input that makes use of the vulnerability in the system under test (SUT) and violates the property of an asset. Vulnerabilities can often be exploited in different ways. One concrete exploit selects a specific asset and a specific property, and makes use of the vulnerability to violate the property for the selected asset.

A *threat* is the potential cause of an unwanted incident that harms or reduces the value of an asset. For instance, a threat may be a hacker, power outages, or malicious insiders. An *attack* is defined by the steps a malicious or inadvertently incorrectly behaving entity performs to the end of turning a threat into an actual corruption of an asset's properties. This is usually done by exploiting a vulnerability.

Security aspects can be considered on the network, operating system, and application level. Each level has its own security threats and corresponding security requirements to deal with them. Typical threats on the network level are distributed denial-of-service or network intrusion. On the operating system level, all types of malware cause threats. Finally, on the application level threats typical threats are related to access control or are application type specific like Cross-Site Scripting in case of web applications. All levels of security can be subject to tests.

Security testing simulates attacks and employs other kinds of *penetration testing* attempting to compromise the security of a system by playing the role of a hacker trying to attack the system and exploit its vulnerabilities [21]. Security testing requires specific expertise which makes it difficult and hard to automate [22]. By identifying risks in the system and creating tests driven by those risks, security vulnerability testing can focus on parts of a system implementation in which an attack is likely to succeed.

Risks are often used as a guiding factor to define security test processes. For instance, Potter and McGraw [22] consider the process steps creating security misuse cases, listing normative security requirements, performing architectural risk analysis, building risk-based security test plans, wielding static analysis tools, performing security tests, performing penetration testing in the final environment, and cleaning up after security breaches. Also the Open Source Security Testing Methodology Manual (OSSTMM) [23] and the OWASP Testing Guide [10] take risks into account for their proposed security testing activities.

3.2 Secure Software Development Life Cycle

Testing is often started very late in the software development life cycle shortly before it is deployed. It has turned out that this is a very ineffective and inefficient practice. One of the best methods to prevent security bugs from appearing in production applications is to improve the software development life cycle by including security in each of its phases, thereby extending it to a secure software development life cycle. A *software development life cycle* is a series of steps, or phases, that provide a model for the development and life cycle management of an application or piece of software. It is a structure imposed on the development of software artifacts. A generic software development life cycle model considering testing as an orthogonal dimension comprises the phases analysis, design, development, deployment, and maintenance [10]. Each phase delivers specific artifacts, ie, the analysis phase results in requirements, design provides design models, development delivers code, deployment results in a running system, and finally all artifacts are maintained.

A secure software development life cycle takes security aspects into account in each phase of software development. A crucial concept within the secure software development life cycle is risk. A *risk* is the likelihood of an unwanted incident and its consequence for a specific asset [24]. Taking into account the negative nature of many security requirements, the concept of risk can be employed to direct the selection or application of security counter-measures like testing [22, 24]. In all phases of the secure software development process, but especially at the design level [25], risk analyses provide effective means to guide security testing and thus detect faults and vulnerabilities.

Major security development processes are the Security Development Life cycle (SDL) [26] from Microsoft and the Open Software Assurance Maturity Model (OpenSAMM) [27] from OWASP.

Microsofts SDL is an established security life cycle for software development projects pursuing the following major principles [26]:

- Secure by Design: Security is a built-in quality attribute affecting the whole software life cycle.
- Security by Default: Software systems are constructed in a way that potential harm caused by attackers is minimized, eg, software is deployed with least necessary privilege.
- Secure in Deployment: software deployment is accompanied by tools and guidance supporting users and/or administrators.

- Communications: software developers are prepared for occurring threats communicating openly and timely with users and/or administrators.

The SDL is composed of security practices attached with the major activities of a software life cycle, ie, requirements, design, implementation, verification, and deployment in case of SDL, which are extended by the two activities training and response. For instance, the security practice "establish security requirements" is attached to requirements analysis, "use threat modeling" to design, "perform static analysis" to implementation, "perform fuzz testing" to verification, and "certify release and archive" to release.

Similar to the SDL, OpenSAMM attaches security practices to core activities, ie, governance, construction, verification, and deployment in case of OpenSAMM, within the software development life cycle. For instance, verification includes the security practices design review, code review, as well as (dynamic) security testing.

In particular, OpenSAMM attaches each security practice with three maturity levels and a starting point of zero:

- Level 0: Implicit starting point representing the activities in the practice being unfulfilled
- Level 1: Initial understanding and ad-hoc provision of security practice
- Level 2: Increase efficiency and/or effectiveness of the security practice
- Level 3: Comprehensive mastery of the security practice at scale

For each security practice and maturity level, OpenSAMM does not only define the objectives and activities, but also gives support to achieve this particular level. This comprises assessment questions, success metrics, costs, and personnel needed to achieve the targeted maturity level.

4. SECURITY TESTING

In this section, we cover basic concepts of security testing and the integration of security testing in the secure software development life cycle.

4.1 Basic Concepts

Security testing is testing of security requirements related to security properties like confidentiality, integrity, availability, authentication, authorization, and nonrepudiation.

Security testing identifies whether the specified or intended security properties are, for a given set of assets of interests, correctly implemented. This can be done by trying to show conformance with the security properties, similar to requirements-based testing; or by trying to address known vulnerabilities, which is similar to traditional fault-based, or destructive, testing. Intuitively, conformance testing considers well defined, expected inputs. It tests if the system satisfies the security properties with respect to these well-defined expected inputs. In contrast, addressing known vulnerabilities means using malicious, nonexpected input data that is likely to exploit the considered vulnerabilities.

As mentioned in the previous section, security requirements can be positive and functional, explicitly defining the expected security functionality of a security mechanism, or negative and nonfunctional, specifying what the application should not do. This classification of security requirements also impacts security testing. For *positive security requirements, classical testing techniques* can be applied, whereas for *negative security requirements* (a combination of) *additional measures* like risk analyses, penetration testing, or vulnerability knowledge bases are essential. This classification is also reflected in by classification in the literature as provided by Tian-yang et al. [11] as well as by Potter and McGraw [28].

According to Tian-yang et al. [11] two principal approaches can be distinguished, ie, *security functional testing* and *security vulnerability testing*. Security functional testing validates whether the specified security requirements are implemented correctly, both in terms of security properties and security mechanisms. Security vulnerability testing addresses the identification of unintended system vulnerabilities. Security vulnerability testing uses the simulation of attacks and other kinds of *penetration testing* attempting to compromise the security of a system by playing the role of a hacker trying to attack the system and exploit its vulnerabilities [21]. Security vulnerability testing requires specific expertise which makes it difficult and hard to automate [28]. By identifying risks in the system and creating tests driven by those risks, security vulnerability testing can focus on parts of a system implementation in which an attack is likely to succeed.

Potter and McGraw [28] distinguish between *testing security mechanisms* to ensure that their functionality is properly implemented, and *performing risk-based security testing* motivated by understanding and simulating the attacker's approach. Testing security mechanisms can be performed by standard test organizations with classical functional test techniques, whereas risk-based security testing requires specific expertise and sophisticated analysis [28].

For security vulnerability testing approaches, Shahriar and Zulkernine [29] propose seven comparison criteria, ie, *vulnerability coverage, source of test cases, test case generation method, testing level, test case granularity, tool automation* as well as *target applications*. Tool automation is further refined into the criteria *test case generation, oracle generation,* and *test case execution*. The authors classify 20 informally collected approaches according to these criteria. The main aim of the criteria is support for security practitioners to select an appropriate approach for their needs. Therefore Shahriar and Zulkernine blend abstract criteria like source of test cases or test case generation method with technological criteria like tool automation or target applications.

Differing from classical software testing, where black- and white-box test design are nowadays considered very similar, ie, in both cases testing proceeds from abstract models [8], the distinction is essential for security testing. White-box testing performs testing based on information about how the software has been designed or coded, and thus enables testing from an internal software producer point of view [7]. Black-box testing relies only on the input/output behavior of the software, and thus enables to mimic external attacks from hackers. The classification into white- and black-box testing is also pointed out by Bachmann and Brucker [12], who additionally classify security testing techniques due to execution (dynamic vs static testing) and automation (manual vs automated testing).

In addition, due to the critical role of negative security requirements, classical testing which focuses on testing functional requirements and security testing differ. It seems desirable that security testing directly targets security properties, as opposed to taking the detour of functional tests of security mechanisms. As the former kind of (nonfunctional) security properties describe all executions of a system, testing them is intrinsically hard. Because testing cannot show the absence of faults, an immediately useful perspective directly considers the *violation* of these properties. This has resulted in the development of specific testing techniques like penetration testing that simulates attacks to exploit vulnerabilities. Penetration tests are difficult to craft because tests often do not directly cause observable security exploits, and because the testers must think like an attacker [28], which requires specific expertise. During penetration testing, testers build a mental model of security properties, security mechanisms, and possible attacks against the system and its environment. Specifying security test models in an explicit and processable way, results in a *model-based security testing approach*. In such an approach, security test models provide guidance for the systematic specification and documentation of security test objectives and security test cases, as well as for their automated generation and evaluation.

(Functional) testing normally focuses on the *presence of some correct behavior but not the absence of additional behavior*, which is implicitly specified by

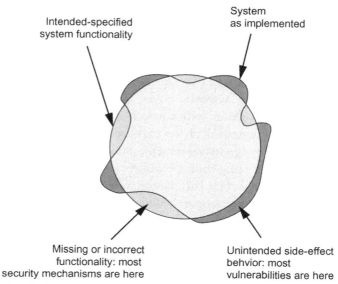

Figure 2 Most faults in security mechanisms are related to missing or incorrect functionality, most vulnerabilities are related to unintended side-effect behavior *(adapted from Thompson [30])*.

negative requirements. Testing routinely misses hidden action and the result is dangerous side effect behaviors that ship with a software. Fig. 2 illustrates this side effect nature of most software vulnerabilities that security testing has to cope with [30].

The circle represents an application's intended functionality including security mechanisms, which is usually defined by the requirements specification. The amorphous shape superimposed on the circle represents the application's actual, implemented functionality. In an ideal system, the coded application would completely overlap with its specification, but in practice, this is hardly ever the case. The areas of the circle that the coded application does not cover represents typical functional faults (ie, behavior that was implemented incorrectly and does not conform to the specification), especially also in security mechanisms. Areas that fall outside of the circular region represent unindented and potentially dangerous functionality, where most security vulnerabilities lay. The mismatch between specification and implementation shown in Fig. 2 leading to faults in security mechanisms and vulnerabilities can be reduced by taking security and especially security testing aspects into account early and in all phases of the software development life cycle as discussed in Section 4.2.

4.2 Security Testing in the Secure Software Development Life cycle

As mentioned before, testing within the security life cycle plays the role to validate and verify security requirements. Due to the negative nature of many security requirements and the resulting broad range of subordinate requirements, also testing activities cover a broad range of scopes and employed methods. In keeping with research and experience, it is essential to take testing into account in all phases of the secure software development life cycle, ie, analysis, design, development, deployment, as well as maintenance. Thus, security testing must be holistic covering the whole secure software development life cycle [12]. In concrete terms, Fig. 3 shows a recommended distribution of static and dynamic testing efforts among the phases of the secure software development life cycle according to Ref. [10]. It shows that security testing should be balanced over all phases, with a focus on the early phases, ie, analysis, design, and implementation.

To provide support for the integration of security testing into all phases of the secure software development process, major security development processes (see Section 3.2), consider the integration of testing. In the Security Development Life cycle (SDL) [26] from Microsoft practices with strong interference with testing efforts are the following:

- SDL Practice #2 (Requirements): Establish Security and Privacy Requirements

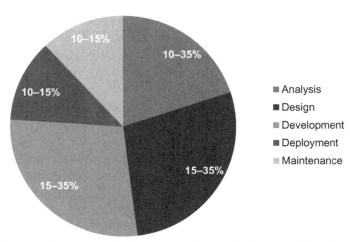

Figure 3 Proportion of test effort in secure software development life cycle according to Ref. [10].

- SDL Practice #4 (Requirements): Perform Security and Privacy Risk Assessments
- SDL Practice #5 (Design): Establish Design Requirements
- SDL Practice #7 (Design): Use Threat Modeling
- SDL Practice #10 (Implementation): Perform Static Analysis
- SDL Practice #11 (Verification): Perform Dynamic Analysis
- SDL Practice #12 (Verification): Perform Fuzz Testing
- SDL Practice #13: Conduct Attack Surface Review
- SDL Practice #15: Conduct Final Security Review

In OpenSAMM [27] from OWASP, the verification activity includes the security practices design review, code review, as well as (dynamic) security testing.

The OWASP Testing Guide [10] and the OWASP Code Review Guide [31] provide a detailed overview of the variety of testing activities of web application security. While the Testing Guide has a focus on black-box testing, the Code Review Guide is a white-box approach focusing on manual code review. Overall, the Testing Guide distinguishes 91 different testing activities split into 11 subcategories (ie, information gathering, configuration and deployment management testing, identity management testing, authentication testing, authorization testing, session management testing, data validation testing, error handling, cryptography, business logic testing, as well as client side testing). Applying security testing techniques to web applications is covered in Section 6.

The OWASP testing framework workflow, which is also contained in the OWASP Testing Guide, contains checks and reviews of respective artifacts in all secure software development phases, creation of UML and threat models in the analysis and design phases, unit and system testing during development and deployment, penetration testing during deployment, as well as regression testing during maintenance. Proper security testing requires a mix of techniques as there is no single testing technique that can be performed to effectively cover all security testing and their application within testing activities at unit, integration, and system level. Nevertheless, many companies adopt only one security testing approach, for instance penetration testing [10].

Fig. 4 abstracts from concrete security testing techniques mentioned before, and classifies them according to their test basis within the secure software development life cycle.

Model-based security testing is grounded on requirements and design models created during the analysis and design phase. *Code-based testing and*

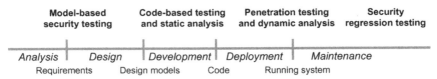

Figure 4 Security testing techniques in the secure software development life cycle.

static analysis is based on source and byte code created during development. *Penetration testing and dynamic analysis* is based on running systems, either in a test or production environment. Finally, *security regression testing* is performed during maintenance. We also apply this classification to structure the discussion of security testing techniques in the following section.

5. SECURITY TESTING TECHNIQUES

This section discusses the security testing techniques model-based testing, code-based testing and static analysis, penetration testing and dynamic analysis as well as regression testing in detail. For each testing technique, basic concepts as well as current approaches are covered.

5.1 Model-Based Security Testing

In model-based testing (MBT) manually selected algorithms automatically and systematically generate test cases from a set of models of the system under test or its environment [19]. MBT is an active area of research [32, 33] and offers big potential to improve test processes in industry [14, 19, 34]. Its prospective benefits include early and explicit specification and review of system behavior, better test case documentation, the ability to automatically generate useful (regression) tests and control test coverage, improved maintenance of test cases as well as shorter schedules and lower costs [19].

Process. The process of MBT consists of three main steps integrated into the overall process of test design, execution, and evaluation. (1) A model of the SUT and/or its environment is built from informal requirements, existing specification documents, or a SUT. The resulting model of the SUT dedicated to test generation is often called *test model*. (2) If they are executable, one execution trace of such a model acts as a test case: input and expected output for an SUT. Because there are usually infinitely many and infinitely long execution traces, models can therefore be used to generate an infinite number of tests. To cut down their number and length, *test selection criteria* are applied. These guide the generation of tests. (3) Once the test model and the test selection criteria are defined, a set of test cases is generated from the test model as determined by the chosen test selection criteria. Test generation is typically performed automatically. The generated test cases are traces of the model and thus in general at a higher level than the events or actions of an SUT. Therefore, the generated test cases are further refined to a more concrete level or adapted to the SUT to support their automated execution.

Model-based security testing. Model-based security testing (MBST) is an MBT approach that validates software system requirements related to security properties. It combines security properties like confidentiality, integrity, availability, authentication, authorization, and nonrepudiation with a model of the SUT and identifies whether the specified or intended security features hold in the model.

Both MBT and MBST have in common, that the input artifact is a model and not the SUT. Therefore the abstraction gap between the model and the SUT has to be addressed. In particular, an identified (security) issue at the model level does not automatically confirm an (security) issue at the SUT. Therefore an additional step is needed to map an abstract test case to an executable test case that can be executed on the SUT.

Selection criteria: "Good" test cases. Arguably, "good" test cases detect potential, rather than actual, defects with good cost effectiveness [35]. Potential defects need to be described by defect hypotheses. In order to turn these hypotheses into operational adequacy criteria [36], they need to be captured by some form of explicit defect model [35, 37, 38]. One form of defect is a fault, understood as the root cause of an incorrect system state (error) or incorrect system output (failure). As we show below, vulnerabilities can be understood as faults.

In addition to explicit models of (the functionality of) the system under test, model-based security testing usually makes use of one or more of the three following models for test selection: properties, vulnerabilities, and attackers. *Models of an attacker* encode an attacker's behavior: the data they need, the different steps they take, the way they craft exploits. Attacker models can be seen as models of the environment of a system under test, and knowledge about a targeted vulnerability usually is left implicit. In contrast, *models of vulnerabilities* explicitly encode weaknesses in a system or a model of the system. In this sense, they can be seen as faults that are used for the generation of "good" test case generation (see above). Finally, *properties* describe desired characteristics of a model, or an implementation, and they include confidentiality, availability, integrity, and so on. Models of properties are needed to describe the properties of an asset that are supposed not to be violated: they describe what exactly the security tester targets, and what an exploit is supposed to exploit.

It is noteworthy that all forms of security testing, model-based or not, always work with an implicit or explicit hypothesis about a potential vulnerability.

Vulnerabilities as Faults. Frequently, as a reaction to known relevant threats, assets are protected by explicit security mechanisms. Mechanisms include input sanitization, Address Space Layout Randomization (ASLR), encryption of password files, but also intrusion detection systems and access control components. Mechanisms are components of a system and can always be syntactically recognized: there is a piece of code (the mechanism) that is supposed to protect the asset; or there is no such piece of code. A vulnerability is a special kind of fault with security implications. It is defined as the absence of a correctly functioning mechanism. This can mean both (1) that there is no mechanism at all (eg, no input sanitization takes place which can lead to buffer overflows or SQL Injections) and (2) that the mechanism does not work correctly, ie, is partially or incorrectly implemented, for instance, if an access control policy is faulty.

Security testing can then be understood in three seemingly different ways: (1) to test if specific security properties of an *asset* can be violated (properties and property models); (2) to test the functionality of a *mechanism* (attacker models); and (3) to directly try to exploit a *vulnerability* (vulnerability models). The boundaries are blurred, however: With the above definition of vulnerabilities as the absence of effectively working defense mechanisms, and the observation that attacker models always involve implicit or explicit hypotheses on vulnerabilities, activities (2) and (3) are close to identical. In practice, they only differ in terms of the perspective that the tester takes: the mechanism or the vulnerability. Because the above definition also binds vulnerabilities to—possibly unspecified—assets, the goal of activities (2) and (3) always is activity (1). It hence seems hard to provide a crisp conceptual distinction between the three activities of (1) testing security properties, (2) testing security mechanisms, and (3) testing for vulnerabilities.

Classification of model-based (security) testing. Several publications have been published that propose taxonomies and classifications of existing MBT [32, 33] and MBST approaches [39, 40]. We will focus on the classification proposed by Schieferdecker *et al.* [40] considering different perspectives used in securing a system. The authors claim that MBST needs to be based on different types of models and distinguish three types of input models for security test generation, ie, *architectural and functional models, threat, fault and risk models,* as well as *weakness and vulnerability models.* Architectural and functional models of the SUT are concerned with security requirements and their implementation. They focus on the expected system behavior. Threat, fault and risk models focus on what can go wrong, and concentrate on causes and consequences of system failures, weaknesses or vulnerabilities. Weakness and vulnerability models describe weaknesses or vulnerabilities by themselves.

In the following, we exemplary describe selected approaches, that make use of different models according to the classification of Schieferdecker *et al.*

5.1.1 A Model-Based Security Testing Approach for Web Applications

An approach that makes use of functional, fault, and vulnerability models according to Schieferdecker *et al.* is presented by Büchler *et al.* [41]. They published a semiautomatic security testing approach for web applications from a secure model. The authors assume there is a formal model $\mathcal{M}$ for the specification of the System under Test (SUT). This model is secure as it does not violate any of the specified security goals (eg, confidentiality and authenticity). Thus, a model-checker will report $\mathcal{M} \models \varphi$ for all security properties φ defining the security goals of the model. The model is built using abstract messages that are defined by the modeler. These messages represent common actions a user of the web application can perform. The idea is that these abstract messages are sent to the server to tell it which actions the client wants to perform, eg, log in to the web application, view profiles of different users, delete profiles, update profiles, and so on. Thus, the modeler does not care about details at the browser/protocol level but only about abstract messages that represent web application actions.

To make use of such a secure model, Büchler *et al.* [41] define semantic mutation operators that represent common, well-known vulnerabilities at source code level. Semantic mutation operators are an abstraction that these vulnerabilities so that they can be injected into the model. After having applied a mutation operator to an original model, the model checker may provide a trace from this mutated model that violates a security property. This trace is called an *attack trace* because it shows which sequence of abstract messages have to be exchanged in order to lead the system to a state where the security property is violated. Since abstract attack traces are at the same level of abstraction as the input model, they need to be instantiated to turn them operational. The approach proposes a multistep instantiation since web applications are usually accessed via a browser. In the first step, abstract messages are translated into abstract browser actions. The second step is a mapping from these browser actions to executable API calls to make them operational in a browser. Finally, a test execution engine executes the operationalized test cases on the SUT to verify, if the implementation of the model suffers from the same vulnerability as reported by the model checker at the abstract level.

5.1.2 A Model-Based Framework for Security Policy Specification, Deployment, and Testing

Mouelhi *et al.* [42] propose an approach based on architectural, functional, and fault models and focus on security policies. They propose a model-based approach for the specification, deployment, and testing of security policies in Java applications. The approach starts with a generic security meta-model of the application. It captures the high level·access control policy implemented by the application and is expressed in a dedicated domain-specific language. Before such a model is further used, the model is verified to check the soundness and adequacy of the model with respect to the requirements. Afterwards the model is automatically transformed to policy decision points (PDP). Since such PDPs are usually not generated from scratch but are based on existing frameworks, the output of the transformation is, for instance, an XACML (Extended Access Control Markup Language) file that captures the security policy. This transformation step is essential in MBT since an identified security issue at model level does not automatically imply the same issue at implementation level, nor does a model without security issues automatically imply the same on the implementation. Mouelhi *et al.* make use of mutations at the model level to ensure that the implementation conforms to the initial security model. An existing test suite is executed on an implementation generated from a mutated security model. If such mutants are not detected by the existing test suite, it will be adapted to cover the mutated part of the security model as well. Finally the test objective is to check that the implementation (security policy) is synchronized with the security model.

5.1.3 Risk-Based Security Testing

In the following, we consider approaches that are based on risk models. Risk-based testing in general is a type of software testing that explicitly considers risks of the software system as the guiding factor to solve decision problems in all phases of the test process, ie, test planning, design, implementation, execution, and evaluation [1, 43, 44]. It is based on the intuitive idea to focus testing activities on those areas that trigger the most critical situations for a software system [45]. The precise understanding of risks as well as their focused treatment by risk-based testing has become one of the cornerstones for critical decisions within complex software development projects and recently gained much attention [44]. Lately, the international standard ISO/IEC/IEEE 29119 Software Testing [17] on testing techniques, processes, and documentation even explicitly considers risks as an integral part of the test planning process. In the following, we describe three risk-based approaches to security testing in more detail.

Grossmann *et al.* [46] present an approach called Risk-Based Security Testing that combines risk analysis and risk-based test design activities based on formalized security test patterns. The involved security test patterns are formalized by using a minimal test design strategies language framework which is represented as a UML profile. Such a (semi-)formal security test pattern is then used as the input for a test generator accompanied by the test design model out of which the test cases are generated. The approach is based on the CORAS method [24] for risk analysis activities. Finally, a tool prototype is presented which shows how to combine the CORAS-based risk analysis with pattern-based test generation.

Botella *et al.* [47] describe an approach to security testing called Risk-Based Vulnerability Testing, which is guided by risk assessment and coverage to perform and automate vulnerability testing for web applications. Risk-Based Vulnerability testing adapts model-based testing techniques using a pattern-based approach for the generation of test cases according to previously identified risks. For risk identification and analysis, the CORAS method [24] is utilized. The integration of information from risk analysis activities with the model-based test generation approach is realized by a test purpose language. It is used to formalize security test patterns in order to make them usable for test generators. Risk-Based Vulnerability Testing is applied to security testing of a web application.

Zech *et al.* [48, 49] propose a new method for generating negative security tests for nonfunctional security testing of web applications by logic programming and knowledge engineering. Based on a declarative model of the system under test, a risk analysis is performed and used for derivation of test cases.

5.2 Code-Based Testing and Static Analysis

Many vulnerabilities can only be detected by looking at the code. While traditionally not understood as a testing technique, *static analysis* of the program code is an important part of any security development process, as it allows to detect vulnerabilities at early stages of the development life cycle where fixing of vulnerabilities is comparatively cheap [50]. In Microsoft's SDL [26], SAST is part of the *implementation* phase to highlight that this technique should be applied as soon as the first line of code is written. Note that in this section, we only discuss purely static approaches, ie, approaches that do not require an executable test system. Thus, we discuss hybrid approaches, ie, approaches that combine static analysis with dynamic testing (such as concolic testing) in Section 5.3.

Code reviews can either be done manually or automated. The latter is often called static code analysis (SCA) or Static Application Security Testing (SAST). Moreover, we can either analyze the source code (ie, the code that was written by a developer) of the program or the compiled source code (ie, binaries or byte-code). As they are closely related, we discuss them not separately. From a software vendor's perspective who is aiming at building secure software, the analysis on the source code is preferred over a binary analysis, as the source code analysis is more precise and can provide detailed recommendations to developers on how to fix a vulnerability on the source code level.

5.2.1 Manual Code Review

Manual code review is the process by which an expert is reading program code "line-by-line" to identify vulnerabilities. This requires expertise in three areas: the application architecture, the implementation techniques (programming languages, frameworks used to build the application), as well as security. Thus, a good manual code review should start with a threat model or at least an interview with the developers to get a good understanding of the application architecture, its attack surface, as well as the implementation techniques. After this, the actual code review can start in which code is, guided by the identified attack surface, manually analyzed for security vulnerabilities. Finally, the results of the analysis are reported back to development to fix the identified vulnerabilities as well as to educate architects and developers to prevent similar issues in the future. Overall, manual code reviews are a tedious process that requires skill, experience, persistence, and patience.

5.2.2 Static Application Security Testing

Automated *static program analysis* for finding security vulnerabilities, also called *Static Application Security Testing* (SAST) [51], is an attempt to automated code reviews: in principle, a SAST tool analyses the program code of a software component (eg, an application or a library) automatically and reports potential security problems (potential vulnerabilities). This limits the manual effort to reviewing the reported problems and, thus, increases the scalability (ie, the amount of program code that can be analyzed in a certain amount of time) significantly. Moreover, on the one hand, SAST tools "encapsulate" most of the required security expertise and, thus, they can (and should) be used by developers that are not necessarily security experts. On the other hand, SAST tools only report vulnerabilities they are looking for and, thus, there is still a need for a small team of experts that configures the SAST tools correctly [52, 53].

For computing the set of potential security problems in a program, a SAST tool mainly employs two different types of analysis:

1. *Syntactic checks* such as calling insecure API functions or using insecure configuration options. An example of this class would be an analysis of Java programs for calls to `java.util.random` (which does not provide a cryptographically secure random generator).

2. *Semantic checks* that require an understanding of the program semantics such as the data flow or control flow of a program. An example of this class would be an analysis checking for direct (not sanitized) data-flows from an program input to a SQL statement (indicating a potential SQL Injection vulnerability).

As SAST tools work on overapproximations of the actual program code as well as apply heuristics checks, the output of a SAST tool is a list of *potential* security vulnerabilities. Thus, or each finding, an human expert is necessary to decide:

- If the finding represents a vulnerability, ie, a weakness that can be exploited by an attacker (*true positive*), and, thus, needs to be fixed.
- If the finding cannot be exploited by an attacker (*false positive*) and, thus, does not need to be fixed.

Similarly, if an SAST tool does not report security issues, this can have two reasons:

- The source code is secure (*true negative*)
- The source code has security vulnerability but due to limitations of the tool, the tool does not report a problem (*false negative*).

There are SAST tools available for most of the widely used programming language, eg, FindBugs [54] that is able to analyzes Java byte code and, thus, can analyze various languages running on the Java Virtual Machine. There are also specializes techniques for Java programs (eg, [55]), or C/C++ (eg, [56]) as well as approaches that work on multiple languages (eg, [57]). For a survey on static analysis methods, we refer the reader elsewhere [51, 58]. Moreover, we discuss further static analysis techniques in the context of a small case study in Section 6.

Besides the fact that SAST tools can be applied very early in the software development life cycle as well as the fact that source code analysis can provide detailed fix recommendations, SAST has one additional advantages over most dynamic security testing techniques: SAST tools can analyze all control flows of a program. Therefore, SAST tools achieve, compared to dynamic test approaches, a significant higher coverage of the program under test and, thus, produce a significant lower false negative rate. Thus, SAST is a very effective method [59] for detecting programming related vulnerabilities early in the software development life cycle.

5.3 Penetration Testing and Dynamic Analysis

In contrast to white-box security testing techniques (see Section 5.2), black-box security testing does not require access to the source code or other development artifacts of the application under test. Instead, the security test is conducted via interaction with the running software.

5.3.1 Penetration Testing

A well-known form of black-box security testing is *Penetration Testing*. In a penetration test, an application or system is tested from the outside in a setup that is comparable to an actual attack from a malicious third party. This means, in most settings the entity that is conducting the test has potentially only limited information about the system under test and is only able to interact with the system's public interfaces. Hence, a mandatory prerequisite for this approach is a (near) productive application, that is feature complete and sufficiently filled with data, so that all implemented workflows can be executed during the test. Penetration tests are commonly done for applications that are open for networked communication.

The NIST Technical Guide to Information Security Testing and Assessment [60] partitions the penetration testing process in four distinct phases (see Fig. 5):

1. *Planning:* No actual testing occurs in this phase. Instead, important side conditions and boundaries for the test are defined and documented. For instance, the relevant components of the applications that are subject of the test are determined and the nature/scope of the to be conducted tests and their level of invasiveness.

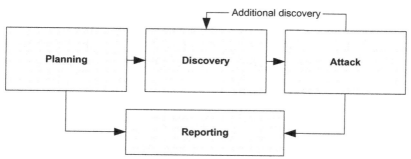

Figure 5 Phases of a penetration test [60].

2. *Discovery:* This phase consists of a steps. First, all accessible external interfaces of the system under test are systematically discovered and enumerated. This set of interfaces constitutes the system's initial *attack surface.* The second part of the discovery phase is vulnerability analysis, in which the applicable vulnerability classes that match the interface are identified (eg, Cross-Site Scripting for HTTP services or SQL Injection for applications with database back end). In a commercial penetration test, this phase also includes the check if any of the found components is susceptible to publicly documented vulnerabilities which is contained in precompiled vulnerability databases.

3. *Attack:* Finally, the identified interfaces are tested through a series of attack attempts. In these attacks, the testers actively attempts to compromise the system via sending attack payloads. In case of success, the found security vulnerabilities are exploited in order to gain further information about the system, widen the access privileges of the tester and find further system components, which might expose additional interfaces. This expanded attack surface is fed back into the discovery phase, for further processing.

4. *Reporting:* The reporting phase occurs simultaneously with the other three phases of the penetration test and documents all findings along with their estimated severeness.

5.3.2 Vulnerability Scanning

In general penetration tests are a combination of manual testing through security experts and the usage of *black-box vulnerability scanners.* Black-box web vulnerability scanners are a class of tools that can be used to identify security issues in applications through various techniques. The scanner queries the application's interfaces with a set of predefined attack payloads and analyses the application's responses for indicators if the attack was successful and, if this is not the case, hints how to alter the attack in the subsequent tries. Bau *et al.* [4] as well as Adam *et al.* [61] provide overviews of recent commercial and academic black-box vulnerability scanners.

5.3.3 Dynamic Taint Analysis

An important variant of black-box testing is an analysis technique called *taint analysis*. A significant portion of today's security vulnerabilities are *string-based code injection vulnerabilities* [62], which enable the attacker to inject syntactic content into dynamically executed programming statements, which—in the majority of all cases—leads to full compromise of the vulnerable execution context. Examples for such vulnerabilities include SQL Injection [63] and Cross-Site Scripting [64]. Such injection vulnerabilities can be regarded as information flow problems, in which unsanitized data paths from untrusted sources to security sensitive sinks have to be found. To achieve this, a well established approach is *(dynamic) data tainting*. Untrusted data is outfitted with *taint* information on runtime, which is only cleared, if the data passes a dedicated sanitization function. If data which still carries taint information reaches a security sensitive sink (eg, an API that converts string data into executable code), the application can react appropriately, for instance through altering, autosanitization the data or completely stopping the corresponding process. If taint tracking is utilized in security testing, the main purpose is to notify the tester that insecure data flows, that likely lead to code injection, exist. Unlike static analysis, that also targets the identification of problematic data flows, dynamic taint analysis is conducted transparently while the application under test is executed. For this, the execution environment, eg, the language runtime, has to be made taint aware, so that the attached taint information of the untrusted data is maintained through the course of program execution, so that it can reliably be detected when tainted data ends up in security sensitive sinks.

5.3.4 Fuzzing

Fuzzing or *fuzz testing* is a dynamic testing technique that is based on the idea of feeding random data to a program "until it crashes." It was pioneered in the late 1980s by Barton Miller at the University of Wisconsin [65]. Since then, fuzz testing has been proven to be an effective technique for finding vulnerabilities in software. While the first fuzz testing approaches where purely based on randomly generated test data (random fuzzing), advances in symbolic computation, model-based testing, as well as dynamic test case generation have lead to more advanced fuzzing techniques such as mutation-based fuzzing, generation-based fuzzing, or gray-box fuzzing.

Random fuzzing is the simplest and oldest fuzz testing technique: a stream of random input data is, in a black-box scenario, send to the program under test. The input data can, eg, be send as command line options, events, or protocol packets. This type of fuzzing in, in particular, useful for test how a program reacts on large or invalid input data. While random fuzzing can find already severe vulnerabilities, modern fuzzers do have a detailed understanding of the input format that is expected by the program under test.

Mutation-based fuzzing is one type of fuzzing in which the fuzzer has some knowledge about the input format of the program under test: based on existing data samples, a mutation-based fuzzing tools generated new variants (mutants), based on a heuristics, that it uses for fuzzing. there are a wide range of mutation-based fuzzing approaches available for different domains. We refer the interested reader elsewhere for details [66, 67].

Generation-based fuzzing uses a model (of the input data or the vulnerabilities) for generating test data from this model or specification. Compared to pure random-based fuzzing, generation-based fuzzing achieves usually a higher coverage of the program under test, in particular if the expected input format is rather complex. Again, for details we refer the interested reader elsewhere [68, 69].

Advanced fuzzing techniques combine several of the previously mentioned approaches, eg, use a combination of mutation-based and generation-based techniques as well as observe the program under test and use these observations for constructing new test data. This turns fuzzing into a gray-box testing technique that also utilizes symbolic computation that is usually understood as a technique used for static program analysis. Probably the first and also most successful application of gray-box fuzzing is SAGE from Microsoft [70, 71], which combines symbolic execution (a static source code analysis technique) and dynamic testing. This combination is today known as concolic testing and inspired several advanced security testing eg, [72, 73], as well as functional test approaches.

5.4 Security Regression Testing

Due to ever changing surroundings, new business needs, new regulations, and new technologies, a software system must evolve and be maintained, or it becomes progressively less satisfactory [74]. This makes it especially challenging to keep software systems permanently secure as changes either in the system itself or in its environment may cause new threats and vulnerabilities [75]. A combination of regression and security testing called security regression testing, which ensures that changes made to a system do not harm its security, are therefore of high significance and the interest in such approaches has steadily increased [76]. Regression testing techniques ensure that changes made to existing software do not cause unintended effects on unchanged parts and changed parts of the software behave as intended [77]. As requirements, design models, code or even the running system can be changed, regression testing techniques are orthogonal to the security testing techniques discussed in the previous sections.

Yoo and Harman [78] classify regression testing techniques into three categories: test suite minimization, test case prioritization and test case selection.

Test suite minimization seeks to reduce the size of a test suite by eliminating redundant test cases from the test suite.

Test case prioritization aims at ordering the execution of test cases in the regression test suite based on a criterion, for instance, on the basis of history, coverage, or requirements, which is expected to lead to the early detection of faults or the maximization of some other desirable properties.

Test case selection deals with the problem of selecting a subset of test cases that will be used to test changed parts of software. It requires to select a subset of the tests from the previous version, which are likely to detect faults, based on different strategies. Most reported regression testing techniques focus on this regression testing technique [78]. The usual strategy is to focus on the identification of modified parts of the SUT and to select test cases relevant to them. For instance, the *retest-all* technique is one naive type of regression test selection by reexecuting all tests from the previous version on the new version of the system. It is often used in industry due to its simple and quick implementation. However, its capacity in terms of fault detection is limited [79]. Therefore, considerable amount of work is related to the development of effective and scalable selective techniques.

In the following, we discuss available security testing approaches according to the categories minimization, prioritization, and selection. The selected approaches are based on a systematic classification of security regression testing approaches by Felderer and Fourneret [76].

5.4.1 Test Suite Minimization

Test suite minimization seeks to reduce the size of a test suite by eliminating test cases from the test suite based on a given criterion. Current approaches on minimization [80–82] address vulnerabilities.

Toth et al. [80] propose an approach that applies automated security testing for detection of vulnerabilities by exploring application faults that may lead to known malware, such as viruses or worms. The approach considers only failed tests from the previous version revealing faults for rerun in a new system version after fault fixing.

He et al. [81] propose an approach for detecting and removing vulnerabilities for minor releases of web applications. In their approach, only strong-association links between pages from a previous version, optimized through iterations, are selected for exploration of web pages that contain vulnerabilities.

Finally, Garvin et al. [82] propose testing of self-adaptive system for already known failures. The authors avoid reproducing already known failures by considering only those tests for execution that exercise the known failures in previous versions.

5.4.2 Test Case Prioritization

Test case prioritization is concerned with right ordering of test cases that maximizes desirable properties, such as early fault detection. Also, current approaches to prioritization [83–85] address only vulnerabilities.

Huang et al. [83] propose a prioritization technique for security regression testing. Their technique gathers historical records, whose most effective execution order is determined by a genetic algorithm.

Yu et al. [84] propose fault-based prioritization of test cases, which directly utilizes the knowledge of their capability to detect faults.

Finally, Viennot et al. [85] propose a mutable record-replay system, which allows a recorded execution of an application to be replayed with a modified version of the application. Their execution is prioritized by defining a so called d-optimal mutable replay based on a cost function measuring the difference between the original execution and the mutable replay.

5.4.3 Test Case Selection

Test case selection approaches choose a subset or all test cases to test changed parts of software. As for classical regression testing [78], also for security regression testing most approaches fall into this category [76].

These approaches test both, security mechanisms and vulnerabilities. Several subset-based approaches [86–90] and retest-all approaches [91–94] have been proposed.

Felderer et al. [86] provide a UML-based approach for regression testing of security requirements of type authentication, confidentiality, availability, authorization, and integrity. Tests, represented as sequence diagrams, are selected based on test requirements changes. Kassab et al. [87] propose an approach to improve regression testing based on nonfunctional requirements ontologies. Tests are selected based on change and impact analysis of nonfunctional requirements, such as security, safety, performance, or reliability. Each test linked to a changed or modified requirement is selected for regression testing. Anisetti et al. [88] propose an approach for providing test evidence for incremental certification of security requirements of services. This approach is based on change detection in the service test model, which will determine if new test cases need to be generated, or existing ones to be selected for reexecution on the evolved service. Huang et al. [89] address security regression testing of access control policies. This approach selects tests if they cover changed elements in the policy. Finally, Hwang et al. [90] propose three safe coverage-based selection techniques for testing evolution of security policies, each of which includes a sequence of rules to specify which subjects are permitted or denied to access which resources under which conditions. The three techniques are based on two coverage criteria, ie, (1) coverage of changed rules in the policy, and (2) coverage of different program decisions for the evolved and the original policy.

Vetterling et al. [91] propose an approach for developing secure systems evaluated under the Common Criteria [95]. In their approach, tests covering security requirements are created manually and represented as sequence diagrams. In case of a change, new tests are written if necessary and then all tests are executed on the new version. Bruno et al. [92] propose an approach for testing security requirements of web service releases. The service user can periodically reexecute the test suite against the service in order to verify whether the service still exhibits the functional and nonfunctional requirements. Kongsli [93] proposes the use of so called misuse stories in agile methodologies (for instance, extreme programming) to express vulnerabilities related to features and/or functionality of the system in order to be able to perform security regression testing. The author suggests that test execution is ideal for agile methodologies and continuous integration. Finally, Qi et al. [94] propose an approach for regression fault-localization in web applications. Based on two programs, a reference program and a modified program, as well as input failing on the modified program, their approach uses symbolic execution to automatically synthesize a new input that is very similar to the failing input and does not fail. On this basis, the potential cause(s) of failure are found by comparing control flow behavior of the passing and failing inputs and identifying code fragments where the control flows diverge.

6. APPLICATION OF SECURITY TESTING TECHNIQUES

In this section, we make a concrete proposal on how to apply the security test techniques (and the tools implementing them) to a small case study: a business application using a three tiered architecture. We focus on security testing techniques that detect the most common vulnerability types that were disclosed in the Common Vulnerabilities and Exposures (CVE) index [5] over the period of the last 15 years (see Fig. 6). This clearly shows that the vast majority of vulnerabilities, such as XSS, buffer overflows, are still caused by programming errors. Thus, we focus in this section on security testing techniques that allow to find these kind of vulnerabilities.

For instance, we exclude techniques for ensuring the security of the underlying infrastructure such as the network configuration, as, eg, discussed in Refs. [96, 97] as well as model-based testing techniques (as discussed in Section 5.1) that are in particular useful for finding logical security flaws. While a holistic security testing strategy makes use of all available security testing strategies, we recommend to concentrate efforts first on techniques for the most common vulnerabilities. Furthermore, we also do not explicitly discuss retesting after changes of the system under test, which is addressed by suitable (security) regression testing approaches (as discussed in Section 5.4).

6.1 Selection Criteria for Security Testing Approaches

When selecting a specific security testing method and tool, many aspects need to be taken into account, eg:

- *Attack surface*: different security testing methods find different attack and vulnerability types. Many techniques are complementary so it is advisable to use multiple security testing methods together to efficiently detect a range of vulnerabilities as wide as possible.
- *Application type*: different security testing methods perform differently when applied to different application types. For example, a method that performs well against a mobile application may not be able to perform as well against three-tier client-server applications.

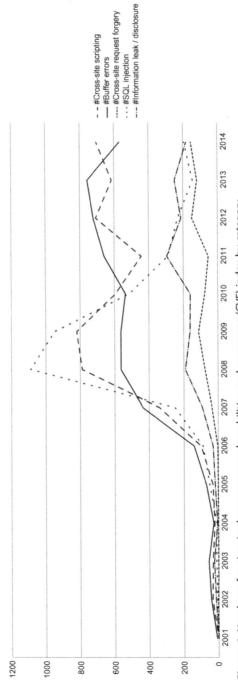

Figure 6 Number of entires in the common vulnerabilities and exposures (CVE) index by category.

- *Performance and resource utilization:* different tools and methods require different computing power and different manual efforts.
- *Costs for licenses, maintenance, and support:* to use security testing tools efficiently in a large enterprise, they need to be integrated into, eg, bug tracking or reporting solutions—often they provide their own server applications for this. Thus, buying a security testing tool is usually not a one-time effort—it requires regular maintenance and support.
- *Quality of results:* different tools that implement the same security testing technique provide a different quality level (eg, in terms of fix recommendations or false positives rates).
- *Supported technologies:* security testing tools usually only support a limited number of technologies (eg, programming languages, interfaces, or build systems). If these tools support multiple technologies, they do not necessary support all of them with the same quality. For example, a source analysis tool that supports Java and C might work well for Java but not as well for C.

In the following, we focus on the first two aspects: the attack surface and the application type. These two aspects are, from a security perspective the first ones to consider for selecting the best combinations of security testing approaches for a specific application type (product). In a subsequent step, the other factors need to be considered for selecting a specific tool that fits the needs of the actual development as well as the resource and time constraints.

6.2 A Three-Tiered Business Application

In this chapter, we use a simple multitiered business application, eg, for booking business travels, as a running example. This architecture is, on the first hand, very common for larger applications and, on the other hand, covers a wide variety of security testing challenges.

Let us assume that we want to plan the security testing activities for business application that is separated into three tiers:

- *First tier:* A front-end that is implemented as rich-client using modern web development techniques, ie, HTML5 and JavaScript, eg, using frameworks such as AngularJS or JQuery.
- *Second tier:* A typical middle-tier implemented in Java (eg, using Java Servlets hosted in an application server such as Apache Tomcat).
- *Third tier:* A third-party database that provides persistency for the business data that is processed in the second tier.

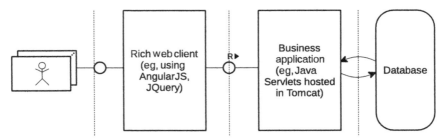

Figure 7 Architecture of example application.

Fig. 7 illustrates this example architecture where the dotted vertical lines mark the trust boundaries of the application.

6.2.1 The First Tier: Web Applications

Web applications are predominantly affected by code injection vulnerabilities, such as SQL Injection [63] or Cross-Site Scripting (XSS) [64]. This is shown in Fig. 6: as it can be seen, besides buffer overflows (and similar memory corruption vulnerabilities), which in general do not occur in Web applications, injection vulnerabilities represent the vast majority of reported issues.

In consequence, security testing approaches for Web applications are primarily concerned with detection of such code injection vulnerabilities. In the remainder of this section, we utilize the field of Web applications as a case study in security testing and comprehensively list academic approaches in this area.

6.2.1.1 Code-Based Testing and Static Analysis

As introduced in Section 5.2, static analysis of source code is a powerful tool to detect vulnerabilities in source code. Static analysis allows to analyze the code of a given application without actually executing it. To detect injection vulnerabilities with such an approach, in most cases the static analysis attempts to approximate the data flows within the examined source code. This way, data flows from *sources* that can be controlled by the attacker (eg, the incoming HTTP request) into security sensitive *sinks* (eg, APIs that create the HTTP response of send SQL to the database).

Different mechanisms and techniques proposed in the program analysis literature can be applied to Web applications. The actual implementation of such an analysis can utilize different techniques such as model checking, data-flow analysis, or symbolic execution, typically depending on the desired precision and completeness. Three different properties are relevant for the analysis phase. First, the static analysis of the source code itself can be performed on different levels, either only within a given function (*intraprocedural analysis*) or the interaction of functions can be analyzed as well (*interprocedural analysis*). Second, the execution context can be examined in detail or neglected, which then typically reduces the precision of the analysis. A third aspect of static analysis deals with the way how the flow of data or code is analyzed.

One of the first tools in this area was *WebSSARI* [98], a code analysis tool for PHP applications developed by Huang *et al.* based on a CQual-like type system [99, 100].

Pixy is a static taint analysis tool presented by Jovanovic *et al.* for automated identification of XSS vulnerabilities in PHP web applications [101, 102]. The tool performs an interprocedural, context-sensitive, and flow-sensitive data flow analysis to detect vulnerabilities in a given application. Combined with a precise alias analysis, the tool is capable of detecting a variety of vulnerabilities. In a similar paper, Livshits and Lam demonstrated how a context-sensitive pointer alias analysis together with string analysis can be realized for Java-based web applications [55].

Xie and Aiken introduced a static analysis algorithm based on so-called block and function summaries to detect vulnerabilities in PHP applications [103]. The approach performs the analysis in both an intraprocedural and an interprocedural way. Dahse and Holz refined this approach and demonstrated that a fine-grained analysis of built-in PHP features and their interaction significantly improves detection accuracy [104, 105].

Wasserman and Su implemented a static code analysis approach to detect XSS vulnerabilities caused by weak or absent input validation [106]. The authors combined work on taint-based information flow analysis with string analysis previously introduced by Minamide [107].

A tool for static analysis of JavaScript code was developed by Saxena *et al.* [108]. The tool named Kudzu employs symbolic execution to find client-side injection flaws in Web applications. Jin *et al.* employ static analysis[109] to find XSS vulnerabilities within HTML5-based mobile applications. Interestingly, they found new ways to conduct XSS attacks within such apps by abusing the special capabilities of mobile phones.

Further static analysis approaches to detect injection vulnerabilities have been proposed by Fu *et al.*[110], Wassermann and Su [111], and Halfond *et al.* [112]

6.2.1.2 Dynamic Analysis and Black-Box Testing

A complementary approach is dynamic analysis, in which a given application is executed with a particular set of inputs and the runtime behavior of the application is observed. Many of these approaches employ dynamic taint tracking and consist of two different components. A detection component to identify potentially vulnerable data flows and a validation component to eliminate false positives.

SECUBAT [113] is a general purpose Web vulnerability scanner that also has XSS detection capabilities. To achieve its goals, SECUBAT employs three different components: a crawling component, an attack component, and an analysis component. Whenever the crawling component discovers a suspicious feature, it passes the page under investigation to the attack component, which then scans this page for web forms. If a form is found, appropriate payloads are inserted into the fields of the form and submitted to the server. The response of the server is then interpreted by the analysis component. SNUCK [114] is another dynamic testing tool. In a first step, SNUCK uses a legitimate test input to dynamically determine a possible injection and the corresponding context via XPATH expressions. Based on the determined context, the tool chooses a set of predefined attack payloads and injects them into the application.

While SECUBAT and SNUCK focus on server-side security problems, FLASHOVER [115] focuses on a client-side problem. More specifically, FLASH-OVER detects client-side reflected XSS in Adobe Flash applets. It does so by decompiling the source code and statically detecting suspicious situations. Then it constructs an attack payload and executes the exploit via dynamic testing.

Recently, Bau *et al.* [4] and Doupe *et al.* [61] prepared comprehensive overviews on commercial and academic black-box vulnerability scanners and their underlying approaches.

6.2.1.3 Taint Tracking

As discussed previously, most Web-specific security vulnerabilities can predominantly be regarded as information flow problems, caused by unsanitized data paths from untrusted sources to security sensitive sinks. Hence, taint tracking (see Section 5.3.3) is a well-established method to detect injection vulnerabilities.

Dynamic taint tracking was initially introduced by Perl in 1989 [116] and since then has been adopted for numerous programming languages and frameworks [117]. Subsequent works describe finer grained approaches towards dynamic taint propagation. These techniques allow the tracking of untrusted input on the basis of single characters. For instance, Nguyen-Tuong *et al.* [118] and Pietraszek and Vanden Berghe [119] proposed fine grained taint propagation for the PHP runtime to detect various classes of injection attacks, such as SQL Injection or XSS. Based on dynamic taint propagation, Su and Wassermann [120] describe an approach that utilizes specifically crafted grammars to deterministically identify SQL injection attempts.

The first taint tracking paper that aimed at automatically generating Cross-Site Scripting attacks was authored by Martin *et al.* [121]. The presented mechanism expects a program adhering to the Java Servlet specification and a taint-based vulnerability specification as an input, and generates a valid Cross-Site Scripting or SQL Injection attack payload with the help of dynamic taint tracking and model checking. While this approach requires a security analyst to manually write a vulnerability specification, Kieyzun *et al.* focus on the fully automatic generation of taint-based vulnerability payloads [122]. Furthermore, they extend the dynamic tainting to the database. Hence, as opposed to the first approach, this approach is able to also detect server-side persistent XSS vulnerabilities.

Besides server-side injection vulnerabilities, Web applications are also susceptible to injection problems on the client-side, ie, Cross-Site Scripting problems caused by insecure JavaScript executed in the browser [123]. Through making the browser's JavaScript engine taint-aware, this vulnerability class can be detected during testing: Lekies *et al.* implemented a browser-based byte-level taint-tracking engine to detect reflected and persistent client-side XSS vulnerabilities [124]. By leveraging the taint information, their approach is capable of generating a precise XSS payload matching the injection context. A similar approach was taken by FLAX [125], which also employs taint tracking in the browser. Instead of using an exploit generation technique, FLAX utilizes a sink-aware fuzzing technique, which executes variations of a predefined list of context-specific attack vectors.

6.2.2 The Second Tier: Java-Based Server Applications

Also the second tier, ie, the Java-based business application, is predominantly affected by code injection vulnerabilities, such as SQL Injection [63] or Cross-Site Scripting [64]. Even if we secure the front-end against these attacks, we cannot rely on these protection as an attacker might circumvent the front-end by attacking the second tier directly (eg, using WSDL-based,

RESTful, or OData-based interfaced). Thus, we need to apply the same standards for secure development also to the second tier.

6.2.2.1 Code-Based Testing and Static Analysis

There are many static analysis approaches available for languages tradition-ally used for server systems, eg, C/C++ or Java; both in the academic world as well as commercial offerings. Commercial tools are at least available since 10 years [57, 126] and used widely since at least 5 years [52, 53]. Due to space reason, we only discuss a few selected works for Java: most notability, FindBugs [54] is a "ready-to-run" tool that finds a large number of potential security vulnerabilities in Java programs and, moreover, can be considered the first widely used static analysis tool for Java that included security checks. Already in 2005, Livshits presented a method based on taint propagation for finding data-flow related vulnerabilities in Java programs [55]. Tripp *et al.* [127] improved this idea to make it applicable to large scale programs by using a optimized pointer analysis as prerequisite for building the call graph. An alternative to using a call-graph-based tainting analysis, there are also approaches, such as [128] that are based on slicing. Moreover, there are two different Open Source frameworks available that for building own static analysis tools for Java: Wala [129], which itself is written in Java, and Swaja [130], which is written in OCaml.

6.2.2.2 Penetration Testing and Dynamic Analysis

From an implementation perspective, the most important dynamic testing approach is—besides manual penetration testing—fuzzing. As we imple-ment the second tier, we focus on gray-box testing approaches that combine white- and black-box testing. The most well known and industrially proven approach is SAGE [71], which is used by Microsoft. Besides SAGE, there are also other approaches that share the same basic concept: using instrumenta-tion or static analyses of the implementation to improve the quality, effi-ciency, or effectiveness of dynamic security testing. For example, Bekrar *et al.* [72] uses a binary taint analysis to increase the fuzz testing coverage while [131] uses symbolic execution to achieve the same goal. Gray-box fuzzing is also successfully applied to commercial operating system [132].

When using a gray-box testing technique on a multitier architecture, one can decide to only test the second tier in isolation or to test all tiers "at once." In the latter case, only selected tiers might be subject to taint tracking or sym-bolic execution, as already such a partial covering of the implementation with white-box techniques allows to improve the testing results. Moreover, even partial application of white-box techniques helps to diagnose the root cause of an vulnerability and, thus, usually helps to minimize the time required for fixing a vulnerability.

Until recently, thus gray-box testing approaches where not generally available in commercial security testing solutions. This has changed: first vendors are staring to integrate similar techniques in their tools, using the *Interactive Security Application Testing* (ISAT).

6.2.3 The Third Tier: Back-End Systems

In our example, we assume that the back-end system (ie, the database) is supplied by a third-party vendor. Therefore, we only have access to the systems as black-box. Still, we need to security test it as we are implementing stored procedures (SQL) on top of it as well as need to configure its security (eg, to ensure proper access control and a secure and trustworthy communication to the second tier). Moreover, we might want to assess the overall implementation-level security of the externally developed product.

6.2.3.1 Security Testing the Implementation

For increasing our confidence in the security of the database, a third-party component, itself, we can apply manual penetration testing as well as fuzzing for checking for buffer overflows in the interfaces that are exposed via the network. As we assume that we only have access to the binary, we can only use black-box fuzzers such as presented by Woo *et al.* [133] or gray-box fuzzers that are based on binary analysis, eg, [134].

Moreover, all code that we develop on top of the core database, ie, stored procedures written in an SQL-dialect such as PL/SQL should be analyzed for injection attacks using dedicated static analysis approaches such as Ref. [135] (also many commercially available static analysis tools support the analysis of SQL dialects). Moreover, we can apply several dynamic security testing approaches that specialize on testing SQL Injections: Appelt *et al.* [136] present a mutation-based testing approach for finding SQL Injections while Wang *et al.* [137] use a model-based fuzzing approach. For an experience report on using fuzzers for finding SQL Injections see Ref. [138].

6.2.3.2 Security Testing the Configuration

Finally, even if all software components are implemented securely, we still need to ensure that the actual configuration used during operations is also secure. While we touch this topic only very briefly, we want to emphasize that it is important to test the secure configuration of the communication channels, the access control of all tiers, as well as to keep the systems up to date by patching known vulnerabilities. Testing the security of the communication channels includes approaches that check the correct validation of SSL/TLS certificates (eg, Frankencerts [139]) as well as protocol fuzzers such as SNOOZE [140] or SECFUZZ [141]. For testing the correct access control, various model-based approaches (eg, [142–144]) haven been applied to case studies of different size. Finally, tools like Nessus [145] that rather easily allow to scan networks for applications with known vulnerabilities and, thus, applications that need to be updated or patched.

7. SUMMARY

In this chapter, we provided an overview of recent security testing techniques and their practical application in context of a three-tiered business application. For this purpose, we first summarized the required background on software testing and security engineering. Testing consists of static and dynamic life cycle activities concerned with evaluation of software products and related artifacts. It can be performed on the component, integration, and system level. With regard to accessibility of test design artifacts white-box testing (ie, deriving test cases based on design and code information) as well as black-box testing (ie, relying only on input/output behavior of software) can be distinguished. Security testing validates software system requirements related to security properties of assets that include confidentiality, integrity, availability, authentication, authorization, and nonrepudiation. Security requirements can be positive and functional, explicitly defining the expected security functionality of a security mechanism, or negative and nonfunctional, specifying what the application should not do. Due to the negative nature of many security requirements and the resulting broad range of subordinate requirements, it is essential to take testing into account in all phases of the secure software development life cycle (ie, analysis, design, development, deployment as well as maintenance) and to combine different security testing techniques.

For a detailed discussion of security testing techniques in this chapter, we therefore classified them according to their test basis within the secure software development life cycle into four different types: (1) *model-based security testing* is grounded on requirements and design models created during the analysis and design phase, (2) *code-based testing and static analysis* on source and byte code created during development, (3) *penetration testing and dynamic analysis* on running systems, either in a test or production environment, as well as (4) *security regression testing* performed during maintenance. With regard to model-based security testing, we considered testing based on architectural and functional models, threat, fault and risk models, as well as weakness and vulnerability models. Concerning, code-based testing and static analysis we took manual code reviews as well as static application security testing into account. With regard to penetration testing and dynamic analysis, we considered penetration testing itself, vulnerability scanning, dynamic taint analysis, as well as fuzzing. Concerning security regression testing, we discussed approaches to test suite minimization, test case prioritization, and test case selection. To show how the discussed security testing techniques could be practically applied, we discuss their usage for a three-tiered business application based on a web client, an application server, as well as a database back end.

Overall, this chapter provided a broad overview of recent security testing techniques. It fulfills the growing need for information on security testing techniques to enable their effective and efficient application. Along these lines, this chapter is of value both for researchers to evaluate and refine existing security testing techniques as well as for practitioners to apply and disseminate them.

ACKNOWLEDGMENTS

The work was supported in part by the research projects QE LaB—Living Models for Open Systems (FFG 822740) and MOBSTECO (FWF P 26194-N15).

REFERENCES

[1] I. Schieferdecker, J. Grossmann, M. Schneider, Model-based security testing, in: Proceedings 7th Workshop on Model-Based Testing, 2012.

[2] ISO/IEC, ISO/IEC 9126-1:2001 software engineering—product quality—Part 1: quality model, 2001.

[3] ISO/IEC, ISO/IEC 25010:2011 systems and software engineering—systems and software quality requirements and evaluation (SQuaRE)—system and software quality models 2011.

[4] J. Bau, E. Bursztein, D. Gupta, J. Mitchell, State of the art: automated black-box web application vulnerability testing, in: 2010 IEEE Symposium on Security and Privacy (SP), IEEE, 2010, pp. 332–345.

[5] MITRE, Common vulnerabilities and exposures, http://cve.mitre.org.

[6] NIST, The economic impacts of inadequate infrastructure for software testing, 2002 (available at www.nist.gov/director/planning/upload/report02-3.pdf [accessed April 7, 2015]).

[7] P. Bourque, R. Dupuis (Eds.), Guide to the Software Engineering Body of Knowledge Version 3.0 SWEBOK, IEEE, 2014, http://www.computer.org/web/swebok.

[8] P. Ammann, J. Offutt, Introduction to Software Testing, Cambridge University Press, Cambridge, UK, 2008.

[9] ISTQB, Standard glossary of terms used in software testing. Version 2.2, Tech. Rep., ISTQB 2012.

[10] OWASP Foundation, OWASP Testing Guide v4, https://www.owasp.org/index. php/OWASP_Testing_Project (accessed March 11, 2015).

[11] G. Tian-yang, S. Yin-sheng, F. You-yuan, Research on software security testing, World Acad. Sci. Eng. Technol. 69 (2010) 647–651.

[12] R. Bachmann, A.D. Brucker, Developing secure software: a holistic approach to security testing, Datenschutz und Datensicherheit (DuD) 38 (4) (2014) 257–261.

[13] ISO/IEC, Information technology—open systems interconnection—conformance testing methodology and framework, 1994 (international ISO/IEC multi-part standard No. 9646).

[14] M. Utting, B. Legeard, Practical Model-Based Testing: A Tools Approach, Morgan Kaufmann Publishers Inc., San Francisco, CA, 2007, ISBN 0123725011.

[15] J. Zander, I. Schieferdecker, P.J. Mosterman, Model-Based Testing for Embedded Systems, vol. 13, CRC Press, 2012.

[16] IEEE, IEEE standard glossary of software engineering terminology, Institute of Electronical and Electronics Engineers, Washington, DC, 1990 (IEEE Std 610121990).

[17] ISO, ISO/IEC/IEEE 29119 software testing, 2013 (available at http://www. softwaretestingstandard.org/ [accessed April 7, 2015]).

[18] IEEE, IEEE standard for software and system test documentation, 2008 (IEEE Std 829-2008).

[19] I. Schieferdecker, Model-based testing, IEEE Softw. 29 (1) (2012) 14–18.

[20] Committee on National Security Systems, National Information Assurance Glossary, Tech. Rep. 4009, Committee on National Security Systems, 2010.

[21] B. Arkin, S. Stender, G. McGraw, Software penetration testing, IEEE Secur. Priv. 3 (1) (2005) 84–87.

[22] B. Potter, G. McGraw, Software security testing, IEEE Secur. Priv. 2 (5) (2004) 81–85.

[23] P. Herzog, The open source security testing methodology manual 3, 2010, http:// www.isecom.org/research/osstmm.html (accessed April 11, 2015).

[24] M.S. Lund, B. Solhaug, K. Stolen, Model-Driven Risk Analysis, Springer, 2011.

[25] D. Verdon, G. McGraw, Risk analysis in software design, IEEE Secur. Priv. 2 (4) (2004) 79–84.

[26] M. Howard, S. Lipner, The Security Development Lifecycle: SDL: A Process for Developing Demonstrably More Secure Software, Microsoft Press, 2006, ISBN 0735622140.

[27] OWASP, OpepSAMM, http://www.opensamm.org/ (accessed March 30, 2015).

[28] B. Potter, G. McGraw, Software security testing, IEEE Secur. Priv. 2 (5) (2004) 81–85.

[29] H. Shahriar, M. Zulkernine, Automatic testing of program security vulnerabilities, in: 33rd Annual IEEE International Computer Software and Applications Conference, 2009, COMPSAC'09, vol. 2, IEEE, 2009, pp. 550–555.

[30] H.H. Thompson, Why security testing is hard, IEEE Secur. Priv. 1 (4) (2003) 83–86.

[31] OWASP Foundation, OWASP Code Review Guide v1.1, https://www.owasp.org/ index.php/Category:OWASP_Code_Review_Project (accessed March 11, 2015).

[32] A.C. Dias-Neto, G.H. Travassos, A picture from the model-based testing area: concepts, techniques, and challenges, Adv. Comput. 80 (2010) 45–120.

[33] M. Utting, A. Pretschner, B. Legeard, A taxonomy of model-based testing approaches, Softw. Test. Verif. Reliab. 22 (2) (2012) 297312.

[34] W. Grieskamp, N. Kicillof, K. Stobie, V. Braberman, Model-based quality assurance of protocol documentation: tools and methodology, Softw. Test. Verif. Reliab. 21 (1) (2011) 55–71.

[35] A. Pretschner, Defect-based testing, in: Dependable Software Systems Engineering, IOS Press, 2015, http://www.iospress.nl/book/dependable-software-systems-engineering/.

[36] H. Zhu, P.A.V. Hall, J.H.R. May, Software unit test coverage and adequacy, ACM Comput. Surv. 29 (4) (1997) 366–427, ISSN 0360-0300.

[37] L.J. Morell, A theory of fault-based testing, IEEE Trans. Softw. Eng. 16 (8) (1990) 844–857, ISSN 0098-5589.

[38] A. Pretschner, D. Holling, R. Eschbach, M. Gemmar, A generic fault model for quality assurance, in: A. Moreira, B. Schätz, J. Gray, A. Vallecillo, P. Clarke (Eds.), Model-Driven Engineering Languages and Systems, Lecture Notes in Computer Science, vol. 8107, Springer, Berlin, ISBN 978-3-642-41532-6, 2013, pp. 87–103.

[39] M. Felderer, B. Agreiter, P. Zech, R. Breu, A classification for model-based security testing, in: The Third International Conference on Advances in System Testing and Validation Lifecycle (VALID 2011), 2011, pp. 109–114.

[40] I. Schieferdecker, J. Grossmann, M. Schneider, Model-based security testing, in: Proceedings 7th Workshop on Model-Based Testing, 2012.

[41] M. Büchler, J. Oudinet, A. Pretschner, Semi-automatic security testing of web applications from a secure model, in: 2012 IEEE Sixth International Conference on Software Security and Reliability (SERE), IEEE, 2012, pp. 253–262.

[42] T. Mouelhi, F. Fleurey, B. Baudry, Y. Traon, A model-based framework for security policy specification, deployment and testing, in: Proceedings of the 11th International Conference on Model Driven Engineering Languages and Systems, MoDELS '08, Toulouse, France, Springer, Berlin, ISBN 978-3-540-87874-2, 2008, pp. 537–552.

[43] P. Gerrard, N. Thompson, Risk-Based e-Business Testing, Artech House Publishers, 2002.

[44] M. Felderer, I. Schieferdecker, A taxonomy of risk-based testing, Int. J. Softw. Tools Technol. Transf. 16 (5) (2014) 559–568.

[45] M.-F. Wendland, M. Kranz, I. Schieferdecker, A systematic approach to risk-based testing using risk-annotated requirements models, in: The Seventh International Conference on Software Engineering Advances, ICSEA 2012, 2012, pp. 636–642.

[46] J. Grossmann, M. Schneider, J. Viehmann, M.-F. Wendland, Combining risk analysis and security testing, in: Leveraging Applications of Formal Methods, Verification and Validation. Specialized Techniques and Applications, Springer, 2014, pp. 322–336.

[47] J. Botella, B. Legeard, F. Peureux, A. Vernotte, Risk-based vulnerability testing using security test patterns, in: Leveraging Applications of Formal Methods, Verification and Validation. Specialized Techniques and Applications, Springer, 2014, pp. 337–352.

[48] P. Zech, M. Felderer, B. Katt, R. Breu, Security test generation by answer set programming, in: 2014 Eighth International Conference on Software Security and Reliability, IEEE, 2014, pp. 88–97.

[49] P. Zech, M. Felderer, R. Breu, Security risk analysis by logic programming, in: Risk Assessment and Risk-Driven Testing, Springer, 2014, pp. 38–48.

[50] M.P. Gallaher, B.M. Kropp, The economic impacts of inadequate infrastructure for software testing, Tech. Rep. Planning Report 02-03, National Institute of Standards & Technology 2002.

[51] B. Chess, J. West, Secure Programming with Static Analysis, first ed., Addison-Wesley Professional, Boston, MA, 2007, ISBN 9780321424778.

[52] A. Bessey, K. Block, B. Chelf, A. Chou, B. Fulton, S. Hallem, C. Henri-Gros, A. Kamsky, S. McPeak, D. Engler, A few billion lines of code later: using static analysis to find bugs in the real world, Commun. ACM 53 (2010) 66–75, ISSN 0001-0782.

[53] A.D. Brucker, U. Sodan, Deploying static application security testing on a large scale, in: S. Katzenbeisser, V. Lotz, E. Weippl (Eds.), GI Sicherheit 2014, Lecture Notes in Informatics, vol. 228, GI, ISBN 978-3-88579-622-0, 2014, pp. 91–101.

[54] N. Ayewah, D. Hovemeyer, J.D. Morgenthaler, J. Penix, W. Pugh, Experiences using static analysis to find bugs, IEEE Softw. 25 (2008) 22–29 (special issue on software development tools, September/October (25:5)).

[55] V.B. Livshits, M.S. Lam, Finding security errors in java programs with static analysis, in: Proceedings of the 14th Usenix Security Symposium, 2005, pp. 271–286.

[56] D. Evans, Static detection of dynamic memory errors, SIGPLAN Not. 31 (1996) 44–53, ISSN 0362-1340.

[57] B. Chess, G. McGraw, Static analysis for security, IEEE Secur. Priv. 2 (6) (2004) 76–79, ISSN 1540-7993.

[58] M. Pistoia, S. Chandra, S.J. Fink, E. Yahav, A survey of static analysis methods for identifying security vulnerabilities in software systems, IBM Syst. J. 46 (2) (2007) 265–288, ISSN 0018-8670.

[59] R. Scandariato, J. Walden, W. Joosen, Static analysis versus penetration testing: a controlled experiment, in: Proceedings of the 24th IEEE International Symposium on Software Reliability Engineering, IEEE, 2013, pp. 1–10.

[60] K. Scarfone, M. Souppaya, A. Cody, A. Orebaugh, Technical guide to information security testing and assessment, Special Publication 800-115, National Institute of Standards and Technology (NIST) 2008.

[61] A. Doupe, M. Cova, G. Vigna, Why Johnny can't pentest: an analysis of black-box Web vulnerability scanners, in: DIMVA 2010, 2010.

[62] M. Johns, Code injection vulnerabilities in web applications—Exemplified at cross-site scripting, Ph.D. thesis, University of Passau, 2009.

[63] W.G. Halfond, J. Viegas, A. Orso, A classification of SQL-injection attacks and countermeasures, in: Proceedings of the IEEE International Symposium on Secure Software Engineering, IEEE, 2006, pp. 65–81.

[64] J. Grossman, R. Hansen, P. Petkov, A. Rager, Cross Site Scripting Attacks: XSS Exploits and Defense, Syngress, 2007 (Seth Fogie).

[65] B.P. Miller, L. Fredriksen, B. So, An empirical study of the reliability of UNIX utilities, Commun. ACM 33 (12) (1990) 32–44, ISSN 0001-0782.

[66] S. Rawat, L. Mounier, Offset-aware mutation based fuzzing for buffer overflow vulnerabilities: few preliminary results, in: Fourth International IEEE Conference on Software Testing, Verification and Validation, ICST 2012, Berlin, Germany, 21-25 March, 2011 Workshop Proceedings, 2011, pp. 531–533.

[67] F. Duchene, S. Rawat, J. Richier, R. Groz, KameleonFuzz: evolutionary fuzzing for black-box XSS detection, in: Fourth ACM Conference on Data and Application Security and Privacy, CODASPY'14, San Antonio, TX, USA, March 03-05, 2014, 2014, pp. 37–48.

[68] D. Yang, Y. Zhang, Q. Liu, BlendFuzz: a model-based framework for fuzz testing programs with grammatical inputs, in: 11th IEEE International Conference on Trust, Security and Privacy in Computing and Communications, TrustCom 2012, Liverpool, United Kingdom, June 25-27, 2012, 2012, pp. 1070–1076.

[69] J. Zhao, Y. Wen, G. Zhao, H-Fuzzing: a new heuristic method for fuzzing data generation, in: Proceedings of the 8th IFIP International Conference Network and Parallel Computing NPC 2011, Changsha, China, October 21-23, 2011, 2011, pp. 32–43.

[70] P. Godefroid, M.Y. Levin, D.A. Molnar, Automated whitebox fuzz testing, in: Proceedings of the Network and Distributed System Security Symposium, NDSS 2008, San Diego, California, USA, 10th February-13th February 2008, The Internet Society, 2008.

[71] P. Godefroid, M.Y. Levin, D.A. Molnar, SAGE: whitebox fuzzing for security testing, Commun. ACM 55 (3) (2012) 40–44.

[72] S. Bekrar, C. Bekrar, R. Groz, L. Mounier, A taint based approach for smart fuzzing, in: 2012 IEEE Fifth International Conference on Software Testing, Verification and Validation, Montreal, QC, Canada, April 17-21, 2012, 2012, pp. 818–825.

[73] H.J. Abdelnur, R. State, O. Festor, Advanced fuzzing in the VoIP space, J. Comput. Virol. 6 (1) (2010) 57–64.

[74] M.M. Lehman, Software's future: managing evolution, IEEE Softw. 15 (1) (1998) 40–44.

[75] M. Felderer, B. Katt, P. Kalb, J. Jürjens, M. Ochoa, F. Paci, L.M.S. Tran, T.T. Tun, K. Yskout, R. Scandariato, F. Piessens, D. Vanoverberghe, E. Fourneret, M. Gander, B. Solhaug, R. Breu, Evolution of security engineering artifacts: a state of the art survey, Int. J. Secur. Softw. Eng. 5 (4) (2014) 48–97.

[76] M. Felderer, E. Fourneret, A systematic classification of security regression testing approaches, Int. J. Softw. Tools Technol. Transf. (2015) 1–15.

[77] H.K.N. Leung, L. White, Insights into regression testing (software testing), in: Proceedings Conference on Software Maintenance 1989, IEEE, 1989, pp. 60–69.

[78] S. Yoo, M. Harman, Regression testing minimisation, selection and prioritisation: a survey, Softw. Test. Verif. Reliab. 1 (1) (2010) 121–141.

[79] E. Fourneret, J. Cantenot, F. Bouquet, B. Legeard, J. Botella, SeTGaM: generalized technique for regression testing based on UML/OCL models, in: 2014 Eighth International Conference on Software Security and Reliability (SERE), 2014, pp. 147–156.

[80] G. Tóth, G. Kőszegi, Z. Hornák, Case study: automated security testing on the trusted computing platform, in: Proceedings of the 1st European Workshop on System Security, EUROSEC '08, Glasgow, Scotland, ACM, ISBN 978-1-60558-119-4, 2008, pp. 35–39.

[81] T. He, X. Jing, L. Kunmei, Z. Ying, Research on strong-association rule based web application vulnerability detection, in: 2nd IEEE International Conference on Computer Science and Information Technology, 2009, ICCSIT 2009, 2009, pp. 237–241.

[82] B.J. Garvin, M.B. Cohen, M.B. Dwyer, Using feature locality: can we leverage history to avoid failures during reconfiguration? in: Proceedings of the 8th Workshop on Assurances for Self-adaptive Systems, ASAS '11, Szeged, Hungary, ACM, ISBN 978-1-4503-0853-3, 2011, pp. 24–33.

[83] Y.-C. Huang, K.-L. Peng, C.-Y. Huang, A history-based cost-cognizant test case prioritization technique in regression testing, J. Syst. Softw. 85 (3) (2012) 626–637, ISSN 0164-1212, http://www.sciencedirect.com/science/article/pii/S0164121211002780 (novel approaches in the design and implementation of systems/software architecture).

[84] Y.T. Yu, M.F. Lau, Fault-based test suite prioritization for specification-based testing, Inf. Softw. Technol. 54 (2) (2012) 179–202, http://www.sciencedirect.com/science/article/pii/S0950584911001947.

[85] N. Viennot, S. Nair, J. Nieh, Transparent mutable replay for multicore debugging and patch validation, in: Proceedings of the Eighteenth International Conference on Architectural Support for Programming Languages and Operating Systems, ASPLOS '13, Houston, Texas, USA, ACM, 2013, pp. 127–138.

[86] M. Felderer, B. Agreiter, R. Breu, Evolution of security requirements tests for service-centric systems, in: Engineering Secure Software and Systems: Third International Symposium, ESSoS 2011, Springer, 2011, pp. 181–194.

[87] M. Kassab, O. Ormandjieva, M. Daneva, Relational-model based change management for non-functional requirements: approach and experiment, in: 2011 Fifth International Conference on Research Challenges in Information Science (RCIS), 2011, pp. 1–9.

[88] M. Anisetti, C.A. Ardagna, E. Damiani, A low-cost security certification scheme for evolving services, in: 2012 IEEE 19th International Conference on Web Services (ICWS), 2012, pp. 122–129.

[89] C. Huang, J. Sun, X. Wang, Y. Si, Selective regression test for access control system employing RBAC, in: J.H. Park, H.-H. Chen, M. Atiquzzaman, C. Lee, T.-h. Kim, S.-S. Yeo (Eds.), Advances in Information Security and Assurance, Lecture Notes in Computer Science, vol. 5576, Springer, Berlin, ISBN 978-3-642-02616-4, 2009, pp. 70–79.

[90] J. Hwang, T. Xie, D. El Kateb, T. Mouelhi, Y. Le Traon, Selection of regression system tests for security policy evolution, in: Proceedings of the 27th IEEE/ACM International Conference on Automated Software Engineering, ACM, 2012, pp. 266–269.

[91] M. Vetterling, G. Wimmel, A. Wisspeintner, Secure systems development based on the common criteria: the PalME project, in: Proceedings of the 10th ACM SIGSOFT Symposium on Foundations of Software Engineering, SIGSOFT '02/FSE-10, Charleston, South Carolina, USA, ACM, 2002, pp. 129–138.

[92] M. Bruno, G. Canfora, M. Penta, G. Esposito, V. Mazza, Using test cases as contract to ensure service compliance across releases, in: B. Benatallah, F. Casati, P. Traverso (Eds.), Service-Oriented Computing—ICSOC 2005, Lecture Notes in Computer Science, vol. 3826, Springer, Berlin, ISBN 978-3-540-30817-1, 2005, pp. 87–100.

[93] V. Kongsli, Towards agile security in web applications, in: Companion to the 21st ACM SIGPLAN Symposium on Object-Oriented Programming Systems, Languages, and Applications, OOPSLA '06, Portland, Oregon, USA, ACM, New York, NY, ISBN 1-59593-491-X, 2006, pp. 805–808.

[94] D. Qi, A. Roychoudhury, Z. Liang, K. Vaswani, DARWIN: an approach to debugging evolving programs, ACM Trans. Softw. Eng. Methodol. 21 (3) (2012) 19:1–19:29.

[95] ISO/IEC, ISO/IEC 15408-1:2009 information technology—security techniques—evaluation criteria for IT security—part 1: introduction and general model, 2009.

[96] N. Bjørner, K. Jayaraman, Checking cloud contracts in Microsoft Azure, in: Proceedings of the 11th International Conference Distributed Computing and Internet Technology ICDCIT 2015, Bhubaneswar, India, February 5-8, 2015, 2015, pp. 21–32.

[97] A.D. Brucker, L. Brügger, B. Wolff, Formal Firewall Conformance Testing: An Application of Test and Proof Techniques, Softw. Test. Verif. Reliab. 25 (1) (2015) 34–71.

[98] Y.-W. Huang, F. Yu, C. Hang, C.-H. Tsai, D.-T. Lee, S.-Y. Kuo, Securing web application code by static analysis and runtime protection, in: International Conference on the World Wide Web (WWW), WWW '04, New York, NY, USA, ACM, New York, NY, ISBN 1-58113-844-X, 2004, pp. 40–52.

[99] J.S. Foster, M. Fähndrich, A. Aiken, A theory of type qualifiers, SIGPLAN Not. 34 (5) (1999).

[100] J.S. Foster, T. Terauchi, A. Aiken, Flow-sensitive type qualifiers, SIGPLAN Not. 37 (5) (2002).

[101] N. Jovanovic, C. Kruegel, E. Kirda, Pixy: a static analysis tool for detecting web application vulnerabilities (short paper), in: IEEE Symposium on Security and Privacy, SP '06, IEEE Computer Society, Washington, DC, ISBN 0-7695-2574-1, 2006, pp. 258–263.

[102] N. Jovanovic, C. Kruegel, E. Kirda, Precise alias analysis for static detection of web application vulnerabilities, in: Workshop on Programming languages and analysis for security, PLAS '06, Ottawa, Ontario, Canada, ACM, New York, NY, ISBN 1-59593-374-3, 2006, pp. 27–36.

[103] Y. Xie, A. Aiken, Static detection of security vulnerabilities in scripting languages, in: USENIX Security Symposium, vol. 15, 2006, pp. 179–192.

[104] J. Dahse, T. Holz, Static detection of second-order vulnerabilities in web applications, in: Proceedings of the 23rd USENIX Security Symposium, 2014.

[105] J. Dahse, T. Holz, Simulation of built-in PHP features for precise static code analysis, in: ISOC-NDSS, 2014.

[106] G. Wassermann, Z. Su, Static detection of cross-site scripting vulnerabilities, in: ICSE '08, Leipzig, Germany, ACM, New York, NY, ISBN 978-1-60558-079-1, 2008, pp. 171–180.

[107] Y. Minamide, Static approximation of dynamically generated web pages, in: International Conference on the World Wide Web (WWW), 2005.

[108] P. Saxena, D. Akhawe, S. Hanna, F. Mao, S. McCamant, D. Song, A symbolic execution framework for javaScript, in: IEEE Symposium on Security and Privacy, SP '10, IEEE Computer Society, Washington, DC, ISBN 978-0-7695-4035-1, 2010, pp. 513–528.

[109] X. Jin, X. Hu, K. Ying, W. Du, H. Yin, G.N. Peri, Code injection attacks on HTML5-based mobile apps: characterization, detection and mitigation, in: 21st ACM Conference on Computer and Communications Security (CCS), 2014.

[110] X. Fu, X. Lu, B. Peltsverger, S. Chen, K. Qian, L. Tao, A static analysis framework for detecting SQL injection vulnerabilities, in: 31st Annual International Computer Software and Applications Conference, 2007, COMPSAC 2007, vol. 1, IEEE, 2007, pp. 87–96.

[111] G. Wassermann, Z. Su, Sound and precise analysis of web applications for injection vulnerabilities, in: Proceedings of Programming Language Design and Implementation (PLDI'07), San Diego, CA, 2007.

[112] W.G.J. Halfond, A. Orso, P. Manolios, Using positive tainting and syntax-aware evaluation to counter SQL injection attacks, in: Proceedings of the 14th ACM SIGSOFT International Symposium on Foundations of Software Engineering, ACM, 2006, pp. 175–185.

[113] S. Kals, E. Kirda, C. Kruegel, N. Jovanovic, SecuBat: a web vulnerability scanner, in: International Conference on the World Wide Web (WWW), WWW '06, Edinburgh, Scotland, ACM, New York, NY, ISBN 1-59593-323-9, 2006, pp. 247–256.

[114] F. d'Amore, M. Gentile, Automatic and context-aware cross-site scripting filter evasion, Department of Computer, Control, and Management Engineering Antonio Ruberti Technical Reports 2012.

[115] S.V. Acker, N. Nikiforakis, L. Desmet, W. Joosen, F. Piessens, FlashOver: automated discovery of cross-site scripting vulnerabilities in rich internet applications, in: ASIACCS, 2012.

[116] L. Wall, T. Christiansen, J. Orwant, Programming Perl, third ed., O'Reilly, Sebastopol, CA, 2000.

[117] E.J. Schwartz, T. Avgerinos, D. Brumley, All you ever wanted to know about dynamic taint analysis and forward symbolic execution (but might have been afraid to ask), in: IEEE Symposium on Security and Privacy, 2010.

[118] A. Nguyen-Tuong, S. Guarnieri, D. Greene, J. Shirley, D. Evans, Automatically hardening web applications using precise tainting, in: 20th IFIP International Information Security Conference, 2005.

[119] T. Pietraszek, C.V. Berghe, Defending against injection attacks through context-sensitive string evaluation, in: Recent Advances in Intrusion Detection (RAID2005), 2005.

[120] Z. Su, G. Wassermann, The essence of command injection attacks in web applications, in: Proceedings of POPL'06, 2006.

[121] M. Martin, M.S. Lam, Automatic generation of XSS and SQL injection attacks with goal-directed model checking, in: USENIX Security Symposium, SEC'08, San Jose, CA, USENIX Association, Berkeley, CA, 2008, pp. 31–43.

[122] A. Kieyzun, P.J. Guo, K. Jayaraman, M.D. Ernst, Automatic creation of SQL injection and cross-site scripting attacks, in: ICSE '09, IEEE Computer Society, Washington, DC, ISBN 978-1-4244-3453-4, 2009, pp. 199–209.

[123] A. Klein, DOM Based Cross Site Scripting or XSS of the Third Kind, 2005, http://www.webappsec.org/projects/articles/071105.shtml.

[124] S. Lekies, B. Stock, M. Johns, 25 million flows later-large-scale detection of DOM-based XSS, in: ACM Conference on Computer and Communications Security (CCS), 2013.

[125] P. Saxena, S. Hanna, P. Poosankam, D. Song, FLAX: systematic discovery of client-side validation vulnerabilities in rich web applications, in: ISOC-NDSS, The Internet Society, 2010.

[126] G. McGraw, Software Security: Building Security In, Addison-Wesley Professional, 2006, ISBN 0321356705.

[127] O. Tripp, M. Pistoia, S.J. Fink, M. Sridharan, O. Weisman, TAJ: effective taint analysis of web applications, SIGPLAN Not. 44 (2009) 87–97, ISSN 0362-1340.

[128] B. Monate, J. Signoles, Slicing for security of code, in: TRUST, 2008, pp. 133–142.

[129] WALA, T. J. Watson Libraries for Analysis, http://wala.sf.net.

[130] L. Hubert, N. Barré, F. Besson, D. Demange, T.P. Jensen, V. Monfort, D. Pichardie, T. Turpin, Sawja: static analysis workshop for Java, in: FoVeOOS, 2010, pp. 92–106.

[131] I. Haller, A. Slowinska, M. Neugschwandtner, H. Bos, Dowsing for overflows: a guided fuzzer to find buffer boundary violations, in: Proceedings of the 22nd USENIX Conference on Security, SEC'13, Washington, DC, USENIX Association, Berkeley, CA, ISBN 978-1-931971-03-4, 2013, pp. 49–64.

[132] S.B. Mazzone, M. Pagnozzi, A. Fattori, A. Reina, A. Lanzi, D. Bruschi, Improving Mac OS X security through gray box fuzzing technique, in: Proceedings of the Seventh European Workshop on System Security, EuroSec '14, Amsterdam, The Netherlands, ACM, New York, NY, ISBN 978-1-4503-2715-2, 2014, pp. 2:1–2:6.

[133] M. Woo, S.K. Cha, S. Gottlieb, D. Brumley, Scheduling black-box mutational fuzzing, in: Proceedings of the 2013 ACM SIGSAC Conference on Computer & Communications Security, CCS '13, Berlin, Germany, ACM, New York, NY, ISBN 978-1-4503-2477-9, 2013, pp. 511–522.

[134] A. Lanzi, L. Martignoni, M. Monga, R. Paleari, A smart fuzzer for x86 executables, in: Third International Workshop on Software Engineering for Secure Systems, 2007, SESS '07: ICSE Workshops 2007, 2007, pp. 7–7.

[135] G. Buehrer, B.W. Weide, P.A.G. Sivilotti, Using parse tree validation to prevent SQL injection attacks, in: Proceedings of the 5th International Workshop on Software Engineering and Middleware, SEM '05, Lisbon, Portugal, ACM, New York, NY, ISBN 1-59593-205-4, 2005, pp. 106–113.

[136] D. Appelt, C.D. Nguyen, L.C. Briand, N. Alshahwan, Automated testing for SQL injection vulnerabilities: an input mutation approach, in: Proceedings of the 2014 International Symposium on Software Testing and Analysis, ISSTA 2014, San Jose, CA, USA, ACM, New York, NY, ISBN 978-1-4503-2645-2, 2014, pp. 259–269.

[137] J. Wang, P. Zhang, L. Zhang, H. Zhu, X. Ye, A model-based fuzzing approach for DBMS, in: 2013 8th International Conference on Communications and Networking in China (CHINACOM), IEEE Computer Society, Los Alamitos, CA, 2013, pp. 426–431.

[138] R. Garcia, Case study: experiences on SQL language fuzz testing, in: Proceedings of the Second International Workshop on Testing Database Systems, DBTest '09, Providence, Rhode Island, ACM, New York, NY, ISBN 978-1-60558-706-6, 2009, pp. 3:1–3:6.

[139] C. Brubaker, S. Jana, B. Ray, S. Khurshid, V. Shmatikov, Using frankencerts for automated adversarial testing of certificate validation in SSL/TLS implementations, in: Proceedings of the 2014 IEEE Symposium on Security and Privacy, SP '14, IEEE Computer Society, Washington, DC, ISBN 978-1-4799-4686-0, 2014, pp. 114–129.

[140] G.Banks, M. Cova, V. Felmetsger, K.C. Almeroth, R.A. Kemmerer, G. Vigna, SNOOZE: toward a stateful netwOrk prOtocol fuzZEr, in: Proceedings of the 9th International Conference Information Security ISC 2006, Samos Island, Greece, August 30-September 2, 2006, 2006, pp. 343–358.

[141] P. Tsankov, M.T. Dashti, D.A. Basin, SECFUZZ: fuzz-testing security protocols, in: 7th International Workshop on Automation of Software Test, AST 2012, Zurich, Switzerland, June 2-3, 2012, 2012, pp. 1–7.

[142] A. Bertolino, Y.L. Traon, F. Lonetti, E. Marchetti, T. Mouelhi, Coverage-based test cases selection for XACML policies, in: 2014 IEEE Seventh International Conference on Software Testing, Verification and Validation, Workshops Proceedings, March 31 - April 4, 2014, Cleveland, Ohio, USA, 2014, pp. 12–21.

[143] A.D. Brucker, L. Brügger, P. Kearney, B. Wolff, An approach to modular and testable security models of real-world health-care applications, in: ACM symposium on Access Control Models and Technologies (SACMAT), Innsbruck, Austria, ACM Press, New York, NY, ISBN 978-1-4503-0688-1, 2011, pp. 133–142.

[144] E. Martin, Testing and analysis of access control policies, in: 29th International Conference on Software Engineering—Companion, 2007, ICSE 2007, 2007, pp. 75–76.

[145] R. Rogers, R. Rogers, Nessus Network Auditing, second ed., Syngress Publishing, Burlington, MA, 2008, ISBN 9780080558653, 9781597492089.

ABOUT THE AUTHORS

Michael Felderer is a senior researcher and project manager within the Quality Engineering research group at the Institute of Computer Science at the University of Innsbruck, Austria. He holds a Ph.D. and a habilitation in computer science. His research interests include software and security testing, empirical software and security engineering, model engineering, risk management, software processes, and industry-academia collaboration. Michael Felderer has coauthored more than 70 journal, conference, and workshop papers. He works in close cooperation with industry and also transfers his research results into practice as a consultant and speaker on industrial conferences.

Matthias Büchler is a Ph.D. student at the Technische Universität München. He holds a master's degree in computer science (Information Security) from the Swiss Federal Institute of Technology Zurich (ETHZ). His research interests include information security, security modeling, security engineering, security testing, domain specific languages, and usage control.

Martin Johns is a research expert in the Product Security Research unit within SAP SE, where he leads the Web application security team. Furthermore, he serves on the board of the German OWASP chapter. Before joining SAP, Martin studied Mathematics and Computer Science at the Universities of Hamburg, Santa Cruz (CA), and Passau. During the 1990s and the early years of the new millennium he earned his living as a software engineer in German companies (including Infoseek Germany, and TC Trustcenter). He holds a Diploma in Computer Science from University of Hamburg and a Doctorate from the University of Passau.

Achim D. Brucker is a research expert (architect), security testing strategist, and project lead in the Security Enablement Team of SAP SE. He received his master's degree in computer science from University Freiburg, Germany and his Ph.D. from ETH Zurich, Switzerland. He is responsible for the Security Testing Strategy at SAP. His research interests include information security, software engineering, security engineering, and formal methods. In particular, he is interested in tools and methods for modeling, building, and validating secure and reliable systems. He also participates in the OCL standardization process of the OMG.

Ruth Breu is head of the Institute of Computer Science at the University of Innsbruck, leading the research group Quality Engineering and the competence center QE LaB. She has longstanding experience in the areas of security engineering, requirements engineering, enterprise architecture management and model engineering, both with academic and industrial background. Ruth is coauthor of three monographs and more than 150 scientific publications and serves the scientific community in a variety of functions (eg Board Member of FWF, the Austrian Science Fund, Member of the NIS Platform of the European Commission).

Alexander Pretschner holds the chair of Software Engineering at Technische Universität München. Research interests include software quality, testing, and information security. Master's degrees in computer science from RWTH Aachen and the University of Kansas and Ph.D. degree from Technische Universität München. Prior appointments include a full professorship at Karlsruhe Institute of Technology, an adjunct associate professorship at Kaiserslautern University of Technology, a group manager's position at the Fraunhofer Institute of Experimental Software Engineering in Kaiserslautern, a senior scientist's position at ETH Zurich, and visiting professorships at the Universities of Rennes, Trento, and Innsbruck.

> CHAPTER TWO

Recent Advances in Model-Based Testing

Mark Utting*, Bruno Legeard[†,‡], Fabrice Bouquet[†],
Elizabeta Fourneret[†], Fabien Peureux[†,‡], Alexandre Vernotte[†]
*University of the Sunshine Coast, QLD, Australia
[†]Institut FEMTO-ST, UMR CNRS 6174, Besançon, France
[‡]Smartesting Solutions & Services, Besançon, France

Contents

Advances in Computers, Volume 101
ISSN 0065-2458
http://dx.doi.org/10.1016/bs.adcom.2015.11.004

Abstract

This chapter gives an overview of the field of model-based testing (MBT), particularly the recent advances in the last decade. It gives a summary of the MBT process, the modeling languages that are currently used by the various communities who practice MBT, the technologies used to generate tests from models, and discusses best practices, such as traceability between models and tests. It also briefly describes several findings from a recent survey of MBT users in industry, outlines the increasingly popular use of MBT for security testing, and discusses future challenges for MBT.

1. INTRODUCTION

Broadly speaking, model-based testing (MBT) is about designing tests from some kind of *model* of the system being tested and its environment. In this sense, all test design is based on some mental model, so could perhaps be called model-based testing. But it is common, and more useful, to use the term *model-based testing* to refer to:

- more formal models (expressed in some machine-readable, well-defined, notation);
- more formal test generation (we are interested in test generation algorithms that are automatic, or are capable of being automated);
- and more automated execution (the generated tests must be sufficient precise that they are capable of being executed automatically).

Testing is an important, but painful and costly, part of the software development lifecycle. So the promise, or hope, of MBT is that if we can only obtain a model from somewhere (preferably at zero cost), then all those tests will be able to be generated automatically, and executed automatically, in order to find all the faults in the system, at greatly reduced cost and effort.

That is obviously a silver bullet, a dream that cannot be true. The truth about MBT lies somewhere between that dream, and the other extreme: a pessimistic dismissal that it could be of no help whatsoever. This chapter aims to shine some light on the current reality of MBT, the range of practices, the use of MBT in industry, some of the recent MBT research and tool advances that have happened in the last decade, and new application areas where MBT is being applied.

We first set the scene with an overview of MBT: the process, the people, the range of MBT practices, and a brief history. Then in Section 3 we discuss current usage of MBT, particularly in industry, in Section 4 we discuss recent advances in the languages used for the test models, in Section 5 we review recent advances in the test generation technologies, in Section 6 we discuss the use of MBT for security testing, which is a recent growth area in the use of MBT, and finally we conclude and discuss future challenges for MBT.

2. MBT OVERVIEW

MBT refers to the process and techniques for the automatic derivation of test cases from models, the generation of executable scripts, and the manual or automated execution of the resulting test cases or test scripts.

Therefore, the key tenets of MBT are the modeling principles for test generation, the reusability of requirements models, the test selection criteria, the test generation strategies and techniques, and the transformation of abstract tests into concrete executable tests.

The essence of MBT is to bridge the domain and product knowledge gap between the business analysts and test engineers. Models are expected to be true representations of business requirements and to associate those requirements with the different states that the product will take as it receives various inputs. Ideally, the models will cover all of the business requirements and will be sufficiently complete to thus ensure near 100% functional coverage.

2.1 MBT Process

Fig. 1 shows a typical MBT process, which starts from the requirements phase, goes through modeling for test generation, and ends in test management and test automation. The main four stages of this process are: (1) designing models for test generation; (2) selecting test generation criteria; (3) generating the tests; and then (4) executing the tests, either manually or automatically. We briefly discuss each of these stages. Table 1 shows some common MBT terminology.

1. *Designing models for test generation.* The models, generally called MBT models, represent the expected behavior and some process workflow of the system under test (SUT), in the context of its environment, at a given abstraction level. The purpose of modeling for test generation is to make explicit the control and observation points of the system, the expected dynamic behavior or workflows to be tested, the equivalence classes of system states, and the logical test data. The model elements and the requirements can be linked in order to ensure bidirectional traceability between the three main artifacts: the requirements, the MBT model, and the generated test cases. MBT models must

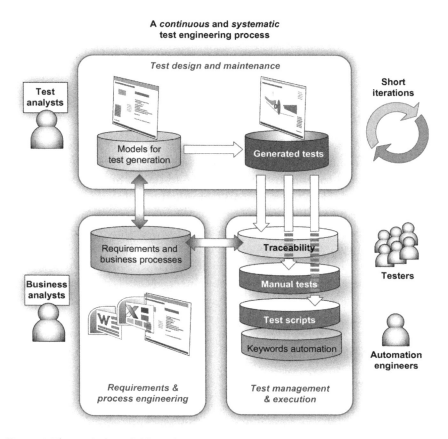

Figure 1 The typical model-based testing process.

be precise and complete enough to allow the automated derivation of tests from these models.

2. *Selecting some test selection criteria.* There are usually an infinite number of possible tests that can be generated from an MBT model, so the test analyst has to apply some test selection criteria to select the pertinent tests, or to ensure satisfactory coverage of the system behaviors. One common kind of test generation criteria is based on structural model coverage, using well-known test design strategies [1], for instance equivalence partitioning, process cycle coverage or pairwise testing. Another useful kind of test strategy ensures that the generated test cases cover all the requirements and business processes, possibly with more tests generated for requirements and processes that have a higher level of risk. In this

Table 1 Terminology Glossary of Model-Based Testing Terms Following ISTQB
Software Resting Glossary of Rerms v3.0

Term	Definition
MBT model	Any model used in model-based testing.
Model coverage	The degree, expressed as a percentage, to which model elements are planned to be or have been exercised by a test suite.
Offline MBT	Model-based testing approach whereby test cases are generated into a repository for future execution.
Online MBT	Model-based testing approach whereby test cases are generated and executed simultaneously.
Model-based testing	Testing based on or involving models.
Test adaption layer	The layer in a test automation architecture that provides the necessary code to adapt test scripts on an abstract level to the various components, configuration or interfaces of the SUT.
Test model	A model describing testware that is used for testing a component or a system under test.
Test selection criteria	The criteria used to guide the generation of test cases or to select test cases in order to limit the size of a test.

way, MBT can be used to implement a risk and requirements-based testing approach. For example, for a noncritical application, the test analyst may choose to generate just one test for each of the nominal behaviors in the model and each of the main error cases; but for the more critical requirements, the test analyst could apply more demanding coverage criteria such as process cycle testing, to ensure that the businesses processes associated with that part of the MBT models are more thoroughly tested.

3. *Generating the tests.* This is a fully automated process that generates the required number of test cases from the MBT models on the basis of the test selection criteria configured by the test analyst. Each generated test case is typically a sequence of SUT actions, with input parameters and expected output values for each action. These generated test sequences are similar to the test sequences that would be designed manually using an action-word approach [2]. They are easily understood by humans and are complete enough to be directly executed on the SUT by a manual tester. The purpose of automated test generation is to generate

fully complete and executable tests: MBT models should make it possible to compute the input parameters and the expected results. Data tables may be used to link abstract values from the model with concrete test values. To make the generated tests executable, a further phase automatically translates each abstract test case into a concrete (executable) script, using a user-defined mapping from abstract data values to concrete SUT values, and a mapping from abstract operations to GUI actions or API calls of the SUT. For example, if the test execution is via the GUI of the SUT, then the action words could be linked to the graphical object map using a test robot. If the test execution of the SUT is API based, then the action words need to be implemented on this API. This could be a direct mapping or a more complex automation layer. The expected results for each abstract test case are translated into oracle code that will check the SUT outputs and decide on a test pass/fail verdict. The tests generated from MBT models may be structured into multiple test suites, and published into standard test management tools. Maintenance of the test repository is done by updating the MBT models, then automatically regenerating and republishing the test suites into the test management tool.

4. *Executing manually or automatically the tests.* The generated tests can be executed either manually or in an automated test execution environment. Either way, the result is that the tests are executed on the SUT, and that tests either pass or fail. The failed tests indicate disparity between the actual SUT results and the expected ones, as designed in the MBT models, which then need to be investigated to decide whether the failure is caused by a bug in the SUT, or by an error in the model and/or the requirements. Experience shows that MBT is good at finding SUT errors, but is also highly effective at exposing requirements errors [3, 4], even before executing a single test (thanks to the modeling phase). In the case of automated test execution, test cases can be executed either offline, most commonly used, or online. With offline execution, the test cases are first generated, and then in a second step, they are executed on the system under test. With online execution, the test execution results influence the path taken by the test generator through the model, so test case generation and execution are combined into one step.

This process is highly incremental and helps to manage test case life cycle when the requirements change. MBT generators are able to manage the evolution of the test repository with respect to the change in the requirements that have been propagated to the test generation model.

2.2 Test Repository and Test Management Tools

The purpose of generating tests from MBT models is to produce the test repository (see Fig. 2). This test repository is typically managed by a test management tool. The goal of such a tool is to help in the organizing and executing of test suites (groups of test cases), both for manual and automated test execution.

In the MBT process, the test repository documentation is fully managed by the automated generation (from MBT models): documentation of the test design steps, requirements traceability links, test scripts and associated documentation are automatically provided for each test case. Therefore, the maintenance of the test repository is done only through the maintenance of MBT models and then regeneration from these models.

2.3 Requirements Traceability

A key element of the added value of MBT is the automation of bidirectional traceability between requirements and test cases. Bidirectional traceability is the ability to determine links between two parts of the software development process. The starting point of the MBT process is the various functional descriptions of the tested application, such as use cases, functional requirements, and descriptions of business processes. To be effective, requirements traceability implies that the requirements repository is structured enough so

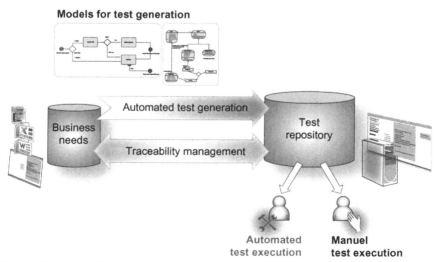

Figure 2 Relationship between requirements and test repositories.

that each individual requirement can be uniquely identified. It is desirable to link these requirements to the generated tests, and to link each generated test to the requirements that it tests.

A best practice in MBT, provided by most of the tools on the market, is to link the model elements to the related test requirements. These links in the MBT models enable the automatic generation and maintenance of a traceability matrix between requirements and test cases.

2.4 Actors and Roles in the MBT Process

The MBT process involves four main roles (see Fig. 3).

1. *Business analysts* (or *subject matter experts*) are the reference persons for the SUT requirements, business processes and business needs. They refine the specification and clarify the testing needs based on their collaboration with the test analysts. In agile environments, they contribute in definition and discussion of user stories and attend sprint meetings to make sure that the evolving user stories are properly developed in the models. Their domain knowledge and experience allow them to easily understand dependencies between different modules and their impact on the MBT models and to provide useful input to test analysts during reviews of MBT models.

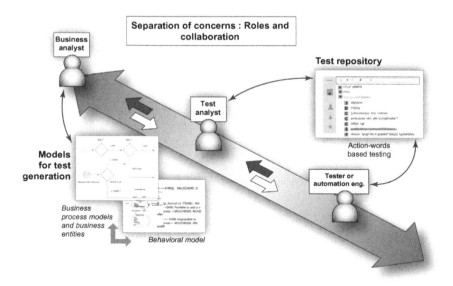

Figure 3 Main roles in the model-based testing process.

2. *Test analysts* design the MBT models, based on interaction with customers and business analysts or subject matter experts. They use the test generation tool to automatically generate tests that satisfy the test objectives and produce a repository of tests. Test analysts are also in charge of reviewing the manual test cases generated through models and validating the correctness and coverage of the tests.

3. *Test engineers* (or testers) are in charge of manual execution of tests, relying on the available information in the test repository, which is generated by the test analysts based on MBT models.

4. *Test automation engineers* are in charge of the automated execution of tests, by linking the generated tests to the system under test. The input for the test automation engineers is the specification of the adaptation layer and action words, defined in the test generation model and to be implemented. This is delivered by the test analysts.

Test analysts are in charge of the test repository quality, which concerns the requirements coverage and the detection of defects. On the one hand, they interact with the subject matter experts, which makes the quality of their interaction crucial. On the other hand, the test analysts interact with the testers in order to facilitate manual test execution or with the test automation engineers to facilitate automated test execution (implementation of keywords). This interaction process is highly iterative.

2.5 Characteristics of MBT Approaches

This section is adapted from the Utting, Pretschner, and Legeard paper on a taxonomy of MBT approaches [5]. Generally speaking, taxonomies in software engineering help clarify the key issues of a field and show the possible alternatives and directions. They can be used to classify tools and to help users to see which approaches and tools fit their specific needs more closely. It is exactly what we are doing here: we are proposing seven different characteristics that describe key aspects of MBT. These characteristics follow the main phases of the MBT process (modeling, test generation, test execution). They are defined by concepts that are largely, but not entirely, independent of each other: for instance, if a project is concerned with combinatorial testing of business rules managed by a business rules management system, this is likely to limit its choice of modeling paradigm. If the target is GUI testing of a web application, test selection criteria will likely be linked with the coverage of the GUI operations.

Fig. 4 gives an overview of seven characteristics of MBT approaches.

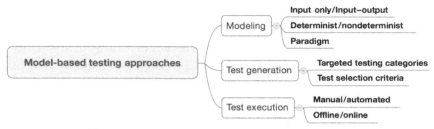

Figure 4 A simplified taxonomy of model-based testing.

Table 2 Input–Output Models Characteristics

Characteristic	Attributes
Model: Input only or input–output	Input only
	Input–output

2.5.1 Modeling: Input only or Input–Output

The first characteristic is the type of models used for test generation, which can be reduced to a binary decision: do the models specify only the inputs to the SUT, or do they specify the expected input–output behavior of the SUT? (Table 2).

The input-only models have the disadvantage that the generated tests will not be able to act as an oracle and are incapable of verifying the correctness of the SUT functional behavior. Input models can be seen as models of the environment. Pure business process models that represent some user workflows (but not the expected behavior) are a prominent example; Domain modeling with combinatorial algorithms such as pairwise, is another one. Generated tests from input-only models are incomplete and must be manually completed before execution.

Input–output models of the SUT not only model the allowable inputs that can be sent to the SUT, but must also capture some of the intended behavior of the SUT. That is, the model must be able to predict in advance the expected outputs of the SUT for each input, or at least be able to check whether an output produced by the SUT is allowed by the model or not. Input–output models make it possible to automatically generate complete tests, including input parameters and expected results for each step.

2.5.2 Modeling: Deterministic or Nondeterministic

This characteristic relates to the determinism vs nondeterminism nature of the model, and how it is supported by the test generation process (Table 3).

Table 3 Determinist/Nondeterminist Models Characteristics

Characteristic	Attributes
Model: Determinist or nondeterminist	Determinist
	Nondeterminist

Nondeterminism can occur in the model and/or the SUT. If the SUT exhibits hazards in the time or value domains, this can often be handled when the verdict is built (which might be possible only after all input has been applied). If the SUT exhibits genuine nondeterminism, as a consequence of concurrency, for instance, then it is possible that test stimuli as provided by the model depend on prior reactions of the SUT. In these cases, the nondeterminism must be catered for in the model, and also in the test cases (they are not sequences anymore, but rather trees or graphs).

2.5.3 Modeling: Paradigm

The third characteristic is what paradigm and notation are used to describe the model (Table 4). There are many different modeling notations that have been used for modeling the behavior of systems for test generation purposes. We retain here only the modeling paradigm used in the domain of enterprise software (see the excellent book of Paul C. Jorgensen entitled "*Modeling software behavior—A Craftman's Approach*" to learn more of these notations [6]:

- *Activity-Based Notations* such as Flowcharts, BPMN, or UML activity diagrams that allow defining sequences of actions and decisions describing a flow.
- *State-Based (or Pre/Post) Notations.* These model a system as a collection of variables, which represent a snapshot of the state of the system, plus some operations that modify those variables.
- *Transition-Based Notations.* These focus on describing the transitions between different states of the system. Typically, they are graphical node-and-arc notations, like finite state machines (FSMs), where the nodes of the FSM represent the major states of the system and the arcs represent the actions or operations of the system. Examples of transition-based notations used for MBT include UML State Machines and labeled transition systems.
- *Decision Tables.* They are used to describe logical relationships, and are a good tool to represent business rules in models for test generation.
- *Stochastic Notations.* These describe a system by a probabilistic model of the events and input values and tend to be used to model environments

Table 4 Modeling Paradigm Characteristics

Characteristic	Attributes
Modeling Paradigm	Activity-based notations
	State-based (or pre/post) notations
	Transition-based notations
	Decision tables
	Stochastic notations

rather than SUTs. For example, statistical modeling, eg, Markov chains is used to model expected usage profiles, so that the generated tests exercise that usage profile.

In practice, several paradigms can be represented in one single notation. For example, the UML notation offers both a transition-based paradigm, with state machine diagrams, and a pre–post paradigm, with the OCL language. The two paradigms can be used at the same time in MBT models and can be composed with business process models in BPMN. This helps to express both the dynamic behavior and some business rules on discrete data types, as well as interesting business scenarios.

2.5.4 Test Generation: Targeted Testing Categories

MBT may address several categories of testing with respect to the software development lifecycle (testing levels), linked to the type of testing activity and also linked to the accessibility and mode of the SUT. Table 5 gives the various subcharacteristics and attributes of this dimension.

2.5.5 Test generation: Test Selection Criteria

As shown in Fig. 5, test cases are automatically generated from the MBT model and from test selection criteria. In practice, the models alone are not sufficient to generate tests because thousands of sequences (and therefore test cases) may be generated by walking through the model. Test selection criteria are defined by the test analyst to guide the automatic test generation so that it produces a good test suite one that fulfills the project test objectives defined for the SUT. The definition of test selection criteria, for a testing project, depends on the project test objectives and on analyzing the risks associated with the software in a Risk-and-Requirements-Based Testing approach.

Table 5 Testing Categories Characteristics

Characteristic	Subcharacteristic	Attributes
Targeted testing categories	Testing levels	Acceptance testing
		System testing
		Integration testing
	Testing types	Risk and requirements based testing
		End-to-end testing
		Regression testing
		Combinatorial testing
	Accessibility modes	GUI-based testing
		API-based testing
		Batch application testing

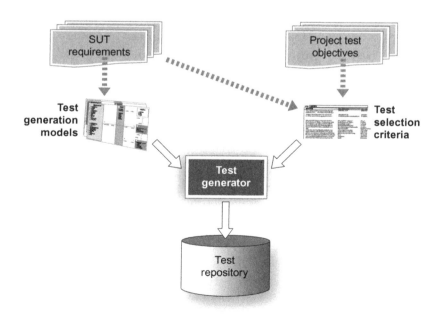

Figure 5 Test selection criteria.

Table 6 Test Selection Criteria Characteristics

Characteristic	Subcharacteristic	Attributes	Example
Test selection criteria	Coverage-based selection criteria	Control flow coverage	Transition-pair coverage
		Data flow coverage	All-uses Coverage
		Decision coverage	Condition/decision coverage
		Data coverage	Boundary values
	Scenario-based selection criteria	Language to express scenarios	UML sequence diagrams

There are two main subcharacteristics to consider, which defines two different families of test selection criteria (Table 6):

• Coverage-based selection criteria This refers to a form of structural coverage on the model elements to achieve the targeted test objectives. For example, if requirements are linked to transitions in UML state machines, then a test selection criterion may be to cover all the transitions linked to a given set of requirements. Thus, requirements coverage is achieved by a structural coverage of transitions of the models.

• Scenario-based selection criteria—Explicit test case specifications where test cases are generated from descriptions of abstract scenarios can obviously be used to control test generation. In addition to the model, the test analyst writes a test case specification in some formal notation, and this is used to determine which tests will be generated.

The difference between the two approaches is that for the first one the definition of the test selection criterion is mainly done by specifying a level of coverage of the elements of the test generation model. This is a great advantage in terms of resilience of the test selection criteria with respect to model changes. The second kind of test selection criteria is more precise because each scenario can be explicitly defined, but, because the definition is done scenario by scenario, scenario-based selection criteria are more fragile with respect to model evolution.

These two kinds of test selection criteria are further refined by more precise attributes, particularly coverage-based selection criteria, which refer to a large set of coverage criteria such as transition-based coverage, data-flow coverage, decision coverage and data coverage. For the scenario-based selection criteria, the attribute is the language to express scenarios. An example of such a language is UML sequence diagrams.

2.5.6 Test Execution: Manual or Automated

The generated test cases may be executed manually or automatically (Table 7). Manual test execution consists of a human tester executing the generated test cases by interacting with the SUT, following the instructions in the test case (documented steps). Automated test execution consists of translating the generated test cases into executable test scripts of some form. For instance, if each generated test case is just a sequence of keywords, it could be executed manually by the testers, or a test automation engineer could write an adaptation layer (program or a library) that automatically reads those keywords and executes them on the system under test. Automatic execution typically requires more work, to develop the adaptation layer, but some of this overhead can be reduced if the adaptor code is reused all along the testing life cycle, for instance for many different tests or for several different versions of the generated tests.

In the case of automated generation of manual test cases, this means that the models for test generation should include one way or another the documentation of abstract operations and attributes. Then, the test generator has to manage the propagation and adaptation of this information in the generated tests.

2.5.7 Test Execution: Offline or Online

The last characteristic deals with test execution and the relative timing of test case generation and test execution: offline MBT or online MBT (Table 8).

With online MBT, the test generation algorithms can react to the actual outputs of the SUT. This is sometimes necessary if the SUT is non-deterministic, so that the test generator can see which path the SUT has

Table 7 Test Execution—Manual/Automated Characteristics

Characteristic	Attributes
Test execution: Manual or automated	Manual testing
	Automated testing

Table 8 Test Execution—Offline/Online Characteristics

Characteristic	Attribute example
Test execution: Offline or online	Offline model-based testing
	Online model-based testing

taken, and follow the same path in the model. In that case, MBT tools interact directly with the SUT and test it dynamically.

Offline MBT means that test cases are generated strictly before they are run. The advantages of offline testing are directly connected to the generation of a test repository. The generated tests can be managed and executed using existing test management tools, which means that fewer changes to the test process are required. One can generate a set of tests once, then execute it many times on the SUT (eg, regression testing). Also, the test generation and test execution can be performed on different machines or in different environments, as well as at different times. Moreover, if the test generation process is slower than test execution, which is often the case, then there are obvious advantages to doing the test generation phase just once.

2.6 A Brief History of MBT

The use of models for test generation has been an area of study from the mid-1970s, with the seminal work of T. S. Chow, from the Bell Laboratories, on testing software design modeled by finite-state machines [7]. This work describes an algorithm for generating tests from this representation of software design. This paper initiated a long series of research work, which is still on-going today, on using finite-state machine representations, state charts and UML state diagrams as a basis for automated test generation. This research stream has been very productive, particularly in testing reactive systems: ie, proposing a large set of automated test generation algorithms, defining test selection criteria, establishing conformance theories, and finally providing research MBT tools that continue to influence the MBT scene.

This interest in MBT increased strongly from 1990 onwards, not only in the academic field by using a large spectrum of formal software requirements and behavior representations for test generation, but also in the industrial field as a response to problems found in designing and maintaining large static test suites. Major scientific foundations of MBT were set up during this period, including test generation algorithms for automating traditional manual test design techniques such as process cycle testing, equivalence classes partitioning or boundary value analysis [4] and also combinatorial test generation techniques such as pairwise techniques [8]. Moreover, the principles of automated bidirectional traceability between requirements and tests were set up at this time.

Early 2000s saw the emergence of MBT as a regular testing practice in the software industry. This implied integrating MBT with key industry standards such as UML and BPMN for the modeling phase, and with the industrial test management and test execution environments to set up a continuous and systematic test engineering process. At the same time, the methodology of MBT was being studied in order to clarify the best practices to go from requirements to models for test generation, for managing the test generation process and to help quality assurance (QA) teams to adopt MBT. This decade was also the period of life-size pilot projects and empirical evidence analysis to confirm the efficiency of MBT practice on testing projects (eg, [3, 4, 9]).

MBT is now in adoption phase in the software testing industry. The next section provides some evidence about the penetration of MBT in industry and the application domains.

3. CURRENT PENETRATION OF MBT IN INDUSTRY

The first experiments with MBT in industry started in the same period as the idea of driving test generation from models appeared in academia, meaning in the 1970s using Finite State Machine models [7]. But the tangible emergence of MBT in industry dates from the early 2000s with the creation of specialized tool providers supporting an effective use of MBT such as Conformiq and Smartesting, and the availability of tools from large companies such as SpecExplorer from Microsoft. So, what more has happened during the last decade? There is clear evidence that MBT is slowly penetrating the testing market, nothing like a tornado, but more like an ink blot strategy. In the rest of this section, we shall review three markers of this slow but palpable penetration:

* The MBT User Survey 2014 results;
* The evolution of the presentation at the ETSI User Conference on MBT (now UCAAT User Conference of Advanced Automated Testing) from 2010 to 2014;
* A certification of competence for MBT: *ISTQB Certified Tester Model-Based Testing*, which is an extension of the foundation level.

3.1 The 2014 MBT User Survey Results

This survey was conducted from mid-June 2014 to early August 2014 [10] to learn about the current motivations, practices and outcomes of MBT in industry. The 2014 MBT User Survey is a follow-up to a similar 2011 survey,[1] and has been conducted under the same conditions and similar dissemination of the information about the survey. This gives some evidence about the penetration of MBT in industry:

- In 2014, exactly 100 MBT practitioners responded, vs 47 in 2011, thus a growth of slightly over 100% can be noticed within the last 3 years.
- In both cases, the respondents were 90% from industry (and 10% from academia), which is due to the fact that the survey was explicitly restricted to practitioners.
- Given the wide-spread dissemination of the survey in professional social-networking groups, software-testing forums, and conferences world-wide, and the typical response rates to external surveys such as this, we estimate that between 2% and 10% of the number of MBT practitioners actually participated in the survey. This suggests that there are between 1000 and 5000 MBT active practitioners worldwide in 2014!

The next MBT User Survey will be conducted again in 2017, which will give another indication of the growth of the number of active MBT practitioners.

One interesting result from the 2014 survey is the level of maturity in the MBT usage. Fig. 6 shows that 48% of the respondents routinely use MBT and 52% are still in the evaluation or trial phase. On average, the respondents had 3 years experience with MBT. This figure shows that we are clearly in an immature area with a lot of newcomers (more than 50%). The obvious

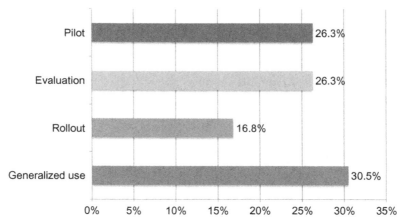

Figure 6 At what stage of MBT adoption is your organization?

---

[1] For the 2011 MBT User Survey, see http://robertvbinder.com/wp-content/uploads/rvb-pdf/arts/MBT-User-Survey.pdf

Table 9 Comparison Between Expectations and Observed satisfaction level

Answer Options	Yes	Partly	No	Don't Know (Yet)	Total
Our test design is more efficient (cheaper tests)	35	29	14	16	94
Our testing is more effective (better tests)	49	24	8	14	95
Models help us to manage the complexity of the system with respect to testing	46	29	5	13	93
Communication between stakeholders has improved	28	26	14	24	92
Models help us to start test design earlier	36	25	9	21	91

question is: what happens after the evaluation and pilot phases? Do the users continue and generalize, or they give-up and stop MBT adoption? It is too early for a definitive answer on this point, but another question of the 2014 MBT User Survey provides us with some information on the level of satisfaction obtained by the respondents.

Table 9 provides a comparison between expectations and observed satisfaction levels, classified by the main types of expectation: cheaper tests, better tests, support to manage complexity of the testing project, support for communication between project stakeholders, and shift left (starting test design earlier).

The results show that, for the majority of respondents, MBT generally fulfils their expectations, and they therefore get the value they are looking for.

This positive vision is consistent with the answers to the next question on how effective has MBT been in their situation (see Fig. 7). A majority of respondents viewed MBT as a useful technology: 64% found MBT moderately or even extremely effective, whereas only 13% rated the method as ineffective. More than 70% of the respondents stated that it is very likely or even extremely likely that they will continue with the method.

Finally, we may have a look at the current distribution of MBT across different areas of industry, as shown in Fig. 8. Nearly 40% of the respondents come from the embedded domain. Enterprise IT accounts for another 30%, web applications for roughly 20%. Other application domains for the SUT are software infrastructure, communications, and gaming. The main lesson learned is that MBT is distributed over the main areas of software applications, with an overrepresentation in the embedded domain.

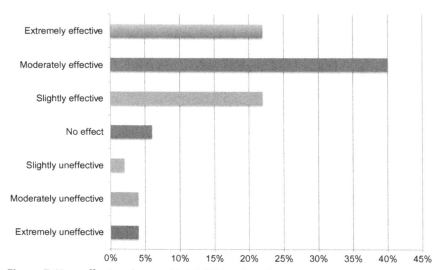

Figure 7 How effective do you think MBT has been?

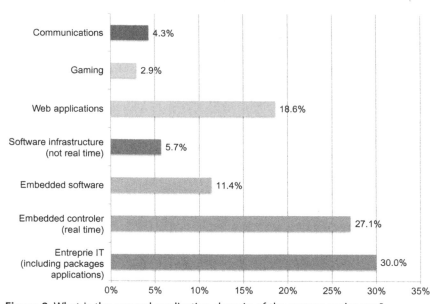

Figure 8 What is the general application domain of the system under test?

3.2 Analysis of the MBT User Conference Presentations

The *MBT User Conference* is an annual conference dedicated to MBT practitioners, sponsored by the ETSI (European Telecom Standard Institute). The conference started its first edition in 2010. In 2013, the conference has been renamed UCAAT (User Conference on Advanced Automated Testing) to broaden the subject area, but it is still a conference consisting for the most part of experience reports on MBT applications. This is a professional conference with more than 80% of people coming from industry, and between 160 and 220 attendees each year, depending mainly on the location (due to the attraction for local people).

Table 10 provides the list of application areas covered during each year of the conference. This confirms the large scope of applications of model-based techniques and tools. The presentations are available on each conference web site (see URL).

These conferences are also good showcases of the diversity of MBT deployment. They show the variety of MBT approaches, in the way that MBT test models are obtained (for instance by reusing existing models or developing specific test models), the nature of such models (variety of languages and notations), and also the way generated tests are executed (offline test execution or online test execution).

3.3 ISTQB Certified Tester MBT extension

Another marker of the penetration of MBT in industry is the upcoming ISTQB certification for model-based testers. ISTQB® (International Software Testing Qualifications Board) is a nonprofit association founded in 2002. ISTQB® has defined the "ISTQB® Certified Tester" certification scheme, with more than 380,000 certifications issued worldwide since the beginning. ISTQB® is an organization based on volunteer work by hundreds of international testing experts.

The ISTQB® scheme has three levels: foundations (basic level), advanced (for test managers and analysts) and expert (for experienced practitioners, which stride for improving the testing process and its automation). The basic level is *ISTQB Certified Tester Foundation Level* with two extensions: one for agile testers (testers embedded in projects using an agile software development process) issued in 2014, and one for model-based testers currently in Beta review phase (June 2015) and expected to be issued in October 2015.

The MBT ISTQB certification is organized as follows:
- ISTQB Certified Tester Foundation Level is a prerequisite
- It consists of 2 days of training
- It covers 38 learning objectives:
  - 9 at cognitive level K1 (remember)
  - 23 at cognitive level K2 (understand)
  - 6 at cognitive level K3 (apply)

Table 10 MBT Application Areas

Conference Year	Web Page	List of Area Covered by Experience Report During the Conference
2011	http://www.model-based-testing.de/mbtuc11/	• Web service protocols • Phone OS • ERP (SAP) applications • Safety-Critical Real-time Systems in Space • Automotive software • Telecom/datacom software • Video system and instant messaging
2012	http://www.elvior.com/model-based-testing-uc-2012	• Music streaming • Industrial Process Control Applications • Telecommunication applications • Defense security components • Bluetooth system • Bank applications • Industrial automation • Street lighting system
2013	http://ucaat.etsi.org/2013/program_conf.html	• ERP (SAP) applications • Banking applications • Music streaming • Telecom software • Automotive applications • Cloud systems • Industrial Automation systems • Railway embedded systems • Phone OS • Nuclear I&C architectures
2014	http://ucaat.etsi.org/2014/Program.html	• Medical devices • Game engine • Car 3D environment and car controller systems • Security components • Web services/internet of Things • IT Finance applications • Telecom/datacom applications

- The content of the syllabus is structured in five chapters, which are the following:
  - Introduction to model-based testing, introduces MBT and discusses its benefits
  - MBT Modeling, gives an overview of modeling languages used in MBT and guidelines for creating MBT models, as a core activity in an MBT approach.
  - Selection Criteria for Test Case Generation, discusses a variety of selection criteria used to drive the test case generation
  - MBT Test Execution, illustrates specific activities related on executing the generated test cases on the system under test
  - Evaluating and deploying an MBT approach, discusses the challenges and gives guidelines for successful introduction of MBT in an enterprise

After successfully passing the certification, it is expected that an ISTQB Certified Model-Based Tester will have acquired the necessary skills to successfully contribute to MBT projects in a given context. This certification will help to disseminate the MBT approach in industry, where the ISTQB certification scheme is very popular. It targets people who have reached a first level of achievement in their software testing career, including Test Engineers, Test Analysts, Technical Test Analysts, and Test Managers, but also software developers who are willing to acquire additional software testing skills.

4. LANGUAGES FOR MBT MODELING ACTIVITIES

This section expands on the "Models for test generation" presented in Fig. 1, by discussing the languages and notations used to build MBT models. There are many paradigms and languages [5] that can be used for the MBT modeling activities. This section gives an overview of the approaches used by three categories of MBT users:

1. the developers or people nearest to the implementation code. In this case, the modeling language is typically a design-by-contract notation that is close to the code. This design-by-contract concept was popularized by Bertrand Meyer with the Eiffel language in 1986.
2. the business people that use business rules to describe the processes being tested—they typically use a graphical notation such as BPMN (with decision tables) or UML to describe the MBT model.

3. the end user. In this case, the tester uses the same interface as the end user of the system being tested. The challenge is how to record and reuse these tests, or generalize them into a model of the system.

4.1 Testing with Contracts

The design-by-contract approach is often considered as unit testing because it is close to the code of the application being tested. Also, there are many discussions about test-driven-development (TDD) vs design-by-contract (DbC). In fact, both techniques are used to help improve the specification of the application. But TDD is for the development team to analyze test cases before code production, whereas DbC is more general in scope, even though it may also be used by the development team. In concrete terms, TDD associates an assertion (true or false) with the expected values returned from a call or action. But in DbC, you can use more complex predicates to describe more sophisticated properties, using a higher level language.

In fact, there are three common usages of contracts. In the first, the program and contract are both translated into logic formulae, which can then be checked for consistency using proof techniques—but this is outside the scope of this chapter, which is about model-based *testing*. A second usage of contracts is to translate the contracts into runtime assertions that can be checked as the application is executed. This is a useful form of testing, but requires separate inputs and sequences of operations to drive the application. The third approach, called *contract-based testing*, was introduced by Aichernig [11] and generates tests of the application from the contracts. In this case, the contracts are being used as the MBT model for the test generation, which is based on:

- using the invariants and preconditions to generate input data for tests;
- using the postconditions to provide the oracle to compute the test verdict during the execution of the tests.

We show in Table 11, some development languages with their associated contract languages. All of these contract languages have been used for test generation purposes.

In the next section, we describe a higher level notation for MBT models, which is further away from the application implementation level.

4.2 Testing Business Rules

As presented in Section 2.6, UML and BPMN are industry standards using for the modeling phase. So, UML is naturally used to realize MBT models

Table 11 Example of Language

Development Language	Contract Language	References
C	ACSL	[12]
C#	Spec#	[13, 14]
Java	JML [17]	Into JMLUnit [15, 16]
		Into UDITA [18]
		Into Java PathFinder [19]
JavaScript	JSConTest	[20, 21]
PHP	Praspel	[22]

and dedicated testing profiles. Often this is done using the *UML Testing Profile*,[2] which has been defined by the Object Modeling Group (OMG), presented for the first time in 2004 [23].

Much research has been performed to establish the range of UML diagrams that can be used to describe the system for testing—two examples are proposed in [24, 25]. The problem is the precise interpretation of the UML diagrams to compute the tests [26]. In some cases, the MBT model expressed using a single kind of UML diagram is not sufficiently precise to use for test generation purposes. Rather than making that diagram more complex, it is often better to add other elements from other kinds of UML diagrams, such as *use cases* [27, 28], *sequence diagrams* [29–32], or *interaction diagrams* [33, 34]. This combination of two (or more) different kinds of diagrams/notations is typically used to allow the test sequences to be specified using one notation, while the details of the inputs and outputs are specified using a different notation.

Another kind of modeling language used for its simplicity is Business Process languages, as outlined by Reijers *et al.* [35], who describe an interesting study on the usage of this language. The language is closer to business rules and allows interaction with all actors. IBM give an overview in [36] and a similar approach is also used with SAP, as described by Mecke [37]. This approach is also useful for testing web services [38–40].

---

[2] http://utp.omg.org

4.3 Testing GUIs

The automation of the test generation and (usually) test execution is one of the main attractions that helps the diffusion of MBT. The desired approach is often to generate tests that interact with the system under test in exactly the same way as the end user does. In fact, we want to test the system using the same interfaces. One of the main domains to use this technique is web-based applications. Execution robots such as Selenium, Watij (for the Java version) or Sahi are the most well known. But the difficulty is *obtaining* the tests that the execution robot can execute. The traditional basic approach is to record the user actions, and simply replay these later. More complex elements can be add as event contexts [41] or parameters. But such recorded test sequences are very low level and fragile [4, page 23], so it is desirable to have higher level approaches to generating the test sequences, which is an area where MBT can contribute.

In recent years, much research has been done on the analysis of GUIs for the purpose of test generation. A popular approach is GUI-ripping [42], where MBT models are constructed from the GUI application automatically, rather than being written manually. For example, the GUITAR framework [43] automatically constructs a tree of all widgets reachable in a GUI, plus an event-flow graph of all the interactions between GUI objects, and then uses these models to generate many short test sequences that find each widget and exercise each event [44]. However, a limitation of GUI ripping is that the generated tests contain fairly weak *oracle checks*, such as just checking that the application does not crash. This is because the automatically generated models do not capture deep semantic knowledge of the expected application behavior. One practical approach for addressing this issue is to manually add stronger oracle checks to the tests after they are generated. An extension of this GUI–ripping approach has also been applied to Android applications [45] and was shown to outperform random testing of Android applications.

Another limitation of GUI–ripping approaches is that when the test generator reaches a widget that requires complex input values, such as an integer or string value, it is not easy to generate meaningful input values. The most common approach is to generate random values, or randomly choose values from a small set of prechosen values. A more sophisticated solution to this problem has been developed by Arlt *et al.* [46], which relies on black-box GUI-ripping testing to reach an input widget, followed by using white-box symbolic execution of the code that handles that input value to determine what input values trigger the different paths through the code.

When applied to four open-source applications, they found that this approach generated tests with better error detection than random generation of input values.

The GUI-ripping approach tends to generate many short tests, which each test just a few events within the GUI. Are there ways of extracting more knowledge of the application, so that it is possible to generate longer and more application-specific test sequences? We briefly describe two extensions of the GUI-ripping approach that show that this is possible.

The first is to combine black–box and white–box models of the application. For example Arlt *et al.* [47] use static analysis of the byte code of the application to determine dependencies between events, so that longer test sequences can be generated to exercise those dependencies. This generates fewer test sequences, and longer test sequences, but matches or improves the error detection rates of pure black-box GUI ripping. On the other hand, the EXSYST test generator for interactive Java programs [48] uses completely different technology (genetic algorithms to search through the massive search space of all event sequences) to generate GUI tests that have high code coverage of the application. It does this by monitoring the branch coverage of the underlying application as the GUI tests are executed, and using that coverage level as the fitness function for the genetic search. Although these two tools use completely different technologies, they both use the technique of observing the execution of the application code (white-box), and connecting those observations to the black-box model of the GUI input events in order to generate smarter and longer input event sequences that can find more GUI faults.

The second approach to improving the depth of the generated test sequences is to base test generation on common user-interface *patterns* [49], such as the *click-login; enter-username; enter-password; click-submit* sequence, followed by the two expected outcomes of either an invalid login message, or correct login as shown by transfer to another page. Such use of patterns goes some way towards incorporating more of the application semantics into the MBT model, which enables richer tests to be generated. A complementary approach to improving the semantic richness of the GUI model is to infer specifications and invariants of the GUI from the traces of GUI executions. This is a challenging task given the infinite space of possible traces, but for example, AutoInSpec [50] does this in a goal-directed way, guided by coverage criteria and by a test suite repair algorithm, and thus finds more invariants than nongoal-directed approaches.

An example of an approach that uses MBT models with even deeper semantic knowledge of the application is the model-driven testing of web applications by Bolis *et al.* [51]. This uses models written as sequential nets of *abstract state machines* (ASM). The models may be developed specifically for testing purposes, or may be adapted from the high-level development models of the application. Either way, the development of such models requires application knowledge and modeling expertise, but the benefit of having the richer models is that they can generate more comprehensive tests that include stronger oracles.

Finally, all these different approaches to automated or semiautomated GUI testing raise the interesting question: which approach is best? Lelli *et al.* [52] have made steps towards answering this question by developing a fault model for GUI faults, validating this against faults found in real GUIs, and developing a suite of GUI mutants that can be used to evaluate the effectiveness of GUI testing tools.

5. TECHNOLOGIES FOR MODEL-BASED AUTOMATED TEST GENERATION

As shown in the previous sections, a key point of MBT is that the generation of test cases is performed from a declarative MBT model that formalizes the behavior of the System Under Test (SUT) in the context of its environment and at a given level of abstraction. The model captures the control and observation points of the SUT, its expected dynamic behavior, the data associated with the tests, and finally the initial state of the SUT. Hence, the MBT model is precise and formal enough to enable unambiguous interpretations, so that the derivation of test cases can be automated [53].

Test generation tools have the task of choosing certain traces of executions. In other words, the model describes a search space containing a large set of execution traces, potentially infinite. The test generation tool must use various algorithms and heuristics, plus guidance from the user (eg, coverage criteria, properties to be guaranteed, and patterns to be applied), to select a subset of execution traces that define test cases. To reduce the cost of software testing, and give a good return on investment, MBT approaches need to support a high degree of automation to automatically and systematically derive the test cases [54].

To address this goal, a large number of MBT tools have been developed in the past few decades, and a lot of research work has been investigated and published. As a result, a significant number of different technologies have emerged to support MBT automation. For very small MBT models and simple SUTs it is possible to generate basic test suites using simple algorithms such as random walks, or the Chinese Postman algorithm[3] [55], but for more complex models with complex data types, test generation quickly becomes a difficult optimization problem. In fact, most real test generation problems are complex enough to be undecidable, which means that no known algorithm can guarantee to find an optimal solution in a reasonable amount of time. For this reason, MBT test generators typically use *heuristic* solvers, which aim to quickly find a test case that satisfies the desired constraints and is close enough to the optimal solution to be acceptable, even though it may not be fully optimal.

The objective of this section is to give an overview of the major test generation technologies used at present to automate the derivation of test cases from MBT models. More precisely, we introduce the following four currently popular and well-used technologies: SAT/SMT solving, constraint programming, search-based algorithms, and model checking. For each of them, we discuss the typical benefits, weaknesses and future challenges that relate to test generation issues.

5.1 SAT and SMT Provers

Initially used for static analysis and program verification, Boolean SATisfiability (SAT) and Satisfiability Modulo Theory (SMT) solvers have received considerable attention during the last decade to automatically derive test cases from MBT models. A SAT prover is a tool that can determine whether there is a solution satisfying a propositional formula represented by a Boolean expression (ie, written only with Boolean variables, parentheses and operators of disjunction, conjunction, and negation). The central algorithm around which the SAT provers are built is called the Davis–Putnam–Logemann–Loveland algorithm [56], *DPLL* for short. It is a complete solving algorithm based on propositional logic formulae in Conjunctive Normal Form and using a backtracking process.

An SMT problem is expressed as a logical first-order formula combining different theories such as equality, linear arithmetic, and bit-vectors. In this way, an SMT problem is a generalization of a SAT problem where the Boolean variables are replaced by predicates using different theories. An SMT prover is thus based on a SAT prover, which is used to solve the logical

---

[3] The Chinese Postman algorithm finds the shortest path that covers all the transitions of a finite state machine.

formulas of first order on a particular theory by using a dedicated decision procedure. As a consequence, an SMT prover attempts to determine if an SMT problem has a solution, and, if a solution exists, returns that solution in the form of a valuation of each of the variables.

Nowadays, the most popular SMT solvers are *Z3* [57], *CVC3* [58], *CVC4* [59], *Yices* [60] and *MathSAT5* [61]. Z3 is an SMT prover developed by Microsoft Research and is part of professional tools such as Visual Studio via the white box code analyzer *Pex* [62]. CVC3, (Cooperating Validity Checker 3), and its successor CVC4 are academic provers developed jointly by the Universities of New York and Iowa. Yices is developed by SRI International's Computer Science Laboratory, and finally, MathSAT5 is the latest version of the MathSat prover, which has been jointly developed by the University of Trento and the FBK-IRST.

For test generation purposes, all the elements of the model such as conditions, assignments and structures (eg, **if–then–else**) are translated into first-order predicates and conjoined. The resulting formula, called an *SMT instance*, describes all the instructions that should be executed along a test case execution path, including the global sequence of SUT operation calls and the local choices within each of those operations. The satisfying instances of this formula correspond to valid input values that enable a desired test case sequence to be activated. This approach can be used to compute input data to activate a particular path in a targeted operation, as well as to provide sequences of operation calls.

For example, Cantenot *et al.* [63] describe a test generation framework, based on SMT solving, from UML/OCL model. This framework is able to translate the UML/OCL model into SMT instances, and various simulation strategies are applied on these SMT instances to compute test sequences. Their paper proposes and compares five different strategies to build the first order formulas used by an SMT instance. Other researchers propose optimizations to improve the test generation performance, including optimizations that exploit the features of the SAT/SMT prover, as well as the form of the first order formulas [64]. These experiments promise to make SAT/SMT test generation techniques as efficient as other existing methods, especially when dealing with Boolean expressions.

However, as underlined by Cristiá and Frydman's experimental feedback about test case generation from Z specifications using the two SMT provers Yices and CVC3 [65], the main weakness regarding the use of SMT provers for test generation purpose, is currently the lack of native decision procedures for the theory of sets. This implies that the representation of sets must be mapped onto some other mathematical structure (such as uninterpreted functions, arrays, lists, etc.), which can result in severely below-average performance. This observation has been recently investigated and confirmed by Cristiá, Rossi and Frydman [66], where experiments have shown that CLP solvers with set constraints can be more effective and efficient than SMT provers for these kinds of problems. The next section introduces such constraint-based approaches.

5.2 Constraint Logic Programming

A constraint system is defined by a set of constraints (properties) that must be satisfied by the solution of the problem being modeled. Such a system can be represented as a Constraint Satisfaction Problem (CSP) [67]. Formally, a CSP is a tuple $\Omega = < X,D,C >$ where X is a set of variables $\{x_1,...,x_n\}$, D is a set of domains $\{d_1,...,d_n\}$, where d_i is the domain associated with the variable x_i, and C is a set of constraints $\{c_1(X_1),...,c_m(X_m)\}$, where a constraint c_j involves a subset X_j of the variables of X. A CSP Ω can be seen as a constraint network whose nodes are the variables of X with their associated domains of D, and whose arcs are the constraints of C. It is such that each variable appearing in a constraint should take its value from its domain.

Hence, a CSP models NP-complete problems as search problems where the corresponding search space is the Cartesian product space $d_1 \times ... \times d_n$ [68]. The solution of a CSP Ω is computed by a labeling function, which provides a set v (called valuation function) of tuples assigning each variable x_i of X to one value from its domain d_i such that all the constraints of C are satisfied. More formally, v is consistent—or satisfies a constraint $c(X)$ of C—if the projection of v on X is in $c(X)$. If v satisfies all the constraints of C, then Ω is a consistent or satisfiable CSP.

Using Logic Programming for solving a CSP has been investigated for many years, especially using Constraint Logic Programming over Finite Domains, written CLP(FD) [69]. This approach basically consists of embedding constraint satisfaction techniques [70] into logic programming languages, by implementing the concept of logical domain variables, which take their value from a finite discrete set of integers.

Test case generation can thus be performed by solving the constraints collected for each path of the model using a constraint solver. The availability of efficient constraint solvers has made it possible to propose lots of automated constraint-based approaches for testing: to compute test data as well as to compute sequences of operation calls, including input values. To this end, the constraint techniques are applied to solve a constraint representation of the MBT model. Basically, this involves mapping each path formalized in the model to a set of constraints: structures (eg, if–then–else statements) define the constraints of the CSP, by manipulating formulas expressed using the variables of the MBT model. In this way, any solution satisfying the CSP defines the test values (input and output values that allow us to solve the oracle problem) and enables us to exercise the corresponding path through the model.

To illustrate this kind of approach, we can cite [71], in which the authors present an original approach and experimental results about using constraint solving to compute functional test cases for controllers for robotic painters. The testing was done within a continuous integration process, so the test generation and execution needed to be fast. The lessons learnt from this industrial experimentation showed that the testing strategy, implemented using the finite domain constraint solving library CLP(FD) [72] of SICStus Prolog, is faster and more effective than current test methodologies currently used in the company, even if this strategy does not ensure a complete coverage (not every possible transition) of the behaviors formalized in the model.

Other work [66], used the **{log}** solver [73, 74] to generate test cases from specifications written in the Z notation, which is based on first-order logic over a set theory. Indeed, to handle the Z notation, the {log} solver is able to manipulate and compute constraint solving on sets using native set structures and primitive operations. As such, it can find solutions of first-order logic formulas involving set-theoretic operators, translated from Z specifications to {log}'s predicates. The feedback of this experiments showed that such a CLP solver over sets is able to tackle two common problems within MBT:

- the elimination of unsatisfiable test objectives, built by partitioning the state space and collecting (dead) path conditions;
- improvement of the computational effectiveness of the reachability problem of finding states verifying the satisfiable test objectives.

However, regarding scalability issues, constraint solvers are not able to reason about a program's environment and may be less scalable with large-scale specification that include a high number of variables linked by complex constraints. Moreover, when a CSP has several solutions, a CLP solver is not able to prioritise them, so just returns the first solution found. Hence, the desirability of the solution may be increased by the use of an objective function. Innovative solutions to respond to this CLP challenge have been addressed by the search-based research and practitioners community. We discuss its challenges in a model-based framework in the next section.

5.3 Search-Based Algorithms

As discussed previously, the desirability of the solution may be increased by the use of an objective function, which requires the solver to find a particular solution (eg, minimize or maximize certain variables) [39]. To solve this optimization problem, a CLP solver would have to find all the solutions, to compare them to each other to be able to select the best one. This computation may involve an extra cost since the solver must explore all the search space if it cannot be sure not to find a better solution that those already computed.

Metaheuristic algorithms, such as search-based algorithms, aim to generate tests and test inputs using this principle (though most of them focus on test input generation). The search-based test generation techniques define a fitness function (or a set of fitness functions) to guide the test generation process. Within MBT, several search algorithms have been proposed focusing in general on evolutionary algorithms or dynamic symbolic execution. Evolutionary algorithms mimic the process of natural evolution. Genetic Algorithms (*GA* for short) are the most commonly used, they are inspired by Darwinian theory: selection, crossover and mutations. UML statemachines are the most frequently used diagram for GA-based approaches [75].

For instance, Doungsa-ard *et al.* [76] view the test data as a chromosome, which represents a sequence of transitions in the state machine. Their fitness function aims to trigger each transition and thus obtain maximal transition coverage in the diagram. Lefticaru and Ipate [77] use also state diagrams but their genetic algorithm is applied for input generation on a chosen path of the state machine. They further evaluated their approach with two other search techniques: simulated annealing and partical swarm optimization. The outcome of their evaluation is that a hybrid technique using simulated annealing and GA combined with local search techniques enables significant improvement of their effectiveness. Ali *et al.* [78], based on their previous work in [79], propose a heuristic approach including GA, (1+1) Evolutionary Algorithm (*EA* for short) and Alternate Variable Method (*AVM* for short). They evaluated their approach on artificial constraints and on an industrial study. Their overall experience showed that the (1+1) EA with their novel heuristics is the most efficient for their studies. In contrast to the previous work that focuses mostly on test data generation, Shirole *et al.* [80] proposed a genetic algorithm to generate feasible paths and test data. They use EA with activity diagrams to produce test scenarios. They also extended their work, by coupling the test generation with genetic algorithms to generate valid and invalid flows of message sequences [81].

To mitigate state exploration problems and the more general combinatorial explosion problems, Albert *et al.* [82] combine search-based algorithms with dynamic symbolic execution, which consists of doing concrete or symbolic executions of the SUT to derive path conditions for feasible paths, in order to simplify the CSP that must be solved. The most famous tools implementing this dynamic symbolic execution strategy are *DART* [83], *CUTE* [84], and *Pex* [85]. This strategy is mostly used for white-box testing, because for black-box testing, it requires computing tests online over the whole SUT, which is often not easily practicable. More details about this strategy, can be found in surveys by Cadar and others [86, 87].

Finally, it should be noted that dynamic symbolic execution is often coupled with model-checking approaches rather than CLP solving. The next section describes how model checking can be used to perform model-based test generation.

5.4 Model Checking

A model checker was initially a tool used to perform formal verification [88]. It takes as input an automaton of a system and a temporal logic property to be satisfied. The model checker visits all the reachable states of the automaton and verifies for each of these states that the temporal logic property is satisfied. If a state does not satisfy the property, it returns the path to reach it, in the form of a sequence of states starting from the initial state. This path thus defines a complete counterexample that illustrates the violation of the property by the automaton.

These basic principles were adapted early on to perform model-based test generation [89]. Basically, in this context, the automaton plays the role of MBT model whereas the temporal logic property defines a particular criterion to be covered. More precisely, the temporal logic property is expressed as the negation of a given test objective: in this way, when the model checker finds a state violating the property (ie, satisfying the test objective), it will return the related counterexample, which thus constitutes a test case covering the given test objective [90].

On the basis of this simple but efficient interpretation, the next challenge is forcing the model checker to find all the possible counterexamples in order to achieve a given coverage criterion of the automaton. This can be done by generating a separate temporal logic property (test objective) for each state that satisfies the coverage criterion, and then running the model checking on each one of those test objectives. Hence, at the end of the whole process, each computed counterexample defines a specific test case, including expected output to assign the test verdict.

Obviously, test generation techniques based on model checking have benefited from the increasing performance of model checkers and from the improved expressiveness of the automata and properties to be verified. For example, some model checkers are able to manipulate timed automata [91], like *UPPAAL* [92], or use a dedicated language to avoid describing a model directly, like *Maude* [93].

To illustrate such MBT approaches based on model checking, we can for example mention the tool-supported methodology proposed in [94]. It consists of translating an initial MBT model, expressed as a Business Process Model, into an algebraic Petri net in order to generate test cases using model checking techniques on an equivalent decision diagram. The test generation is driven by dedicated test intentions, which generate test cases including their oracles according to the transition system. More recently, another toolbox [95], based on UPPAAL, has been developed for generating test cases by applying model checking techniques on networks of timed automata. Finally, it should be noted that, based on the UPPAAL model checker, an online testing tool, called UPPAAL for Testing Real-time systems ONline (*UPPAAL TRON*) [96], supports the generation of test cases from models, and their online execution on the SUT.

Recently, authors in [97] combined formal specification and MBT approaches and evaluated their approach through the EnergyBus standard. They used the TGV tool [98] for verifying formal specification inconsistencies. They further constructed an MBT platform for conformance testing of EnergyBus implementations. This combination of tools and approaches has been applied for the first time in a mandatory step of a new industrial standard introduction, for instance EnergyBus.

Contrary to the TGV tool, which uses dedicated algorithms for test case generation, the authors in [99] expressed the system and its properties as boolean equations, and then used an equation library to check the equations on-the fly. The model checker used on a model with faults produces counter examples, seen as negative abstract test cases.

These technologies, using model-checking techniques to derive test cases, appear to be efficient and well-used solutions to automating MBT approaches. However, since model checkers are not natively devoted to test case generation, these techniques suffer from a lack of improvements with regard to test suite quality and performance [100], such as the native implementation of test coverage strategies. Moreover, they also suffer from the major weakness of model-checking techniques: state space explosion. Indeed, state space explosion remains a critical problem, even if some tools are now capable of handling the state spaces associated with realistic problems. Nevertheless, the performance of model checkers regularly increases due to innovative approaches, and so it makes MBT approaches more and more scalable. Among these innovative approaches, we can mention symbolic model checking [101], which allows the representation of significantly larger state spaces by using ordered binary decision diagrams to represent sets of states and function relations on these states. Finally, bounded model checking [102] is also a very relevant approach for test generation [103]. It aims to accelerate the generation of counterexamples by translating the model-checking problem into a SAT problem, but to achieve this, it does not perform an exhaustive verification.

6. MODEL-BASED SECURITY TESTING

Systems not conforming to security requirements are vulnerable and are more likely to succumb to security attacks and system intrusions. *Security testing* aims to increase the user's confidence in the system, by ensuring its conformance to security requirements.

Various techniques exist to address the challenge of increasing the system's safety and security and thereby increase the user's confidence in the system. According to Schieferdecker, security testing techniques can be grouped into four families [104]:

- vulnerability scanning: network scanners are used to check for active ports on the system and attempt to access those ports;
- static application security testing (SAST): typically the system byte/binary/source code is analyzed for known security threats;
- monitoring: an application monitors and logs traces of the inputs/outputs of the system during its execution;
- dynamic application security testing (DAST): consists of dynamically checking the security requirements.

DAST techniques can be performed using MBT approaches that are customized to security functions and security properties. This is called Model-Based Security Testing (MBST). MBST is a relatively novel and promising field of research. It is especially dedicated to systematic and efficient specification and documentation of security test objectives, security test cases and test suites, as well as automated or semiautomated test generation [105].

According to Tian-Yang *et al.* [106] we can consider two main goals for security testing:

- *Functional security testing* aims to ensure that the security requirements, both in terms of security properties and security functions, are implemented correctly.
- While *vulnerability testing* aims to identify and discover potential vulnerabilities, based on risk and threat analysis, but also based on the information normally given by databases such as the National Vulnerability Database (NVD) or the Common Vulnerabilities Exposure (CVE) database.

Thus, in this section we are interested to provide an overview of Model-Based Security Testing, divided into these two security testing goals. Section 6.1 focuses on the functional security testing techniques (MBFST), and Section 6.2 details techniques for vulnerability testing (MBVT).

6.1 Model-Based Functional Security Testing

Model-Based Functional Security Testing (MBFST) aims on one hand to ensure the secure functioning of the system, which for critical systems is merely dedicated to security, on the other hand to ensure the security requirements, for example confidentiality, integrity, availability, authentication, authorization and nonrepudiation.

The CNSS (Committee on National Security Systems) in their glossary defines these security properties as follows [107]:

- *Confidentiality* is the assurance that information is not disclosed to entities (users, processes, devices) which are not authorized.
- *Integrity* is provided when an entity has not been modified in an unauthorized manner.
- *Authentication* is a security measure of verifying the identity or other attributes claimed by or assumed of an entity (user, process, or device), or to verify the source and integrity of data.
- *Authorization* provides access privileges granted to a user, program, or process.
- *Availability* guarantees the property of being accessible and useable upon demand by an authorized entity.
- *Nonrepudiation* is the assurance that the sender of information is provided with proof of delivery and the recipient is provided with proof of the sender identity, so neither can later deny having processed the information.

In MBFST the models are functional and describe the security functions and the system's expected behavior. In addition, they are enriched with annotations, for example stereotypes or high level scenarios that focus on expressing specific security properties or the security engineer's experience, since security testing is a task that requires a high degree of security-related knowledge. These annotations or scenarios guide further the generation of security related tests.

MBFST proposes techniques and tools using ideas such as selection criteria (static and dynamic), model checking, and robustness techniques (for instance mutation testing or fuzzing). Furthermore, these techniques address security-critical domains such as web services, protocols, legacy systems, smart cards, cryptographic components, etc. All these domains require rigorous testing and validation. Moreover, the approaches have shown that they can be applied to certifications such as Common Criteria. Thus, MBFST remains a challenging and promising approach to security testing, and the creation of more secure and safer critical systems.

In the remaining part of this section we discuss first the three main families of techniques and approaches in MBFST and then we present in detail an MBFST methodology and tools, which has been applied in industry for testing security components.

6.1.1 Test Selection Criteria

Test selection criteria are chosen to guide the automatic test generation so that it produces a good test suite—one that fulfils the test policy defined for the system under test (SUT) [5], as discussed in Section 2.5. We can categorize them into two families: *static* and *dynamic*. In the context of MBT, static selection criteria are related to the structure of the model elements, whereas dynamic selection criteria relate to the dynamic aspects of the system, for instance using the expert's experience.

In MBFST, most of the techniques based on *static test selection criteria* focus on access-control policy testing. For instance Le Traon *et al.* defined new structural test selection criteria for access control policies [108] and test generation based on access control models [109]. Further, they have presented an approach for test generation using a combinatorial testing technique by combining roles, permissions and contexts [110]. Recently, they worked on a tool-supported process for building access-control MBT models from contracts and access-rules [111].

Other work based on static selection criteria focuses in general on privacy properties. Anisetti *et al.* express the privacy properties of a service

(P-ASSERT) and generate test cases based on service models, which is used further in their certification scheme for digital privacy of services [112].

Experience in industry showed that static test selection criteria cannot cover high-level security properties, so to ensure the security of a critical application it is necessary to use *dynamic criteria* in order to produce tests that cover such properties. In general, the test scenarios are expressed in a dedicated language that can be either textual or graphical, describing the sequences of steps (usually operation calls) that can be performed, along with possible intermediate states reached during the unfolding of the scenario. We now briefly describe several approaches that use dynamic test selection criteria.

Mallouli *et al.* provided a formal approach to integrate timed security rules, expressed in the Nomad language, into a TEFSM functional specification of a system. Then they use the TestGen-IF tool to generate test cases, which are later executed on the system using tclwebtest scripts [113].

Another MBFST approach is the one proposed by Julliand *et al.* [114]. They generate test cases based on B-models and use dynamic test selection criteria (also called test purposes) for producing test objectives, represented as regular expressions.

Legeard *et al.*, for security testing of cryptographic components, use an approach based on dynamic test selection criteria: Test Purpose (TP) [115]. The TP language allows one to express high-level scenarios based on security expert experience and it has been successfully deployed and used at the French army computer science department. Moreover, Cabrera *et al.* have created a textual language for expressing high-level user scenarios that takes into account the temporal aspect of the security properties that are written in Temporal OCL (TOCL) [116]. TOCL has been successfully applied for Common Criteria evaluation. These languages, TP and TOCL, are both integrated within the Smartesting CertifyIt Tool and allow users to guide the generation of functional security tests. We discuss these approaches in detail in the last section.

6.1.2 Model Checking

A common technique for generating tests in the security testing is to use a model checker. The model checker produces a trace by providing a counter example for a given property [117]. In the scope of MBFST, Pellegrino *et al.* use a model checker for ASLan and ASLan++[4] to generate abstract test cases

---
[4] http://www.avantssar.eu/

as counter examples for the security properties. To create concrete test cases executable on the system under test they use a test adapter [118].

Jürjens presented an approach to generate traces by injecting faults into UML models, and UMLsec *stereotypes*, used for verification of properties. Furthermore, Fourneret *et al.* applied the UMLsec verification technique for security properties in the domain of a smart card industry, and then based on their transformation into a Test Purpose Language they generate tests covering the security properties [119].

Another approach proposed by Aichernig *et al.* uses a model checking technique on an Input/Output Label Transition System (IOLTS) model to generate test cases. They further inject faults using mutation operators, and generate traces used as test objectives for the TGV tool [120]. Thus, we can also classify this as a robustness technique.

6.1.3 Robustness Techniques

Many MBFST techniques aim to address robustness issues of the system under test. Most of them concern protocol testing and are based on *mutation* or *fuzzing* operators. We briefly describe several examples of each of these model-based techniques for robustness testing.

Mutation testing is quite a large field of study and has been studied over decades, as shown by Jia and Harman in their survey [121]. In the context of MBT it has been applied in various domains, such as security policies, protocols, etc.

In the domain of security policies, Martin and Xie presented a mutation-testing framework for policy specifications in their "eXtensible Access Control Markup Language" (XACML). To generate tests from XACML policies they synthesize inputs to a change-impact analysis tool. Le Traon *et al.* introduced eight mutation operators for the Organization-Based Access Control OrBAC policy [122].

In the domain of protocol robustness, Wimmel and Jurjens apply mutation operators to System Structure Diagrams in AutoFocus, in order to generate test cases based on attack scenarios [123].

Close to their work, Dadeau *et al.* [124], introduced an approach to verify the security of an actual implementation of a security protocol. They generate test cases based on fault-models written in the High-Level Security Protocol Language (HLPSL). They have successfully applied their approach to a set of existing security protocols.

Model-Based Fuzzing uses knowledge about the message structure to semantically generate invalid, unexpected or random messages.

The messages could be generated from scratch—*generation-based fuzzing* or as mutants of valid messages, *mutation-based fuzzing*. Traditionally in fuzzing, messages relate to the invalid input data of tests. Hence in the context of MBFST, fuzzing consists of generating invalid message sequences, referred to as *behavioral fuzzing*.

The DIAMONDS project introduces novel techniques in the research field of model-based security testing and particularly in fuzzing [105]. Shieferdecker *et al.* designed a mutation-based fuzzing approach that uses fuzzing operators on scenario models specified by sequence diagrams. The fuzzing operators perform a mutation of the diagrams resulting in an invalid sequence. Contrary to the previous work, where tests are executed after their generation, referred as offline testing (see Section 2), Shieferdecker *et al.* use online behavioral fuzzing, which generates tests at run time [125].

Another work by Johansson *et al.*, close to the DIAMONDS project, developed T-Fuzz, a generation-based fuzzing framework for protocol implementation testing based on the TTCN-3 language [126]. This approach relies on protocol models used for conformance testing, by reusing the already existing test environment. In addition, they present its successful application to the validation of the Non-Access Stratum (NAS) protocol, used in telecommunication networks for carrying signaling messages.

6.1.4 An Example of Functional Security Testing Technique Based on Dynamic Test Selection

Testing security components is complex and expensive due to their specific nature. On one hand, a security component implements security functions, such as cryptographic algorithms, including symmetric and public-key cyphers. On the other hand, the interaction with the component is allowed through an Application Program Interface (API). These cryptographic APIs allow the exchange of information and access to critical data in a secure way and it is common to define them by specifications to increase security, for example PKCS#11[5] or GlobalPlatform[6].

The CertifyIt tool, produced by Smartesting, offers an industrial solution for Model-Based Functional Security Testing (MBFST). This section gives a short illustration of how the tool combines static and dynamic test selection criteria to support security testing.

---

[5] http://www.emc.com/emc-plus/rsa-labs/standards-initiatives/pkcs-11-cryptographic-token-interface-standard.htm

[6] http://www.globalplatform.org/

The Smartesting MBFST methodology for testing of security components, considers the specification as the entry point. The static view of the system is represented using an MBT model, so the structure of the API, for example cryptographic, is represented by a UML class diagram. In addition, the dynamic view of the system (its behavior) is represented by OCL constraints, which are used to drive test generation. The generated test cases are independent of any code implementation. To concretize and execute the tests on the system under tests different adapter layers can be created for different implementations, each of them being dependent on the system under test.

However, as discussed previously, this classical MBT approach to functional testing is not sufficient to cover security requirements. Thus, recent versions of the tool (eg, CertifyIt version 6.3) improve this process in two directions. First, in order to address the coverage of the security-specific test requirements, it uses properties to represent the security functional aspects of an application. These properties could also be used to evaluate the strength of an already existing test suite in terms of coverage of the security requirements (through the coverage of the properties). Second, it uses the experts knowledge to generate realistic test scenarios that can be quite long, which are expected to reveal more complex weaknesses than single-purpose test cases that cover functional requirements.

More precisely, the tool helps to uncover the potentially dangerous behaviors resulting from the interactions of the application with the security component. Then, in addition to functional testing that targets the coverage of the system's behavior, it supports testing of the security requirements for the system, by combining two dynamic test selection criteria (based on TOCL [116] and Test Purposes (TP) [115]) for generation of test targets and tests that cover the security requirements. The TP language is based on regular expressions, and by combining keywords it allows the test engineers to conceive scenarios in terms of states to be reached and operations to be called [115]. The TOCL language is based on temporal logic and it allows the expression of temporal properties that are composed of two artifacts: a *temporal pattern* and a *scope*. The scopes are defined from events and delimit the impact of the pattern. To define the sequences appropriate for execution, the patterns are applied on a scope and they are defined from event and state properties, expressed by OCL constraints [116].

These TOCL and TP approaches are complementary, since they cover different types of security requirements. On one hand, TP covers security requirements that are required to express specific application scenarios, and they are not able to express the temporal aspects of precedence or succession of events. On the other hand, with TOCL it is possible to capture these temporal aspects in the time axis. However, in both cases, the generated security tests exercise as much as possible the unusual interactions with the security component.

The Smartesting CertifyIt tool further monitors the test coverage of the security requirements expressed in TOCL, and generates new test cases if it is necessary to increase the coverage [116]. Finally, the tool generates a coverage report that ensures the traceability between the specification, the security requirements and the generated tests, so that that coverage report can be used in a product certification. Fig. 9 depicts the TOCL plugin integrated within the CertifyIt tool and shows its features for coverage monitoring and report generation.

To illustrate the approach based on TOCL and the tool, we use the specification of PKCS#11. PKCS#11 defines the API Cryptoki that offers an interface for managing the security and interoperability of security components. The specification defines various security requirements for which we were able to generate test cases, for example: "A user cannot verify a signed-message using the C_Verify operation without login to Cryptoki (using the operation C_Login)." From a testing perspective, this requirement is interpreted as the user must call a C_Login operation before calling C_VerifyInit, which initiates the verification function. The TOCL language allows this requirement to be expressed by two properties: one that defines the nominal case and a second complementary property that defines the "flawed" case.

The first property defines whenever a verification function is performed with success (model behavior @CKR:OK, CKR being a tag to represent a

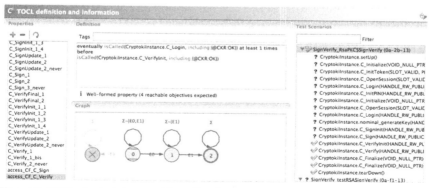

Figure 9 TOCL plugin integrated into CertifyIt.

function return value), it must be preceded by a login operation, performed also with a success. We can distinguish the temporal pattern (*before* the first occurrence of a successful call of C_VerifyInit function) and the scope (*eventually* a successful call of the login function follows the previous event, for instance C_VerifyInit).

eventually isCalled(C_Login, @CKR:OK) **before** isCalled(C_VerifyInit, @CKR:OK)

The second property expresses that when a user is logged out, the user must go through the login state before performing any message verification function.

eventually isCalled(C_Login,@CKR:OK)

between isCalled(C_Logout, @CKR:OK) **and** isCalled(C_VerifyInit, @CKR:OK)

Each TOCL property is translated into an automaton, which allows the coverage of the property to be measured, and also supports the generation of additional tests to augment the coverage of the TOCL property.

Measuring the coverage of a property is based on measuring the coverage of the automaton transitions by each already existing test. This step is illustrated in Fig. 9. The automaton also has an error state, represented by the state containing a cross. If this state is reached by any tests it means that the property is violated, which needs a further investigation to define whether the security property is too restrictively written, or the MBT model contains errors. In the latter case, our experience found that the TOCL properties help in debugging the MBT model. Indeed, MBT models may contain errors, as well as the code, and their correctness is often tackled by researchers and practitioners.

Once the coverage is evaluated, if any transitions of the automaton are not covered, CertifyIt can produce test targets based on the uncovered automaton transitions and then *generate additional abstract test cases* to augment the property coverage.

6.2 Model-Based Vulnerability Security Testing

MBT has proven its efficiency when it comes to test security properties, such as access control policies for instance. However, a large part of what we call security is implied and usually not explicitly specified in a document. This large part is referred as Vulnerability Testing, which consists of defining, identifying, quantifying and prioritizing the security holes (vulnerabilities) in a system, network, or application software. Whereas security properties testing (MBFST) is about "verifying that a given security property or policy is met," vulnerability testing (MBVT) is more about "verifying that users cannot use a system in a way it was not intended to be used." While model-based vulnerability testing may help conduct tests at every infrastructure layer (networks, systems, applications), most papers focus on application-level vulnerabilities, typically for web applications.

Indeed, the mosaic of technologies used in current web applications (eg, HTML5 and JavaScript frameworks) increases the risk of security breaches. This situation has led to significant growth in application-level vulnerabilities, with thousands of vulnerabilities detected and disclosed annually in public databases such as the MITRE CVE—Common Vulnerabilities and Exposures [127]. The most common vulnerabilities found in these databases are a lack of resistance to code injection, such as SQL Injection (SQLI) or Cross-Site Scripting (XSS), which have many variants. This kind of vulnerability frequently appears in the top list of current Web applications attacks.

Application-level vulnerability testing is first performed by developers, but they often lack sufficient in-depth knowledge of recent vulnerabilities and related exploits. This kind of testing can also be performed by companies specialized in security testing, in penetration testing for instance. But they mainly use manual approaches, making the dissemination of their techniques very difficult, and the impact of this knowledge very low. Finally, web application vulnerability scanners can be used to automate the detection of vulnerabilities, but since they often generate many false positives and negatives, human investigation is also required.

In this section, we first provide an overview on Model-Based Vulnerability Testing, which can be grouped into three main families: pattern-based and attack-model-based, model checking, and fuzzing approaches. We then present a pattern-driven and MBT approach for web applications, proposed within the RASEN project.

6.2.1 Pattern-Based and Attack-Model-Based Approaches

The majority of MBT papers have chosen not to represent the behavior of the SUT, but rather the behavior of attackers. Whether these are referred to as *attack-models* or *patterns*, the idea is to model how an malicious individual would conduct an attack, step by step. We now outline several representative example of this approach.

Blome *et al.* [128] describe a model-based vulnerability testing tool called VERA, standing for "VERA Executes the Right Attacks." It is based on the fact that usually the presence of a vulnerability is a prerequisite to deploy an attack, but actually exploiting this vulnerability is time consuming. This approach relies on attacker models, which can be seen as extensions of Mealy finite state machines. These models, if combined with the back-end of the approach, can provide fully automated test scripts. The back-end of the approach is composed of (i) an instantiation library, which is basically a list of nominal and malicious vectors, (ii) a configuration file that contains system-specific information (cookie data such as the session ID, target URL, specific headers, etc.), and (iii) an XML file describing the attacker model to be tested. This approach can address a large variety of vulnerability types like code injection, source disclosure, file enumeration, remote file inclusion (RFI), cross-site request forgery (CSRF), among others.

Bozic and Wotawa [129] present a MBT approach relying on attack patterns to detect web application vulnerabilities such as SQL injections and XSS. An attack pattern is a specification of a malicious attack. Represented by a UML state machine, it specifies the goal, conditions, individual actions and postconditions of the represented attack. Test cases are computed and executed by branching through the states of the state machine and executing the corresponding methods of the SUT. This approach has been implemented as a toolchain using several existing tools, such as Yakindu for the state machine modeling, Eclipse to encapsulate the entire system, and WebScarab for the interpretation of communication between the Web application and clients, and for manual submission of attacks. Experiments have been conducted on three vulnerable applications (DVWA, Mutillidae, and BodgeIt) and one real life application (WordPress Anchor). SQLI and XSS vulnerabilities were found on Mutillidae and DVWA, on various security levels. No vulnerability was found on Wordpress Anchor because an administrator needs to approve each post submitted by users. It requires a more detailed model of the attack.

Wei *et al.* [130] focus on penetration test case inputs and propose a model-based penetration test method for SQL injections. First, they provide attack models using the Security Goal Model notation, which is a modeling method used to describe vulnerabilities, security properties, attacks, and so on. Models are generic and describe goals in a top-down fashion. A typical goal is for instance "steal system information," and is modeled as two sub-parts: error-message utilizing and blind injection. Hence, each top-down path in a model represents an attack process that realizes a certain attack goal. Each top-down successful attack process represents the attack scheme, defined as a triple $< OBJ, INP, OUT >$, OBJ being the attack goal, INP being the attack input, and OUT being the vulnerable response of the Web application. To perform an actual attack, one must instantiate the test case model according to the fingerprint of the web application and use certain coverage criteria to generate executable test cases. The authors created an automated web application SQL injection vulnerability penetration test tool called NKSI scan: it applies the widely used "crawling-attack-analysis" method to detect the SQL injection vulnerability in subject applications. They compared their technique with popular scanners IBM AppScan and Acunetix. Results show that NKSI was able to discover more flaws than those two scanners.

Xu *et al.* [131] present an approach to automate the generation of executable security tests from Threat Model-Implementation Description (TMID) specifications, which consist of threat models represented as Predicate/Transition (PrT) nets and a Model-Implementation Mapping (MIM) description. A threat model describes how a malicious individual may trigger the system under test to violate a security goal. A MIM description maps the individual elements of a threat model to their implementation constructs. Abstract test cases (ie, complete attack paths) are computed in two steps. First a reachability graph is generated from the threat net. It represents all states and state transitions reachable from the initial marking. Then the reachability graph is transformed to a transition tree containing complete attack paths by repeatedly expanding the leaf nodes that are involved in attack paths but do not result from firings of attack transitions. Concrete test cases are derived by automatically composing the attack paths and the MIM description. The approach has been implemented in ISTA, a framework for automated test code generation from Predicate/Transition nets, and experiments have been conducted on two real-world systems. It shows good results with most vulnerabilities being found (90%), whether they are web-related vulnerabilities (XSS, SQLi, CSRF, etc.) or protocol-based vulnerabilities (FTP).

Salva *et al.* [132] present a Model-Based Data Testing approach for Android applications that automatically generates test cases from intent-based vulnerabilities, using vulnerability patterns. It specifically targets the Android Intent Messaging mechanism, whose objective is to allow sharing of actions and data between components using content providers, in order to perform operations. The concern is that attackers may exploit this mechanism to pass on payloads from component to component, infecting the whole system and making their attack more severe. This approach therefore searches for data vulnerabilities inside components. The automated generation of test cases relies on three artifacts: vulnerability patterns, class diagrams, and specifications. Vulnerability patterns are specialized Input–Output Symbolic Transition Systems, which allow formal expression of intent-based vulnerabilities. A pattern formally exhibits intent-based vulnerabilities and helps to define test verdicts. Class diagrams are partially generated from the decompiled Android application under test, and represent Android components with their types and their relationships. They typically provide the Activities (these are Android components that display screens to let users interact with programs) or Services composed with content providers. Specifications are generated from the Android manifest. They express the behavior of components after the receipt of intents combined with content-provider requests. Test case generation is performed by composing the three artifacts. This method has been implemented in a tool called APSET, and has been applied to several real life applications. Results support the effectiveness of the tool, finding vulnerabilities in popular Android applications such as YouTube and Maps.

A pattern-driven and MBT approach has been developed by Vernotte *et al.* [133] for various vulnerability types, technical and logical. The approach relies on attack patterns and a behavioral model of the SUT. The test generator uses attack patterns as guides, and follows each step into the model. If each step has been fulfilled, an abstract test case is computed. A more thorough presentation of this approach may be found in Section 6.2.4.

6.2.2 Model-Checking Approaches

Test cases can also be obtained by using a model checker. Given a website specification/model, a typical model-checking approach will inject faults into the model and use a model checker to generate attack traces. Various techniques have been proposed to detect technical vulnerabilities (XSS, SQLI, CSRF, etc.) as well as logical vulnerabilities (authentication bypass, insecure direct object references, etc.). We shall discuss three examples of such model-checking approaches.

Buchler *et al.* [134] represent the SUT using a secure AVANTSSAR Specification Language (ASLan++) model, where all traces fulfill the specified security properties. A library of fault injection operators has been developed. The goal is to apply a fault injection operator to the model, and use a model checker to report any violated security goal. If a security goal has indeed been violated, the reported trace then constitutes an Abstract Attack Trace (AAT). The attack traces are translated into concrete test cases by using a two-step mapping: the first step is to translate an AAT into WAAL (Web Application Abstract Language) actions, the second step is to translate

WAAL actions into executable code. An attack may be conducted in a fully automated fashion, at the browser level. In some specific cases (disabled input elements, etc.), a test expert may be required to craft HTTP level requests in order to recover from the error. This approach is highly amenable to full automation.

Rocchetto et al. [135] present a formal model-based technique for automatic detection of CSRF during the design phase. It is based on the ASLan++ language to define the several entities involved (client, server) and their interactions. The client is used as an oracle by the attacker, and the model is centered around the web server and extends the work of Dolev–Yao (usually used for security protocol analysis). To generate tests, the model is submitted to the AVANTSSAR platform, which, when a CSRF is found, returns an abstract attack trace reporting the list of steps an attacker has to follow in order to exploit the vulnerability. This technique takes into account that the web server may have some CSRF protection in place, and will try to bypass it. It will typically look for CSRF token-related flaws, for instance if the tokens are unique for each client, and for each client/server interaction. If no attack trace is produced, the specification is considered safe regarding CSRF. The authors assume that attackers can listen to the network and build their attack upon the transactions between a client and the server.

Felmetsger et al. [136] present advances toward the automated detection of application logic vulnerabilities, combining dynamic execution and model checking in a novel way. Dynamic execution allows for the inference of specifications that capture a web applications logic, by collecting likely invariants. A likely invariant is derived by analyzing the dynamic execution traces of the web application during normal operation, and captures constraints on the values of variables at different program points, as well as relationships between variables. The intuition is that the observed, normal behavior allows one to model properties that are likely intended by the programmer. Model checking is used with symbolic inputs to analyze the inferred specifications with respect to the web applications code, and to identify invariants that are part of a true program specification. A vulnerability is therefore any violation of such an invariant. This technique has been implemented in a tool called Waler (Web Application Logic Errors AnalyzeR), which targets servlet-based web applications written in Java. Up to now, Waler detects a restricted set of logic flaws and is currently limited to servlet-based web applications, but was still able to find previously undetected vulnerabilities in real-life applications while producing a low number of false positives.

6.2.3 Fuzzing Approaches

Fuzzing is extensively used in vulnerability testing [137] to introduce malformed data or mutate nominal values to trigger flawed code in applications. Fuzzing techniques are usually very cheap to deploy, do not suffer from false positives, but lack an expected-result model and therefore rely on crashes and fails to assign a verdict. Two main fuzzing techniques exist: mutation based and generation based. Mutation fuzzing consists of altering a sample file or data following specific heuristics, while generation-based fuzzers take the input specification and generate test cases from it. Fuzzing may be used for crafting malicious input data [138], or crafting erroneous communication messages [139].

The approach presented by Duchene [138] consists of modeling the attacker's behavior, and driving this model by a genetic algorithm that evolves SUT input sequences. It requires a state-aware model of the SUT, either derived from an ASLan++ description or inferred from traces of valid/expected SUT execution. This model is then annotated using input taint data-flow analysis, to spot possible reflections. Concrete SUT inputs are generated with respect to an Attack Input Grammar which produces fuzzed values for reflected SUT input parameters. The fitness function depends on the obtained SUT output following the injection of a concrete SUT input. It computes the veracity of an input by looking for correlations, using the string distance between a given input parameter value and a substring of the output. Two genetic operators are used: mutation and cross-over. It is an efficient technique for detecting XSS, as it goes beyond the classical XSS evasion filters that may not be exhaustive. Such a technique also tackles multistep XSS discovery by using a more complex string matching algorithm to generate an annotated FSM, in order to inspect the SUT to find the possibilities of XSS at certain places.

A model-based behavioral fuzzing approach has been designed by Wang et al. [139] to discover vulnerabilities of Database Management Systems (DBMS). A DBMS defines a format rule that specifies packet format and a behavior rule that specifies its semantics and functionality. This approach is based on two main artifacts. The first artifact is a behavioral model, which includes fuzzing patterns and behavioral sequences. This is obtained from a behavior analysis of DBMS (protocol format analysis, attack surface analysis, etc.). A fuzzing pattern expresses the data structure of packets, the needs of security testing, and the design strategy for vulnerability discovery. A behavioral sequence defines the message transfer order between client and DBMS. The second artifact is a DBMS Fuzzer composed of a test instance (a detailed test script based on fuzzing patterns), and a finite state machine model EXT-NSFSM used for semivalid test case generation based on behavioral sequences and test instances. The authors describe a general framework for behavioral fuzzing that has been implemented and used in several experiments. It allows for the generation of thousands of fuzzing instances, and despite a few errors of analysis and script, the tool was able to discover buffer overflow vulnerabilities, 10 of which were not released yet.

6.2.4 Example of a Pattern-Driven and Model-Based Vulnerability Testing Approach

The VESONTIO team from the FEMTO-ST/DISC institute has designed a pattern-driven Model-Based Vulnerability Testing approach, proposed within the framework of the RASEN project, to generate and execute vulnerability test cases. It combines MBT and fuzzing techniques, and drives the test generation by security test patterns resulting from risk assessment. This approach aims to improve the accuracy and precision of vulnerability testing. It is supported by tools that automate the detection of vulnerabilities, particularly in web applications.

The process, shown in Fig. 10, is composed of the four following activities:

1. **The *Modeling* activity.** As for every MBT approach, the modeling activity consists of designing an MBT model that can be used to automatically generate abstract test cases. The PMVT approach, based on the CertifyIt technology, requires a model designed using the UML4MBT notation: UML class diagrams specify the static structure, while state diagrams describe the dynamic behavior of the application (notably the navigation between pages).

   To ease and accelerate this modeling activity, a Domain Specific Modeling Language (DSML) has been developed, called *DASTML*, which allows the global structure of a web application to be modeled. It is composed of three entities: *Page*, *Action* and *Data* with various link possibilities between the three. Only relevant information to vulnerability test case generation is represented, such as the available pages (or screens in case of single-url applications), the available actions on each page, and the user inputs of each action (potentially used to inject an attack vector). An algorithm performs the automatic instantiation of the UML4MBT notation based on a given DASTML model.

2. **The *Test Purpose* design activity.** This activity consists of formalizing a test procedure from each vulnerability test pattern (vTP) that the

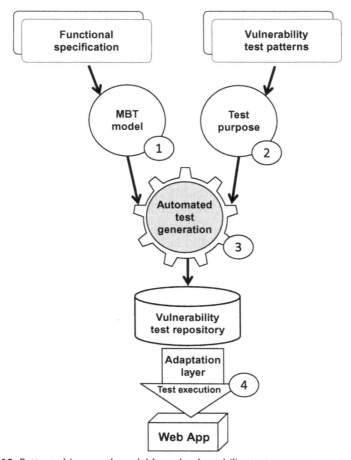

Figure 10 Pattern-driven and model-based vulnerability test process.

generated test cases have to cover. vTPs provide a starting point for security test case derivation by giving information on how to compute appropriate vulnerability test cases depending on the kind of vulnerability. These patterns are typically gathered from public databases such as CVE and OWASP, and from research projects such as the ITEA2 DIAMONDS project.

Because vTPs are informal specifications they need to be translated into a machine-readable language, to allow the automatic computation of test cases by the generation engine. Hence each procedure targeting a dedicated vulnerability is given by a *test purpose*, which is a high-level expression that formalizes a testing objective to drive the automated test generation on the test model. Basically, such a test purpose can be seen as a partial algorithm that defines a sequence of significant steps that has to be executed by the test case scenario. Each step takes the form of a set of operations or behaviors to be covered, or specific state to be reached on the test model, in order to assess the robustness of the application under test with respect to the vulnerability that is being tested. The test purpose language supports complex pattern modeling by making use of OCL constraints to define specific states to reach and data to collect, and "foreach" statements to iterate over enumeration literals (abstract data) and thus unfold a given test purpose into numerous abstract test cases.

3. **The *Test Generation* activity.** The test generation process automatically produces abstract vulnerability test cases, including the expected results. It consists of instantiating the vulnerability test purposes on the test model of the application under test: the test model and the test purposes are both translated into elements and data directly computable by the test generator CertifyIt. Test case generation is performed by instantiating the selected test purposes on the behavioral UML4MBT test model specifying the web application under test.

   Notably, test purposes are transformed into test targets, which are defined by a sequence of intermediate objectives used by the test generation engine. The test targets are then executed on the test model to generate the abstract test cases. In this way, each test purpose produces one or more abstract test cases that verify the test purpose specification, while satisfying the constraints of the behavioral test model.

4. **The *Adaptation, Test Execution and Observation* activity.** The abstract test cases are finally exported into the test execution environment. This consists of automatically creating a JUnit test suite, in which each abstract test case is exported as a JUnit test case skeleton that embeds the test sequence and the observation procedures in order to automate the verdict assignment.

   However, during the modeling activity all data used by the application is modeled at an abstract level. As a consequence, test cases are abstract and cannot be executed directly as they are. To bridge the gap, test engineers must link the abstract data to concrete data in order to provide executable test scripts. It should be emphasized that all abstract operations ("login," "register," "goto_page," and so on) are automatically concretized using basic HTMLUnit primitives. As this sequence of primitives is rather generic, test engineers may have to tweak the generated code if the web application under test requires it.

In summary, the key aspects of this approach are:

1. The formalization of vulnerability test patterns using generic test purposes to drive the test generation engine;
2. The use of a DSML to ease and accelerate the functional modeling of the Web application under test;
3. The full automation of the testing process, including test generation, test execution and verdict assignment.

This PMVT approach has been found to be suitable for a range of vulnerability types, including technical ones (XSS, SQL injections, CSRF) as well as logical ones (authentication bypass, privilege escalation).

7. CONCLUSION AND FUTURE CHALLENGES

This chapter has reviewed the advances in MBT over the last few years. It is apparent that there have been many research advances and tool improvements, so that there is now a rich variety of notations and languages used for expressing the MBT models. Some standard choices of modeling notations are starting to emerge for modeling business applications (notably, UML and BPMN), and the area of GUI ripping has become a popular way of obtaining models for testing GUIs.

The past decade has seen continual improvements both in the MBT algorithms used to generate tests, and in the efficiency and flexibility of the underlying solver technologies used during test generation. These improvements have the incremental effect of allowing the tools to scale to larger problems, and producing better quality test suites. The scope of MBT practice has also expanded to include a wide range of different kinds of security testing, as discussed in Section 6.

But with regards to industry adoption, the progress is slower. The maturity analysis of various topics related to software testing in the industry, by the Trends and Benchmark Switzerland Report from 2013 [140], showed that MBT is placed in the introduction phase. As we have seen before, this is still the case in 2015, even if some evidence shows gradual progress in the dissemination of the approach.

It is of course very difficult to predict the future penetration of MBT into various industry areas. Beside the MBT User Survey 2014 presented in Section 3.1, we need more detailed studies to better understand the kinds of software where MBT is most effective, and the current strengths and weaknesses of the approach. For example, one recent study by Schulze et al. [141] compared the effort and the benefits of manual testing vs

MBT and found that MBT detected significantly more faults, but required more time up-front activities (modeling and implementing test infrastructure). They also noted that MBT was better at detecting functional issues, whereas the manual testing was more efficient for detecting GUI issues. Overall, they concluded that *"MBT detected more issues with higher severity scores with less testing and analysis effort than manual testing. However, it required more initial effort, which eventually would pay off if several versions of the same system would be tested"*.

This study points out one of the key issues regarding the penetration of MBT in industry, which is how to reduce effort when using MBT. Of course, in the MBT process these efforts are mainly related to modeling activities (ie, creation and maintenance of the MBT model). This is also linked with the adaptation of the MBT technologies to current software tester skills (typically ISTQB Foundation Level Certified Testers), who often have no or very few software modeling skills. Consequently, MBT modeling should be adapted to be more easily used by such professional testers.

These aspects may be seen as drivers for the research challenges for the MBT research community. There are several directions we can mention that directly address these aspects of MBT effort reduction and modeling simplification:

Fully or partially automate the creation of the MBT model. In the context of MBT of web applications, and more generally, model-based GUI testing (see Section 4.3), GUI-ripping techniques can automate the construction of the model. This has to be extended to other types of testing by analyzing existing artifacts to provide the right information. One limit of this approach is of course the oracle problem: extracting information from the system under test can help to determine sequence of test actions. But the expected results need to be derived from an external source, not from the buggy application.

Provide DSML to simplify the creation and maintenance of the MBT model. Domain-Specific Modeling Languages adapt the model creation process to the semantics of the application domain. Domain-specific modeling allows using existing domain terminology, with known semantics, and familiar notation in a specific application domain. For example, DSML may be used for ERP MBT, by adapting the modeling language to the targeted business domain, or in the context of aircraft traffic monitoring systems, by specifying MBT models using specific domain concepts such as plane, navigation path and monitoring zone. The use of DSML in MBT may allow faster model development and wider model accessibility, as compared to the use of general-purpose modeling languages.

Better reuse of existing requirements artifacts. At system or acceptance testing levels, testing objectives are strongly related to system requirements (particularly functional requirements). Requirements engineering leads to a large variety of artifacts, which are often very informal such as user stories or use case descriptions [142]. This leads also to structured artifacts like business process models or interface requirements specification. Automating the reuse of such informal artifacts may facilitate and accelerate MBT modeling activities. For example, deriving test cases or partial MBT models from use cases may help to capture the basic flow of events and the alternate flows of events.

Some other practical challenges for the future, particularly for the increased use of MBT in industry, are:

- the portability of models between different MBT tools—even when two tools use similar modeling notations such as UML, they tend to use different subsets of those notations, so models are not immediately transferable between MBT tools. This is likely to improve gradually as certain notations and tools achieve market dominance;
- the training of new MBT users in how to model for testing, and how to use MBT techniques in practice. The proposed ISTQB certified tester extension for MBT is expected to make a big improvement in this area, but learning how to design good MBT models is a nontrivial task, so on-going training, shepherding and support systems will be needed;
- the urgency for further studies that compare the use of MBT with other testing approaches.

REFERENCES

[1] C. Lee, A Practitioner's Guide to Software Test Design, Artech House, Inc., Norwood, MA, 2004.
[2] Q. Hung, H. Michael, K. Brent, Global Software Test Automation: A Discussion of Software Testing for Executives, Happy About, Cupertino, USA, 2006.
[3] A. Pretschner, W. Prenninger, S. Wagner, C. Kühnel, M. Baumgartner, B. Sostawa, R. Zölch, T. Stauner, One evaluation of model-based testing and its automation, in: Proceedings of the 27th International Conference on Software Engineering, ICSE '05, St. Louis, MO, USA, ACM, New York, NY, ISBN 1-58113-963-2, 2005, pp. 392–401, http://dx.doi.org/10.1145/1062455.1062529.
[4] M. Utting, B. Legeard, Practical Model-Based Testing—A Tools Approach, Morgan Kaufmann, San Francisco, CA, 2006, ISBN 0123725011.
[5] U. Mark, P. Alexander, L. Bruno, A taxonomy of model-based testing approaches, Softw. Test. Verif. Rel. 22 (5) (2012) 297–312, ISSN 1099-1689, http://dx.doi.org/10.1002/stvr.456.

[6] P.C. Jorgensen, A Craftsman's Approach, first ed., Auerbach Publications, Boca Raton, FL, 2009.

[7] T.S. Chow, Testing software design modeled by finite-state machines, IEEE Trans. Softw. Eng. 4 (3) (1978) 178–187, ISSN 0098-5589.

[8] Pairwise web site at http://www.pairwise.org/, 2015.

[9] G. Wolfgang, K. Nicolas, S. Keith, B. Victor, Model-based quality assurance of protocol documentation: tools and methodology, Softw. Test. Verif. Rel. 21 (1) (2011) 55–71, ISSN 1099-1689.

[10] R. Binder, L. Bruno, K. Anne, Model-based testing: where does it stand? Commun. ACM 58 (2) (2015) 52–56, ISSN 0001-0782, http://dx.doi.org/10.1145/2697399.

[11] B.K. Aichernig, Contract-based testing, in: Formal Methods at the Crossroads: From Panacea to Foundational Support, Lecture Notes in Computer Science, vol. 2757, Springer, Berlin, ISBN 3-540-20527-6, 2003, pp. 34–48.

[12] P. Baudin, P. Cuoq, J.-C. Filliâtre, C. Marché, B. Monate, Y. Moy, V. Prevosto, ACSL: ANSI/ISO C specification language version 1.7, 2013, http://frama-c.com/download/acsl-implementation-Fluorine-20130601.pdf.

[13] M. Barnett, K.R.M. Leino, W. Schulte, The Spec# programming system: an overview, in: Proceedings of the International Workshop on Construction and Analysis of Safe, Secure and Interoperable Smart Devices (CASSIS'04), Marseille, France, Lecture Notes in Computer Science, vol. 3362, Springer, 2004, pp. 49–69.

[14] J. Jacky, M. Veanes, NModel, online 2006, 2015 (last access March 2015), http://nmodel.codeplex.com/.

[15] Y. Cheon, G.T. Leavens, A simple and practical approach to unit testing: the JML and JUnit way, in: B. Magnusson (Ed.), 16th European Conference on Object-Oriented Programming, ECOOP 2002, Lecture Notes in Computer Science, vol. 2374, Springer, Berlin, ISBN 3-540-43759-2, 2002, pp. 231–255.

[16] D.M. Zimmerman, R. Nagmoti, JMLUnit: the next generation, in: Formal Verification of Object-Oriented Software, Lecture Notes in Computer Science, vol. 6528, Springer, 2010, pp. 183–197.

[17] G.T. Leavens, A.L. Baker, C. Ruby, JML: a notation for detailed design, in: H. Kilov, B. Rumpe, I. Simmonds (Eds.), Behavioral Specifications of Businesses and Systems, Kluwer Academic Publishers, Boston, MA, 1999, pp. 175–188 (36 references).

[18] M. Gligoric, T. Gvero, V. Jagannath, S. Khurshid, V. Kuncak, D. Marinov, Test generation through programming in UDITA, in: ICSE (1), 2010, pp. 225–234, http://doi.acm.org/10.1145/1806799.1806835.

[19] W. Visser, K. Havelund, G.P. Brat, S. Park, F. Lerda, Model checking programs, Autom. Softw. Eng. 10 (2) (2003) 203–232, http://dx.doi.org/10.1023/A:1022920129859.

[20] P. Heidegger, P. Thiemann, JSConTest: contract-driven testing and path effect inference for JavaScript, J. Obj. Technol. 11 (1) (2012) 1–29, http://dx.doi.org/10.5381/jot.2012.11.1.a6.

[21] S. Mirshokraie, Effective test generation and adequacy assessment for javascript-based web applications, in: Proceedings of the 2014 International Symposium on Software Testing and Analysis, ISSTA 2014, San Jose, CA, USA, ACM, New York, NY, ISBN 978-1-4503-2645-2, 2014, pp. 453–456, http://dx.doi.org/10.1145/2610384.2631832.

[22] I. Enderlin, F. Dadeau, A. Giorgetti, A. Ben Othman, Praspel: a specification language for contract-based testing in PHP, in: ICTSS, 2011, pp. 64–79.

[23] P. Baker, Z.R. Dai, J. Grabowski, O. Haugen, E. Samuelsson, I. Schieferdecker, C.E. Williams, The UML 2.0 testing profile, in: Proceedings of the 8th Conference on Quality Engineering in Software Technology (CONQUEST), Nuremberg, Germany, 2004, pp. 181–189.

[24] Z.R. Dai, J. Grabowski, H. Neukirchen, H. Pals, From design to test with UML, in: R. Groz, R.M. Hierons (Eds.), Testing of Communicating Systems, Lecture Notes in Computer Science, vol. 2978, Springer, Berlin, ISBN 978-3-540-21219-5, 2004, pp. 33–49.

[25] V. Sawant, K. Shah, Construction of test cases from UML models, in: K. Shah, V.R. Lakshmi Gorty, A. Phirke (Eds.), Technology Systems and Management, Communications in Computer and Information Science, vol. 145, Springer, Berlin, ISBN 978-3-642-20208-7, 2011, pp. 61–68, http://dx.doi.org/10.1007/978-3-642-20209-4.

[26] J. Cantenot, F. Ambert, F. Bouquet, Test generation with satisfiability modulo theories solvers in model-based testing, Softw. Test. Verif. Rel. 24 (7) (2014) 499–531, ISSN 1099-1689, http://dx.doi.org/10.1002/stvr.1537.

[27] T. Yue, S. Ali, L. Briand, Automated transition from use cases to UML state machines to support state-based testing, in: R.B. France, J.M. Kuester, B. Bordbar, R.F. Paige (Eds.), Modelling Foundations and Applications, Lecture Notes in Computer Science, vol. 6698, Springer, Berlin, ISBN 978-3-642-21469-1, 2011, pp. 115–131, http://dx.doi.org/10.1007/978-3-642-21470-7_9.

[28] S. Nogueira, A. Sampaio, A. Mota, Test generation from state based use case models, Form. Asp. Comput. 26 (3) (2014) 441–490, ISSN 0934-5043, http://dx.doi.org/10.1007/s00165-012-0258-z.

[29] S. Pickin, J.-M. Jezequel, Using UML sequence diagrams as the basis for a formal test description language, in: E.A. Boiten, J. Derrick, G. Smith (Eds.), Integrated Formal Methods, Lecture Notes in Computer Science, vol. 2999, Springer, Berlin, ISBN 978-3-540-21377-2, 2004, pp. 481–500, http://dx.doi.org/10.1007/978-3-540-24756-2_26.

[30] A. Rountev, S. Kagan, J. Sawin, Coverage criteria for testing of object interactions in sequence diagrams, in: M. Cerioli (Ed.), Fundamental Approaches to Software Engineering, Lecture Notes in Computer Science, vol. 3442, Springer, Berlin, ISBN 978-3-540-25420-1, 2005, pp. 289–304, http://dx.doi.org/10.1007/978-3-540-31984-9_22.

[31] A. Tripathy, A. Mitra, Test case generation using activity diagram and sequence diagram, in: K.M. Aswatha, R. Selvarani, T.V.S. Kumar (Eds.), Proceedings of International Conference on Advances in Computing, Advances in Intelligent Systems and Computing, vol. 174, Springer, India, ISBN 978-81-322-0739-9, 2012, pp. 121–129, http://dx.doi.org/10.1007/978-81-322-0740-5_16.

[32] V. Panthi, D. Mohapatra, Automatic Test Case Generation Using Sequence Diagram, in: A. Kumar, M.S. Ramaiah, T.V.S. Kumar (Eds.), Proceedings of International Conference on Advances in Computing, Advances in Intelligent Systems and Computing, vol. 174, Springer, India, ISBN 978-81-322-0739-9, 2012, pp. 277–284, http://dx.doi.org/10.1007/978-81-322-0740-5_33.

[33] R. Kumar, R.K. Bhatia, Interaction diagram based test case generation, in: P.V. Krishna, M.R. Babu, E. Ariwa (Eds.), Global Trends in Information Systems and Software Applications, Communications in Computer and Information Science, vol. 270, Springer, Berlin, ISBN 978-3-642-29215-6, 2012, pp. 202–211, http://dx.doi.org/10.1007/978-3-642-29216-3_23.

[34] A.K. Jena, S.K. Swain, D.P. Mohapatra, Test case creation from UML sequence diagram: a soft computing approach, in: L.C. Jain, S. Patnaik, N. Ichalkaranje (Eds.), Intelligent Computing, Communication and Devices, Advances in Intelligent Systems and Computing, vol. 308, Springer, India, ISBN 978-81-322-2011-4, 2015, pp. 117–126, http://dx.doi.org/10.1007/978-81-322-2012-1_13.

[35] A.H. Reijers, S. van Wijk, B. Mutschler, M. Leurs, BPM in practice: who is doing what? in: R. Hull, J. Mendling, S. Tai (Eds.), Business Process Management, Lecture

Notes in Computer Science, vol. 6336, Springer, Berlin, ISBN 978-3-642-15617-5, 2010, pp. 45–60, http://dx.doi.org/10.1007/978-3-642-15618-2_6.

[36] S.H. Jensen, S. Thummalapenta, S. Sinha, S. Chandra, Test Generation from Business Rules, Tech. Rep. RI14008, IBM Research Report, 2014.

[37] C. Mecke, Automated testing of mySAP business processes, in: D. Meyerhoff, B. Laibarra, R. van der Pouw Kraan, A. Wallet (Eds.), Software Quality and Software Testing in Internet Times, Springer, Berlin, ISBN 978-3-540-42632-5, 2002, pp. 261–279, http://dx.doi.org/10.1007/978-3-642-56333-1_17.

[38] H. Andreas, G. Tobias, G. Volker, F. Holger, Business process-based testing of web applications, in: M. zur Muehlen, J.W. Su (Eds.), Business Process Management Workshops, Lecture Notes in Business Information Processing, vol. 66, Springer, Berlin, ISBN 978-3-642-20510-1, 2011, pp. 603–614, http://dx.doi.org/10.1007/978-3-642-20511-8.

[39] S. Anand, E.K. Burke, T.Y. Chen, J. Clark, M.B. Cohen, W. Grieskamp, M. Harman, M.J. Harrold, P. McMinn, An orchestrated survey of methodologies for automated software test case generation, J. Syst. Softw. 86 (8) (2013) 1978–2001, ISSN 0164-1212, http://dx.doi.org/10.1016/j.jss.2013.02.061.

[40] Y. Wang, N. Yang, Test case generation of web service composition based on CP-nets, J. Softw. 9 (3) (2014). http://ojs.academypublisher.com/index.php/jsw/article/view/jsw0903589595.

[41] X. Yuan, M.B. Cohen, A.M. Memon, GUI interaction testing: incorporating event context, IEEE Trans. Softw. Eng.g 37 (4) (2011) 559–574, ISSN 0098-5589, http://dx.doi.org/10.1109/TSE.2010.50.

[42] A. Memon, I. Banerjee, B.N. Nguyen, B. Robbins, The first decade of GUI ripping: extensions, applications, and broader impacts, in: 20th Working Conference on Reverse Engineering (WCRE), 2013, 2013, pp. 11–20, http://dx.doi.org/10.1109/WCRE.2013.6671275.

[43] A. Memon, B.N. Nguyen, GUITAR, 2015. http://sourceforge.net/projects/guitar/ (last access March 2015).

[44] D.R. Hackner, A.M. Memon, Test case generator for GUITAR, in: Companion of the 30th International Conference on Software Engineering, ICSE Companion '08, Leipzig, Germany, ACM, New York, NY, ISBN 978-1-60558-079-1, 2008, pp. 959–960, http://dx.doi.org/10.1145/1370175.1370207.

[45] D. Amalfitano, A.R. Fasolino, P. Tramontana, S. De Carmine, A.M. Memon, Using GUI ripping for automated testing of android applications, in: Proceedings of the 27th IEEE/ACM International Conference on Automated Software Engineering, ASE 2012, Essen, Germany, ACM, New York, NY, ISBN 978-1-4503-1204-2, 2012, pp. 258–261, http://dx.doi.org/10.1145/2351676.2351717.

[46] S. Arlt, P. Borromeo, M. Schf, A. Podelski, Parameterized GUI Tests, in: B. Nielsen, C. Weise (Eds.), Testing Software and Systems, Lecture Notes in Computer Science, vol. 7641, Springer, Berlin, ISBN 978-3-642-34690-3, 2012, pp. 247–262.

[47] S. Arlt, A. Podelski, C. Bertolini, M. Schaf, I. Banerjee, A.M. Memon, Lightweight static analysis for GUI testing, in: 23rd IEEE International Symposium on Software Reliability Engineering (ISSRE), 2012, IEEE, 2012, pp. 301–310.

[48] F. Gross, G. Fraser, A. Zeller, EXSYST: Search-based GUI testing, in: 34th International Conference on Software Engineering (ICSE), 2012, ISSN 0270-5257, 2012, pp. 1423–1426, http://dx.doi.org/10.1109/ICSE.2012.6227232.

[49] R.M.L.M. Moreira, A.C.R. Paiva, A. Memon, A pattern-based approach for GUI modeling and testing, in: 24th IEEE International Symposium on Software Reliability Engineering (ISSRE), 2013, 2013, pp. 288–297, http://dx.doi.org/10.1109/ISSRE.2013.6698881.

[50] M.B. Cohen, S. Huang, A.M. Memon, AutoInSpec: using missing test coverage to improve specifications in GUIs, in: 23rd IEEE International Symposium on Software Reliability Engineering (ISSRE), 2012, ISSN 1071-9458, 2012, pp. 251–260, http://dx.doi.org/10.1109/ISSRE.2012.33.

[51] F. Bolis, A. Gargantini, M. Guarnieri, E. Magri, L. Musto, Model-driven testing for web applications using abstract state machines, in: M. Grossniklaus, M. Wimmer (Eds.), Current Trends in Web Engineering, Lecture Notes in Computer Science, vol. 7703, Springer, Berlin, ISBN 978-3-642-35622-3, 2012, pp. 71–78.

[52] V. Lelli, A. Blouin, B. Baudry, Classifying and qualifying GUI defects. in: IEEE International Conference on Software Testing, Verification and Validation (ICST 2015), IEEE, April 2015, pp. 1–10, http://dx.doi.org/10.1109/ICST.2015.7102582.

[53] H. Zhu, F. Belli, Advancing test automation technology to meet the challenges of model-based software testing, J. Inform. Softw. Technol. 51 (11) (2009) 1485–1486.

[54] E. Dustin, T. Garrett, B. Gauf, Implementing Automated Software Testing: How to Save Time and Lower Costs While Raising Quality, Addison Wesley Professional, Indianapolis, USA, 2009. ISBN 0-32-158051-6.

[55] H.W. Thimbleby, The directed Chinese postman problem, Soft. Pract. Exp. 33 (11) (2003) 1081–1096, http://dx.doi.org/10.1002/spe.540.

[56] M. Davis, G. Logemann, D. Loveland, A machine program for theorem-proving, Commun. ACM 5 (7) (1962) 394–397.

[57] L. de Moura, N. Bjørner, Z3: an efficient SMT solver, in: 14th International Conference on Tools and Algorithms for the Construction and Analysis of Systems (TACAS'08), Budapest, Hungary, Lecture Notes in Computer Science, vol. 4963, Springer, Berlin, 2008, pp. 337–340.

[58] C. Barrett, C. Tinelli, CVC3, in: 19th International Conference on Computer Aided Verification (CAV'07), Berlin, Germany, 2007, pp. 298–302.

[59] C. Barrett, C.L. Conway, M. Deters, L. Hadarean, D. Jovanovic, T. King, A. Reynolds, C. Tinelli, CVC4, in: 23rd International Conference on Computer Aided Verification (CAV'11), Snowbird, UT, USA, 2011, pp. 171–177.

[60] B. Dutertre, Yices 2.2, in: Computer-Aided Verification (CAV'14), Lecture Notes in Computer Science, vol. 8559, Springer, Berlin, 2014, pp. 737–744.

[61] A. Cimatti, A. Griggio, B. Schaafsma, R. Sebastiani, The MathSAT5 SMT Solver, in: International Conference on Tools and Algorithms for the Construction and Analysis of Systems (TACAS'13), Lecture Notes in Computer Science, vol. 7795, 2013, pp. 93–107.

[62] N. Tillmann, J. de Halleux, Pex white box test generation for .NET, in: Tests and Proofs (TAP'08), Lecture Notes in Computer Science, vol. 4966, Springer, Berlin, 2008, pp. 134–153.

[63] J. Cantenot, F. Ambert, F. Bouquet, Test generation with SMT solvers in model-based testing, STVR, Softw. Test. Verif. Rel. 24 (7) (2014) 499–531.

[64] P. Arcaini, A. Gargantini, E. Riccobene, Optimizing the automatic test generation by SAT and SMT solving for Boolean expressions, in: 26th IEEE/ACM International Conference on Automated Software Engineering (ASE'11), IEEE Computer Society, Washington, DC, 2011, pp. 388–391.

[65] M. Cristiá, C.S. Frydman, Applying SMT solvers to the test template framework, in: 7th Workshop on Model-Based Testing (MBT'12), Tallinn, Estonia, Electronic Proc. in Theoretical Computer Science, vol. 80, 2012, pp. 28–42.

[66] M. Cristiá, G. Rossi, C.S. Frydman, {log} as a test case generator for the test template framework, in: 11th International Conference on Software Engineering and Formal Methods (SEFM'13), Madrid, Spain, Lecture Notes in Computer Science, vol. 8137, 2013, pp. 229–243.

[67] A.K. Macworth, Consistency in networks of relations, J. Artif. Intell. 8 (1) (1977) 99–118.

[68] S.W. Golomb, L.D. Baumert, Backtrack programming, J. ACM 12 (4) (1965) 516–524.

[69] P. van Hentenryck, M. Dincbas, Domains in logic programming, in: Nat. Conf. on Artificial Intelligence (AAAI'86), 1986, pp. 759–765.

[70] E.P.K. Tsang, Foundations of constraint satisfaction. Computation in cognitive science, Academic Press, San Diego, CA, 1993, ISBN 978-0-12-701610-8.

[71] M. Mossige, A. Gotlieb, H. Meling, Testing robot controllers using constraint programming and continuous integration, Inform. Softw. Technol. 57 (2015) 169–185.

[72] M. Carlsson, G. Ottosson, B. Carlson, An open-ended finite domain constraint solver, in: 9th International Symposium on Programming Languages: Implementations, Logics, and Programs (PLILP'97), Springer-Verlag, London, UK, 1997, pp. 191–206.

[73] A. Dovier, C. Piazza, E. Pontelli, G. Rossi, Sets and constraint logic programming, ACM Trans. Program. Lang. Syst. 22 (5) (2000) 861–931.

[74] A. Dovier, C. Piazza, G. Rossi, A uniform approach to constraint-solving for lists, multisets, compact lists, and sets, ACM Trans. Comput. Log. 9 (3) (2008) 1–30.

[75] M. Shirole, R. Kumar, UML behavioral model based test case generation: a survey, SIGSOFT Softw. Eng. Notes 38 (4) (2013) 1–13, ISSN 0163-5948.

[76] C. Doungsa-ard, K. Dahal, A. Hossain, T. Suwannasart, Test data generation from UML state machine diagrams using GAs, in: International Conference on Software Engineering Advances, ICSEA 2007, 2007, pp. 47–47, http://dx.doi.org/10.1109/ICSEA.2007.70.

[77] R. Lefticaru, F. Ipate, Functional Search-based Testing from State Machines, in: 1st International Conference on Software Testing, Verification, and Validation, 2008, 2008, pp. 525–528, http://dx.doi.org/10.1109/ICST.2008.32.

[78] S. Ali, M.Z. Iqbal, A. Arcuri, Improved heuristics for solving OCL constraints using search algorithms, in: Genetic and Evolutionary Computation Conference, GECCO '14, Vancouver, BC, Canada, July 12-16, 2014, 2014, pp. 1231–1238.

[79] S. Ali, M. Zohaib Iqbal, A. Arcuri, L.C. Briand, Generating test data from OCL constraints with search techniques, IEEE Trans. Softw. Eng. 39 (10) (2013) 1376–1402.

[80] M. Shirole, M. Kommuri, R. Kumar, Transition sequence exploration of UML activity diagram using evolutionary algorithm, in: Proceedings of the 5th India Software Engineering Conference, ISEC '12, Kanpur, India, ACM, New York, NY, 2012, pp. 97–100.

[81] M. Shirole, R. Kumar, A hybrid genetic algorithm based test case generation using sequence diagrams, in: S. Ranka, A. Banerjee, K. Biswas, S. Dua, P. Mishra, R. Moona, S.-H. Poon, C.-L. Wang (Eds.), Contemporary Computing, Communications in Computer and Information Science, vol. 94, Springer, Berlin, 2010, pp. 53–63.

[82] E. Albert, M.J.G. de la Banda, M. Gómez-Zamalloa, J.M. Rojas, P. Stuckey, A CLP heap solver for test case generation, Theory Pract. Logic Program. 13 (2013) 721–735 (special Issue 4-5).

[83] P. Godefroid, N. Klarlund, K. Sen, DART: directed automated random testing, in: ACM SIGPLAN Conference on Programming Language Design and Implementation (PLDI'05), Chicago, IL, USA, ACM, New York, NY, 2005, pp. 213–223.

[84] K. Sen, D. Marinov, G. Agha, CUTE: a concolic unit testing engine for C, in: 10th European Software Engineering Conference (ESEC'05), Lisbon, Portugal, ACM, New York, NY, 2005, pp. 263–272.

[85] N. Tillmann, J. De Halleux, Pex: white box test generation for .NET, in: 2nd International Conference on Tests and Proofs (TAP'08), Prato, Italy, Springer-Verlag, Berlin, 2008, pp. 134–153.

[86] C. Cadar, P. Godefroid, S. Khurshid, C.S. Păsăreanu, K. Sen, N. Tillmann, W. Visser, Symbolic execution for software testing in practice: preliminary assessment, in: 33rd International Conference on Software Engineering (ICSE'11), Waikiki, Honolulu, HI, USA, ACM, New York, NY, 2011, pp. 1066–1071.

[87] C. Cadar, K. Sen, Symbolic execution for software testing: three decades later, Commun. ACM 56 (2) (2013) 82–90.

[88] E.M. Clarke, E.A. Emerson, A.P. Sistla, Automatic verification of finite-state concurrent systems using temporal logic specifications, ACM Trans. Program. Lang. Syst. 8 (2) (1986) 244–263.

[89] J. Callahan, F. Schneider, S. Easterbrook, Specification-based testing using model checking, in: SPIN Workshop, Rutgers University, 1996, pp. 1066–1071 (Tech. Report NASA-IVV-96-022).

[90] G. Fraser, F. Wotawa, P.E. Ammann, Testing with model checkers: a survey, Softw. Test. Verif. Rel. 19 (3) (2009) 215–261.

[91] R. Alur, D.L. Dill, A theory of timed automata, Theor. Comput. Sci. 126 (1994) 183–235.

[92] B. Johan, K.G. Larsen, L. Fredrik, P. Paul, Y. Wang, UPPAAL–a tool suite for automatic verification of real-time systems, in: Workshop on Verification and Control of Hybrid Systems III, no. 1066 in Lecture Notes in Computer Science, Springer-Verlag, Berlin, 1995, pp. 232–243.

[93] K. Bae, J. Meseguer, The linear temporal logic of rewriting Maude model checker, in: Rewriting Logic and Its Applications, Lecture Notes in Computer Science, vol. 6381, Springer, Berlin, 2010, pp. 208–225.

[94] D. Buchs, L. Lucio, A. Chen, Model checking techniques for test generation from business process models, in: Reliable Software Technologies, Ada-Europe 2009, Lecture Notes in Computer Science, vol. 5570, Springer, Berlin, 2009, pp. 59–74.

[95] E.P. Enoiu, A. CauÅević, T.J. Ostrand, E.J. Weyuker, D. Sundmark, P. Pettersson, Automated test generation using model checking: an industrial evaluation, Softw. Tools Technol. Transf. (2014) 1–19.

[96] K.G. Larsen, M. Mikucionis, B. Nielsen, Online testing of real-time systems using UPPAAL, in: Formal Approaches to Testing of Software, Linz, Austria, Lecture Notes in Computer Science, vol. 3395, Springer, Berlin, 2004, pp. 79–94.

[97] A. Graf-Brill, H. Hermanns, H. Garavel, A model-based certification framework for the energy bus standard, in: E. Abraham, C. Palamidessi (Eds.), Formal Techniques for Distributed Objects, Components, and Systems, Lecture Notes in Computer Science, vol. 8461, Springer, Berlin, 2014, pp. 84–99.

[98] C. Jard, T. Jéron, TGV: theory, principles and algorithms: a tool for the automatic synthesis of conformance test cases for non-deterministic reactive systems, Int. J. Softw. Tools Technol. Transf. 7 (4) (2005) 297–315, ISSN 1433-2779.

[99] A. Kriouile, W. Serwe, Using a formal model to improve verification of a cache-coherent system-on-chip, in: C. Baier, C. Tinelli (Eds.), Tools and Algorithms for the Construction and Analysis of Systems, Lecture Notes in Computer Science, vol. 9035, Springer, Berlin, 2015, pp. 708–722.

[100] G. Fraser, F. Wotawa, P. Ammann, Issues in using model checkers for test case generation, J. Syst. Softw. 82 (9) (2009) 1403–1418.

[101] K.Y. Rozier, Linear temporal logic symbolic model checking, Comput. Sci. Rev. 5 (2) (2011) 163–203.

[102] A. Biere, A. Cimatti, E.M. Clarke, O. Strichman, Y. Zhu, Bounded Model Checking, in: Advances in Computers, vol. 58, Elsevier, London, 2003, pp. 117–148.

[103] K. Gent, M.S. Hsiao, Functional test generation at the RTL Using Swarm Intelligence and Bounded Model Checking, in: 22nd Asian Test Symposium (ATS'13), Yilan, Taiwan, IEEE Computer Society, 2013, pp. 233–238.

[104] I. Schieferdecker, J. Gromann, A. Rennoch, Model based security testing *selected considerations* (keynote at SECTEST at ICST 2011 (accessed Septmber 25, 2012)), http://www.avantssar.eu/sectest2011/pdfs/Schieferdecker-invited-talk.pdf.

[105] I. Schieferdecker, J. Grossmann, M. Schneider, Model-based security testing, in: Proceedings MBT 2012, 2012, pp. 1–12, http://dx.doi.org/10.4204/EPTCS.80.1.

[106] G. Tian-yang, S. Yin-sheng, F. You-yuan, Research on software security testing, World Acad. Sci. Eng. Technol. 70 (2010) 647–651.

[107] Committee on National Security Systems, CNSS Instruction-4009. National Information Assurance Glossary, 2010.

[108] Y. le Traon, T. Mouelhi, A. Pretschner, B. Baudry, Test-driven assessment of access control in legacy applications, in: 1st International Conference on Software Testing, Verification, and Validation, 2008, 2008, pp. 238–247.

[109] T. Mouelhi, F. Fleurey, B. Baudry, Y. Traon, A model-based framework for security policy specification, deployment and testing, in: Proceedings of the 11th International Conference on Model Driven Engineering Languages and Systems, MoDELS '08, Toulouse, France, Springer-Verlag, Berlin, ISBN 978-3-540-87874-2, 2008, pp. 537–552.

[110] A. Pretschner, T. Mouelhi, Y. le Traon, Model-based tests for access control policies, in: 1st International Conference on Software Testing, Verification, and Validation, 2008, 2008, pp. 338–347.

[111] D. Xu, L. Thomas, M. Kent, T. Mouelhi, Y. Le Traon, A model-based approach to automated testing of access control policies, in: Proceedings of the 17th ACM Symposium on Access Control Models and Technologies, SACMAT '12, Newark, New Jersey, USA, ACM, New York, NY, ISBN 978-1-4503-1295-0, 2012, pp. 209–218.

[112] M. Anisetti, C.A. Ardagna, M. Bezzi, E. Damiani, A. Sabetta, Machine-readable privacy certificates for services, in: R. Meersman, H. Panetto, T. Dillon, J. Eder, Z. Bellahsene, N. Ritter, P. De Leenheer, D. Dou (Eds.), On the Move to Meaningful Internet Systems: OTM 2013 Conferences, Lecture Notes in Computer Science, vol. 8185, Springer, Berlin, ISBN 978-3-642-41029-1, 2013, pp. 434–450.

[113] W. Mallouli, M. Lallali, A. Mammar, G. Morales, A. Cavalli, Modeling and testing secure web applications, in: Web-Based Information Technologies and Distributed Systems, Atlantis Ambient and Pervasive Intelligence, vol. 2, Atlantis Press, Paris, France, 2010, pp. 207–255.

[114] P.-A. Masson, M.-L. Potet, J. Julliand, R. Tissot, G. Debois, B. Legeard, B. Chetali, F. Bouquet, E. Jaffuel, L. Van Aertrick, J. Andronick, A. Haddad, An access control model based testing approach for smart card applications: results of the POSÉ project, J. Inform. Assur. Secur. 5 (1) (2010) 335–351.

[115] J. Botella, F. Bouquet, J.-F. Capuron, F. Lebeau, B. Legeard, F. Schadle, Model-based testing of cryptographic components–lessons learned from experience, in: Sixth IEEE International Conference on Software Testing, Verification and Validation, Luxembourg, Luxembourg, March 18-22, 2013, 2013, pp. 192–201.

[116] F. Dadeau, K.C. Castillos, Y. Ledru, T. Triki, G. Vega, J. Botella, S. Taha, Test generation and evaluation from high-level properties for common criteria evaluations–the TASCCC testing tool, in: Sixth IEEE International Conference on Software Testing, Verification and Validation, Luxembourg, Luxembourg, March 18-22, 2013, 2013, pp. 431–438.

[117] F. Bouquet, F. Peureux, F. Ambert, Model-based testing for functional and security test generation, in: A. Aldini, J. Lopez, F. Martinelli (Eds.), Foundations of Security Analysis and Design VII, Lecture Notes in Computer Science, vol. 8604, Springer International Publishing, Switzerland, ISBN 978-3-319-10081-4, 2014, pp. 1–33.

[118] G. Pellegrino, L. Compagna, T. Morreggia, A tool for supporting developers in analyzing the security of web-based security protocols, in: H. Yenigün, C. Yilmaz,

A. Ulrich (Eds.), Testing Software and Systems, Lecture Notes in Computer Science, vol. 8254, Springer, Berlin, ISBN 978-3-642-41706-1, 2013, pp. 277–282.

[119] E. Fourneret, M. Ochoa, F. Bouquet, J. Botella, J. Jürjens, P. Yousefi, Model-based security verification and testing for smart-cards, in: Sixth International Conference on Availability, Reliability and Security, ARES 2011, Vienna, Austria, August 22-26, 2011, 2011, pp. 272–279.

[120] B.K. Aichernig, M. Weiglhofer, F. Wotawa, Improving fault-based conformance testing, Electron. Notes Theor. Comput. Sci. 220 (1) (2008) 63–77, ISSN 1571-0661.

[121] Y. Jia, M. Harman, An analysis and survey of the development of mutation testing, IEEE Trans. Softw. Eng. 37 (5) (2011) 649–678, ISSN 0098-5589.

[122] Y.L. Traon, T. Mouelhi, B. Baudry, Testing security policies: going beyond functional testing, in: ISSRE 2007, The 18th IEEE International Symposium on Software Reliability, Trollhättan, Sweden, 5-9 November 2007, 2007, pp. 93–102.

[123] G. Wimmel, J. Jürjens, Specification-based test generation for security-critical systems using mutations, in: C. George, H. Miao (Eds.), Formal Methods and Software Engineering, Lecture Notes in Computer Science, vol. 2495, Springer, Berlin, 2002, pp. 471–482.

[124] F. Dadeau, P.-C. Héam, R. Kheddam, Mutation-based test generation from security protocols in HLPSL, in: M. Harman, B. Korel (Eds.), 4th Int. Conf. on Software Testing, Verification and Validation, ICST 2011, Berlin, Germany, IEEE Computer Society Press, 2011, pp. 240–248.

[125] M. Schneider, J. Gromann, I. Schieferdecker, A. Pietschker, Online model-based behavioral fuzzing, in: Sixth IEEE International Conference on Software Testing, Verification and Validation Workshops (ICSTW), 2013, 2013, pp. 469–475.

[126] W. Johansson, M. Svensson, U.E. Larson, M. Almgren, V. Gulisano, T-fuzz: model-based fuzzing for robustness testing of telecommunication protocols, in: Seventh IEEE International Conference on Software Testing, Verification and Validation (ICST), 2014, 2014, pp. 323–332.

[127] MITRE, Common Weakness Enumeration 2015. http://cwe.mitre.org/ (last accessed April 2015).

[128] A. Blome, M. Ochoa, K. Li, M. Peroli, M.T. Dashti, VERA: a flexible model-based vulnerability testing tool, in: Proc. of the 6th Int. Conference on Software Testing, Verification and Validation (ICST'13), IEEE Computer Society, Luxembourg, 2013, pp. 471–478.

[129] J. Bozic, F. Wotawa, Security testing based on attack patterns, in: IEEE Seventh International Conference on Software Testing, Verification and Validation Workshops (ICSTW), 2014, IEEE, 2014, pp. 4–11.

[130] T. Wei, Y. Ju-Feng, X. Jing, S. Guan-Nan, Attack model based penetration test for SQL injection vulnerability, in: 2012 IEEE 36th Annual Computer Software and Applications Conference Workshops (COMPSACW), IEEE, 2012, pp. 589–594.

[131] D. Xu, M. Tu, M. Sanford, L. Thomas, D. Woodraska, W. Xu, Automated security test generation with formal threat models, IEEE Trans. Depend. Secure Comput. 9 (4) (2012) 526–540.

[132] S. Salva, S.R. Zafimiharisoa, Data vulnerability detection by security testing for android applications, in: Information Security for South Africa, 2013, IEEE, 2013, pp. 1–8.

[133] A. Vernotte, F. Dadeau, F. Lebeau, B. Legeard, F. Peureux, F. Piat, Efficient detection of multi-step cross-site scripting vulnerabilities, in: Information Systems Security, Springer, Berlin, 2014, pp. 358–377.

[134] M. Buchler, J. Oudinet, A. Pretschner, Semi-automatic security testing of web applications from a secure model, in: Proc. of the 6th Int. Conference on Software

Security and Reliability (SERE'12), Gaithersburg, MD, USA, IEEE Computer Society, 2012, pp. 253–262.

[135] M. Rocchetto, M. Ochoa, M.T. Dashti, Model-based detection of CSRF, in: ICT Systems Security and Privacy Protection, Springer, Berlin, 2014, pp. 30–43.

[136] V. Felmetsger, L. Cavedon, C. Kruegel, G. Vigna, Toward automated detection of logic vulnerabilities in web applications, in: USENIX Security Symposium, 2010, pp. 143–160.

[137] R. Kaksonen, A. Takanen, Test coverage in model-based fuzz testing, in: Model Based Testing User Conference, Tallinn/Estonia, ETSI, 2012 (invited talk).

[138] F. Duchene, Detection of web vulnerabilities via model inference assisted evolutionary fuzzing, Ph.D. thesis, Grenoble University, 2014 (ph.D. thesis).

[139] J. Wang, T. Guo, P. Zhang, Q. Xiao, A model-based behavioral fuzzing approach for network service, in: Third International Conference on Instrumentation, Measurement, Computer, Communication and Control (IMCCC), 2013, IEEE, 2013, pp. 1129–1134.

[140] Trends and Benchmarks Report Switzerland. Where do we stand where are we going to? Testing 2013, Available from www.swissq.it. 2013, http://www.swissq.it/wp-content/uploads/2013/07/Testing-Trends-and-Benchmarks-2013_Web_En.pdf.

[141] C. Schulze, D. Ganesan, M. Lindvall, R. Cleaveland, D. Goldman, Assessing model-based testing: an empirical study conducted in industry, in: Companion Proceedings of the 36th International Conference on Software Engineering, ICSE Companion 2014, Hyderabad, India, ACM, New York, NY, ISBN 978-1-4503-2768-8, 2014, pp. 135–144, http://dx.doi.org/10.1145/2591062.2591180.

[142] C. Wang, F. Pastore, A. Goknil, L. Briand, Z. Iqbal, Automatic generation of system test cases from use case specifications. in: International Symposium on Software Testing and Analysis, ISSTA'15, Baltimore, Maryland, USA, July 12-17, 2015, ACM, New York, USA, 2015, pp. 385–396, http://dx.doi.org/10.1145/2771783.2771812 (accepted paper, to be published).

ABOUT THE AUTHORS

Mark Utting is a Senior Lecturer in ICT at the University of the Sunshine Coast. Previously, he worked as Senior Research Fellow in software engineering at QUT for several years, developing computer simulations of future Queensland Electricity Networks, and as Associate Professor at the University of Waikato in New Zealand, teaching programming and software engineering. He has also worked in industry, developing next-generation genomics software and manufacturing software. Mark is coauthor of the book "Practical Model-Based Testing: A Tools Approach," as well as more than 60 publications on model-based testing, verification techniques for object-oriented and real-time software, and language design for parallel computing.

Bruno Legeard Professor of Software Engineering at the University of Franche-Comté (France), cofounder and Senior Scientist at Smartesting Solutions & Services, is internationally recognized as an expert and a well-known speaker in the model-based testing field. He has given talks at numerous testing and software engineering conferences. He is experienced in deploying model-based testing solutions both in enterprise information systems area and in the embedded systems field. B. Legeard wrote the seminal book "Practical Model-Based Testing—A Tools Approach," published by Morgan and Kaufmann in 2007, with Dr. Mark Utting. He was also a coleader of the author team developing the recent ISTQB Model-Based Testing certification. He earned his Master of Science Degree in Software Engineering and his PhD in Computer Science from INSA Lyon, France.

Fabrice Bouquet studied computer science and received his PhD from the University of Provence, France in 1999. He is a full Professor of Software Engineering at the University of Franche-Comté, France. He researches the validation of complex systems from requirements to models, including operational semantics, testing, model transformation, functional and nonfunctional properties, with applications in vehicle, aircraft, smart objects, and energy.

Elizabeta Fourneret completed her PhD at INRIA/University of Franche-Comté, France in 2012 in Model-Based Regression Testing of Critical Systems. She is currently a Research Engineer at the Department of Computer Science at the Institut FEMTO ST in Besançon, France. She is interested in developing new solutions and tools for testing and test data generation toward ensuring the system's compliance to given requirements. In this framework, her research activities focus on Model-Based Testing (MBT) approaches that tackle the modeling and testing of critical systems, for instance, systems in the satellite or smartcard industry.

Fabien Peureux received his PhD in Computer Science from the University of Franche-Comté in 2002, where he works since 2003 as Assistant Professor and does his research activities with the FEMTO-ST Institute. Since 2005, he is also senior scientific consultant for the Smartesting company. His main expertise is focused on the automation of validation process in the domains of smartcard applications, information systems, and embedded software, with a particular interest in Model-Based Testing techniques and agile approaches.

Alexandre Vernotte received his PhD at the Institut Femto-ST, Besancon in 2015 in Model-Based Security Testing for Web applications. He recently obtained a postdoc position at the Department of Industrial Information and Control Systems at the Royal Institute of Technology (KTH) in Stockholm, Sweden. His research centers on enterprise system architectures security. His interests also include threat, risk, and behavioral modeling, Model–Based Testing and Model–Based Engineering.

CHAPTER THREE

On Testing Embedded Software

Abhijeet Banerjee*, Sudipta Chattopadhyay†, Abhik Roychoudhury*
*National University of Singapore, Singapore
†Saarland University, Saarbrücken, Germany

Contents

Abstract

For the last few decades, embedded systems have expanded their reach into major aspects of human lives. Starting from small handheld devices (such as smartphones) to advanced automotive systems (such as anti-lock braking systems), usage of embedded systems has increased at a dramatic pace. Embedded software are specialized software that are intended to operate on embedded devices. In this chapter, we shall describe the unique challenges associated with testing embedded software. In particular, embedded software are *required* to satisfy several non-functional constraints, in addition to functionality-related constraints. Such non-functional constraints may include (but not limited to), timing/energy-consumption related constrains or reliability requirements, etc. Additionally, embedded systems are often required to operate in

Advances in Computers, Volume 101
ISSN 0065-2458
http://dx.doi.org/10.1016/bs.adcom.2015.11.005

121

interaction with the physical environment, obtaining their inputs from environmental factors (such as temperature or air pressure). The need to interact with a dynamic, often non-deterministic physical environment, further increases the challenges associated with testing, and validation of embedded software. In the past, testing and validation methodologies have been studied extensively. This chapter, however, explores the advances in software testing methodologies, specifically in the context of embedded software. This chapter introduces the reader to key challenges in testing non-functional properties of software by means of realistic examples. It also presents an easy-to-follow, classification of existing research work on this topic. Finally, the chapter is concluded with a review of promising future directions in the area of embedded software testing.

1. INTRODUCTION

Over the last few decades, research in software testing has made significant progress. The complexity of software has also increased at a dramatic pace. As a result, we have new challenges involved in validating complex, real-world software. In particular, we are specifically interested in testing and validation of embedded software. In this modern world, embedded systems play a major role in human lives. Such software can be found ubiquitously, in electronic systems such as consumer electronics (eg, smartphones, mp3 players, and digital cameras) and household appliances (eg, washing machines and microwave ovens) to automotive (eg, electric cars and antilock braking systems) and avionic applications. Software designed for embedded systems have unique features and constraints that make its validation a challenging process. For instance, unlike Desktop applications, the behavior of an embedded systems often depends on the physical environment it operates in. As a matter of fact, many embedded systems often take their inputs from the surrounding physical environment. This, however, poses unique challenges to testing of such systems because the physical environment may be non-deterministic and difficult to recreate during the testing process. Additionally, most embedded systems are required to satisfy several non-functional constraint such as timing, energy consumption, reliability, to name a few. Failure to meet such constraints can result in varying consequences depending upon the application domain. For instance, if the nature of constraints on the software are hard real time, violation may lead to serious consequences, such as damage to human life and property. Therefore, it is of utmost importance that such systems be tested thoroughly before being put to use. In the proceeding sections, we shall discuss some of the techniques proposed by the software engineering community that are targeted at testing and validation of real life, embedded systems from various application domains and complexities. However, first we shall present an example, inspired from a real life embedded system, that will give the reader an idea on the nature of constraints commonly associated with embedded systems.

Fig. 1 provides the schematic representation of a *wearable fall detection application* [1]. Such an application is used largely in the health care domain to assist the frail or elderly patients. The purpose of the system, as shown in Fig. 1, is to detect a *potential fall* of its wearer and to invoke appropriate safety measures. In order to detect a fall, the system needs to monitor the user's movement. This task is accomplished via a number of sensors, that are positioned at different parts of the patient's body. These sensors detect physical motions and communicate the information via wireless sensor networks. In the scenario when the system detects a potential fall it activates appropriate safety measures, such as informing the health care providers over mobile networks. Testing the fall-detection system is essential to ensure its functional correctness, such as *a potential fall must not go undetected*. However, such a testing requires the inputs from the sensors. To properly test the system, its designers should be able to systematically model the inputs from sensors and the surrounding environment.

Apart from the functional correctness, the fall-detection system also needs to satisfy several non-functional constraints. For instance, the detection of a fall should meet hard timing constraints. In the absence of such constraints, the respective patient might get seriously injured, making the system impractical to use. Moreover, if the application is deployed into a battery operated device, its energy consumption should be acceptable to ensure a graceful degradation of battery life. Finally, due to the presence of unreliable hardware components (eg, *sensors*) and networks (eg, sensor and mobile

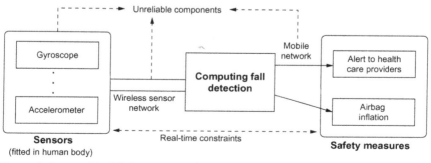

Figure 1 A wearable fall-detection application.

networks), the application should also guarantee that a potential fall of the patient is detected with acceptable reliability.

Non-functional properties of embedded software, such as timing and energy, are extremely sensitive to the underlying execution platform. This makes the testing process complicated, as the underlying execution platform may not be available during the time of testing. Besides, if the embedded software is targeted at multiple execution platforms, its non-functional properties need to be validated for each such platform. To alleviate these issues, a configurable model for the execution platform might be used during the testing process. For instance, such a configurable model can capture the timing or energy behavior of different hardware components. Building such configurable models, however, may turn out challenging due to the complexity of hardware and its (vendor-specific) intellectual properties.

Over the last two decades, numerous methods in software testing have been proposed. These include random testing, search-based testing, and directed testing (eg, based on symbolic execution), among several others. These testing methodologies have focused primarily on the validation of functional properties. Validation of non-functional software properties, have gained attention only recently. In this Chapter, we explore the potential of different testing methodologies in the context of embedded software. For an embedded software, its non-functional aspects play a crucial role in the validation process. We introduce some salient properties of validating typical embedded systems in Section 2. Subsequently, we shall explore the recent advances in testing embedded systems in Section 3. We first categorize all testing methodologies into three broader categories. Such categories reflect the level of abstraction, in which embedded systems are validated. In particular, our first category captures black-box testing, where the system is abstracted away and test inputs are generated via sampling of the input space. The remaining categories either use an abstract model of the system or the actual implementation. We shall discuss that different testing machineries (eg, evolutionary testing and symbolic execution) can be employed for such categories. Based on our categorization of testing embedded systems, we shall argue that no single category can be decided to be superior than others. In general, the choice of abstraction, for testing embedded system, largely depends on the intention of the designer. For instance, if the designer is interested in detecting fine-grained events (eg, memory requests and interrupts), it is recommended to carry out the testing process on the actual implementation (eg, binary code). On the contrary, testing binary code may reveal non-functional bugs too late in the design process, leading to a complete redesign of the software.

Through this chapter, we aim to bring the attention of software engineering community towards the unique challenges involved in embedded software testing. Specifically, testing of non-functional properties is an integral part of validating embedded software. In order to validate non-functional properties, software testing methodologies should explicitly target to discover non-functional bugs, such as the loss of performance and energy. Moreover, in order to test functional properties of embedded software, the designer should be able to simulate the interaction of software with the physical environment. We shall discuss several efforts in recent years to discover functional as well as non-functional bugs in embedded software. In spite of these efforts, numerous challenges still exist in validating embedded software. For instance, non-functional behaviors of embedded software (eg, time and power) can be exploited to discover secret inputs (eg, secret keys in cryptographic algorithms). Testing of timing and energy-related properties is far from being solved, not to mention the immaturity of the research field to validate security constraints in embedded software. We hope this chapter will provide the necessary background to solve these existing challenges in software testing.

2. TESTING EMBEDDED SOFTWARE

Analogous to most software systems, testing embedded software is an integral part of the software development life cycle. To ensure the robustness of embedded software, both its functional and non-functional properties need to be examined. In the following discussion, we outline some salient features that make the testing of embedded systems unique and challenging, compared to traditional software systems.

2.1 Testing Functional Properties

The functionality of software systems capture the way such systems should behave. Therefore, testing functional properties is a critical phase for all applications. Typically, the functionality testing of software aims to discover "buggy" scenarios. For instance, such buggy scenarios may capture the violation of software behavior with respect to the specification or an implementation bug (eg, null pointer dereference and assertion failure). To discover and investigate a buggy scenario, the designer must be provided with appropriate test inputs that trigger the respective bug. Therefore, software testing tools should have a clear domain knowledge of the relevant inputs to the system. For embedded software, the functionality is often (partially) controlled by the physical environment. Such physical environment might include air pressure, temperature, physical movement, among others. Unfortunately, the physical environment, where an embedded software is eventually deployed, is often not present during the testing time. For instance, consider the fall-detection application, which was introduced in the preceding section. It is crucial that the designed software invokes appropriate actions according to the movement of the patient. In the actual working environment, such movements are sampled from sensor inputs. Consider the code fragment in Fig. 2, which reads an accelerometer and takes action accordingly. The function f(buffer) captures a predicate on the values read into the buffer. The else branch of the code fragment exhibits a *division-by-zero* error when buffer[0] = 0. In order to execute the else branch, the test input must, additionally, satisfy the condition f(buffer) = 0. As the value of buffer depends on the physical environment, the inputs from the accelerometer might often need to be simulated via suitable abstractions. Similarly, for embedded software, whose functionality might depend on air pressure or temperature, the testing process should ensure that the respective software acts appropriately in different environmental conditions. In general, to simulate the physical environment, the designer may potentially take the following approaches:

- The physical environment (eg, inputs read from sensors) might be made completely *unconstrained* during the time of testing. This enables the testing of software under all operating conditions of the physical environment. However, such an approach might turn infeasible for complex embedded software. Besides, unconstraining the physical environment might lead to unnecessary testing for irrelevant inputs. Such inputs may include sensor readings (such as -300 K for air temperature readings) that may never appear in the environment where the software is deployed.

```
int x, y, buffer[128];

buffer = read_accelerometer(); //read accelerometer

if (f(buffer))
  Code A; //non-buggy code fragment
else
  y = x/buffer[0]; //buggy code fragment
```

Figure 2 The dependency of functionality on the physical environment.

- The physical environment might be simulated by randomly generating synthetic inputs (eg, generating random temperatures readings). However, such an approach may fail to generate relevant inputs. However, like traditional software testing, search-based techniques might improve the simulation of physical environment via evolutionary methods and metaheuristics.
- With a clear knowledge of the embedded software, the testing process can be improved. For instance, in the fall-detection system, it is probably not crucial to simulate the movement for all possible movement angles. It is, however, important to test the application for some inputs that indicate a fall of the patient (hence, indicating safety) and also for some inputs that does not capture a fall (hence, indicating the absence of false positives). In general, building such abstractions on the input space is challenging and it also requires a substantial domain knowledge of the input space.

We shall now discuss some non-functional properties that most embedded software are required to satisfy.

2.2 Testing Non-functional Properties

In general, most embedded software are constrained via several non-functional requirements. In the following and for the rest of the chapter, we shall primarily concentrate on three crucial properties of embedded software—timing, energy, and reliability.

2.2.1 Timing Constraints

Timing constraints capture the criteria to complete tasks within some time budgets. The violation of such constraints may lead to a complete failure of the respective software. This, in turn, may have serious consequences. For instance, consider the fall-detection application. The computation of a potential *fall* should have real-time constraints. More precisely, the time-frame between the sampling of sensor inputs and triggering an alarming situation should have strict timing constraints. Violation of such constraints may lead to the possibility of detecting a fall *too late*, hence, making the respective software impractical. Therefore, it is crucial that the validation process explicitly targets to discover the violation of timing-related constraints. It is, however, challenging to determine the timing behavior of an application, as the timing critically depends on the execution platform. The execution platform, in turn, may not be available during the testing phase. As a result, the validation of timing-related constraints, may often involve building a timing model of the underlying execution platform. Such a timing model should be able to estimate the time taken by each executed instruction. In general, building such timing models is challenging. This is because, the time taken by each instruction depends on the specific instruction set architecture (ISA) of the processor, as well as the state of different hardware components (eg, cache, pipeline, and interconnect). To show the interplay between the ISA and hardware components, let us consider the program fragment shown in Fig. 3.

In Fig. 3, the `true` leg of the conditional executes an `add` instruction and the `false` leg of the branch executes a `multiply` instruction. Let us assume that we want to check whether this code finishes within some given time budget. In other words, we wish to find out if the execution time of branch with the longer execution time is less than the given time budget. In a typical processor, a multiplication operation generally takes longer than an addition operation. However, if the processor employs a cache between the CPU and the memory, the variable z will be cached after executing the statement $z := 3$. Therefore, the statement $x := x * z$ can be completed without accessing the memory, but the processor may need to access the memory to execute $x := x + y$ (to fetch y for the first time). As a result, even though multiplication is a costly operation compared to addition, in this particular scenario, the multiplication may lead to a faster completion time. This example illustrates that a timing model for an execution platform should carefully consider such interaction between different hardware components.

Once a timing model is built for the execution platform, the respective software can be tested against the given timing-related constraints. Broadly, the validation of timing constraints may involve the following procedures:
• The testing procedure may aim to discover the violation of constraints. For instance, let us assume that for a fall-detection application to be

```
int x, y, z;

z := 3; //z is accessed and put into the cache

if (x > 0)
    x := x + y; //y needs to be fetched from the cache
else
    x := x * z; //all variables are cached
```

Figure 3 The timing interplay between hardware components (eg, caches) and instructions.

practical, the alarming situation must be notified within 1 ms (*cf.* Fig. 1). Such a constraint can be encoded via the assertion: *assert*(*time* $<= 1ms$), where *time* is the time taken by the fall-detection application to compute a potential fall. The value of *time* can be obtained by executing the application directly on the targeted platform (when available) or by using a timing model for the same. The testing process aims to find test inputs that may potentially invalidate the encoded assertions.

- It may, however, turn difficult for a designer to develop suitable assertions that capture timing constraints. In such cases, she might be interested to know the worst-case execution time (WCET) of the software. As the name suggests, WCET captures the maximum execution time of an application with respect to all inputs. Accurately determining the WCET of an application is extremely challenging, especially due to the complex interactions across different software layers (application, operating systems, and hardware) and due to the absence of (proprietary) architectural details of the underlying execution platform. However, WCET of an application can be approximated via systematically testing the software with appropriate inputs. For instance, we shall discuss in Section 3 about the progress in evolutionary testing to discover the WCET.

2.2.2 Energy Constraints

Like timing, energy consumption of embedded software may also need careful consideration. In particular, if the respective software is targeted for a battery-operated device, the energy consumption of the software may pose a serious bottleneck. For instance, if a fall-detection software is battery-operated, the power drained from the battery should be acceptable in a way to trigger the alarming situation. Like timing, the energy consumption of software is also highly sensitive to the underlying execution platform. Therefore, in the absence of the execution platform, an appropriate energy-model needs to be developed. Such an energy model can be used during the test time to estimate the energy consumption of software and to check whether the software satisfies certain energy constraints. Similar to timing constraints, energy constraints can be captured systematically via assertions or via computing the worst case energy consumption (WCEC) of the respective software. The computation of WCEC has similar challenges as the computation of the WCET and therefore, such computations might involve approximations via systematically generating test inputs.

2.2.3 Reliability Constraints

As embedded software often interacts with the physical environment, it needs to reliably capture the data acquired from the physical world. Usually, this is accomplished via sensors (eg, gyroscope and accelerometers), which interacts with the software via communicating the data from the physical world. For instance, in the fall detection application, the data read via the sensors are sent via wireless sensor network. In general, it is potentially infeasible to get the sensor data accurately. This might be due to the inaccuracy of sensor chips or due to potential packet drops in the network. Therefore, the reliability of different software components may pose a concern for a critical embedded software, such as a fall detector. Besides, the reliability of a component and its cost has nontrivial trade-offs. For instance, a more accurate sensor (or a reliable network) might incur higher cost. Overall, the designer must ensure that the respective software operates with an acceptable level of reliability. As an example, in the fall detector, the designer would like to ensure that a physical fall is alarmed with $x\%$ reliability. Computing the reliability of an entire system might become challenging when the system consists of several components and such components might interact with each other (and the physical world) in a fairly complex fashion.

To summarize, apart from the functionality, most embedded software have several non-functional aspects to be considered in the testing process. Such non-functional aspects include timing, energy, and reliability, among others. In general, the non-functional aspects of embedded software may lead to several complex trade-offs. For instance, an increased rate of sampling sensor inputs (which capture the data from the physical world) may increase energy consumption; however, it might increase the reliability of the software in terms of monitoring the physical environment. Similarly, a naive implementation to improve the functionality may substantially increase the energy consumption or it may lead to the loss of performance. As a result, embedded software are required to be systematically tested with respect to their non-functional aspects. In the next section, we shall discuss several testing methodologies for embedded software, with a specific focus on their non-functional properties.

3. CATEGORIZATION OF TESTING METHODOLOGIES

Real-time and embedded systems are used extensively in a wide variety of applications, ranging from automotive and avionics to entertainment and consumer electronics. Depending on the application, the constraints applicable on such systems may range from mission-critical to soft-real time

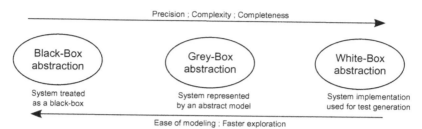

Figure 4 Classification of existing approaches for embedded software testing.

in nature. Additionally, embedded systems often have to interact with the physical environment that may be deterministic or non-deterministic. Such factors imply that embedded systems have to be designed and developed with varying operational requirements and no single testing technique is well suited to all systems. In some scenarios, the system under test (SUT) may be too complex to model and hence, approximate, yet fast sampling-based techniques are suitable. In other scenarios, where the SUT has mission-critical constraints and requires thorough testing, a fine-grained modeling of the system is crucial. In the following paragraphs, we shall categorize and discuss some of the existing works on testing embedded systems, with a specific focus on works being published in the past 5 years. In particular, we categorize all works into following three divisions (as shown in Figure 4):

  Black-Box Abstraction : Such techniques often consider the SUT as a black-box. Test cases are generated by sampling, randomized testing techniques.

  Grey-Box Abstraction : Such techniques do not treat the SUT as a black-box. The SUT is represented by a model, which captures only the information related to the property of interest. Test cases are generated by exploring the search space of the model.

  White-Box Abstraction : Techniques in this category often require the source code or binary of the implemented system for the testing process. In other words, the source code and binary serves as the model of the system. Test cases are generated by searching the input space of the implemented system.

In subsequent sections, we shall elaborate on each of the categorization as described in the preceding paragraphs.

4. BLACK-BOX ABSTRACTION

One of the most simple (but not necessarily effective) approaches of testing complex systems is to uniformly sample its input space. The goal of such sampling is to generate test inputs. As exceedingly simple as such a method might seem, the effectiveness of such uniform (or unguided) sampling remains questionable. When testing a system, in general, the objective is to produce test inputs that bears witnesses to failure of the system. Such a failure might capture the violation of a property of interest. Besides, such violations should be manifested within a certain time budget for testing.[1] Testing approaches, which are purely based on uniform random sampling, clearly do not adhere to the aforementioned criteria. For example, consider a system that expects an integer value as an input. For such a system uniform random sampling may blindly continue to generate test inputs forever without providing any information about the correctness (or in-correctness) of the system. However, there will be systems in the wild that are too complex to model. Such systems require some sort of mechanism by which they can be tested to some extent. For such systems, the sampling based technique, as discussed in the following paragraphs, might be useful.

The work in [2, 3] proposes sampling based techniques to generate failure-revealing test inputs for complex embedded systems. In particular, they focus on generating test inputs that lead to violation of timing-related properties. For these techniques to work, the essential timing-related properties of the system must be formulated via Metric Temporal Logic (MTL). An MTL formula can be, in a broad way, described as a composition of propositional as well as temporal operators. Common examples of propositional operators are *conjunction*, *disjunction*, and *negation*, whereas some example of temporal operators would be *until*, *always*, and *eventually*. Besides, MTL extends the traditional linear temporal logic (LTL) with timing constraints. For instance, consider our example in Fig. 1. Let us consider that a potential fall of the patient must be reported within 100 time units. Such a criteria can be captured via the following MTL formula:

$$\Box(fall \rightarrow \Diamond_{(0,100)} alarm)$$

`fall` captures the event of a potential fall and `alarm` captures the event to notify the health care providers. Besides, the temporal operators $\Box$ and $\Diamond$ capture *always* and *eventually*, respectively. Once the timing-related properties of the system have been identified and encoded as MTL formulas, the next step is to identify test inputs (as shown in Fig. 5), for which the aforementioned formula do not hold true (ie, the system fails).

---

[1] Otherwise, the testing process should terminate with assurance that the system functionality is expected under all feasible circumstances.

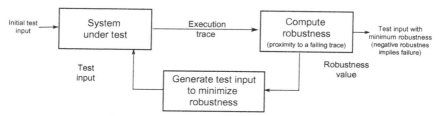

Figure 5 Overview of sampling based test-generation techniques.

The cornerstone of sampling-based approaches lies in the definition of a metric, as often called *robustness metric*. Such a metric represents the distance of a given execution trace (of the SUT, for a given input) from a failure revealing execution trace. The metric is designed in such a manner that if an execution trace has a negative value for the *robustness metric*, then it implies that the respective execution has lead to a violation of some timing-related property. Similarly, a positive value for a robustness metric signifies that the execution satisfies the MTL formulas. In general, the *robustness metric* provides a measure of how robustly an execution trace satisfies the encoded MTL formulas. Once such a metric has been defined, it needs to be decided *whether there exists an input that leads to the violation of the given property*. This decision problem can be transformed into an optimization problem. For instance, this optimization problem might aim to discover the execution with the lowest robustness value. Existing works have discussed a number of ways of solving the optimization (minimizing robustness) problem. For example, the technique of [2] uses Monte-Carlo simulations to solve this optimization problem. An obvious drawback being that the technique of [2] can only give probabilistic guarantees to find failure inducing test inputs. At the same time, an advantage of such a technique is to find execution where the timing-related property was the closest to being violated. Subsequent work in this direction have experimented with other optimization techniques, such as [3] uses Cross-entropy method based optimization and [4] uses ant-colony based optimization, in trying to improve the efficiency of the test-generation process.

5. GREY-BOX ABSTRACTION

This class of techniques work by creating an abstract model of the SUT. As shown in Fig. 6, in general, frameworks discussed in this category require three key components as follows:

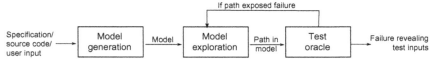

Figure 6 Overview of grey-box abstraction based testing techniques.

- A technique for model generation
- A technique for model exploration (to generate test cases), and
- An oracle for identifying failure-revealing tests

Once the property of interest has been identified, the model of the SUT can be generated through an automatic, semi-automatic or manual approaches. The model can be generated by analyzing the system specification, the source code or the environment. The generated model is then explored using a wide variety of techniques, ranging from random walk of the model to evolutionary or genetic algorithms. Test oracle is a critical component of the framework and it is used to differentiate between the correct and incorrect system execution. A test oracle is used to identify failure-revealing test inputs, while exploring the model of the SUT. The efficacy of the test-generation technique largely depends on the level of abstraction of the model and the efficiency of the exploration algorithm. A coarse-grained model is relatively easy to create and explore, but it may miss some of the important (failure-revealing) scenarios. On the contrary, a very detailed and fine-grained model is difficult to create and explore. However, such a fine-grained model is likely to discover more failure revealing test inputs. Considering the accuracy and precision of abstraction, we further classify the techniques in this category, based on the respective models used for testing. In the following sections, we describe each such model in more details.

5.1 Timed State Machines

Modelings tools, such as Markov chains have been used to model and test systems for a long time. To be more specific, Markov Chain Usage Models (MCUM) can be described as directed graphs, where the nodes of the graph represent the states of the SUT. The nodes of the system are connected by edges, representing events (inputs) that may arrive at a given state of the system. Additionally, edges are annotated with the probability of the occurrence of an event, when the system is in a given state. However MCUMs, by themselves, do not provide a suitable way of representing the timing-related properties of the SUT. Such timing-related properties may require certain events to happen before, after or within a specific deadline. Since timing-related requirements are often an integral part of real-time embedded system (eg, in automotive applications), MCUMs were extended to capture such requirements. One of the earliest such extensions of MCUMs was proposed in [5], where the extended MCUMs are referred to as Timed Usage Models (TUMs). Similar to the conventional MCUMs, all paths, from the start state to the end state in a TUM, represent feasible executions of the SUT. Figure 7A provides a simple example of a timed usage model. However, there also exists some key differences between an MCUM and a TUM that are listed in the following:

- Similar to the conventional MCUMs, a TUM has a set of states to capture the feasible usage of the system. However, in TUM, an additional probability distribution function (*pdf*) is associated with each state. This *pdf* encodes the time, for which the SUT will be in the respective state.
- In TUM, each transition between two states is triggered by a stimulus. Additionally, edges connecting the states are associated with two variables, a transition probability and a probability distribution function (*pdf*) of stimulus time. As the name suggests, the transition probability captures the probability of the respective transition between two states. Therefore, the transition probability has a similar role to that of conventional MCUMs. The *pdf* of the stimulus time represents the duration of execution of the stimulus on the system, at a given state.
- In a deterministic MCUM, there could be at most one transition (from a given state) for a given stimulus. However, in a TUM, the next state not only depends on the stimulus, but also on the duration of the execution of the stimulus. This feature is required to capture timing-related dependencies in the system. Additionally, to maintain consistency, the *pdfs* of stimulus time, originating from a state, do not overlap.

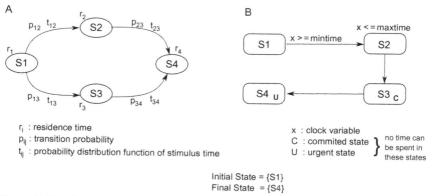

Figure 7 Simple example showing (A) timed usage model and (B) timed automata.

Once the model of the system has been created, a variety of model-exploration techniques can be used to generate test cases. For instance [5] and [6] perform a simple random walk of the TUM model to generate test cases while other works such as [7] and [8], have designed coverage metrics to guide the test-generation process. In particular, works in [7] and [8], combine the usage of TUMs with dependencies between the different components of the SUT. This allows them to generate test cases that not only represent different timing scenarios, but also capture dependencies between critical system components.

Another line of work [9] propose to extend finite state machines model (FSM) to incorporate timing-related constraints. Such a model is most commonly known as *timed automata* (TA). In timed automata, an FSM is augmented with a finite number of clocks. These clocks are used to generate boolean constraints and such constraints are labeled on the edges of the TA. Additionally, clock values can be manipulated and reset by different transitions of the automata. The boolean constraints succinctly captures the criteria for the respective transition being triggered. Timed automata also has the feature to label time-critical states. For instance, states marked as *Urgent* or *Committed* imply that no time can be spent in these states. Besides, while exploring the model, certain states (such as states marked as *Committed*), have priority over other states. These additional features make the process of modeling intuitive and also make the model easier to read. Figure 7B provides a simple example of timed automata. A major difference between the works (eg, works in [5–8]) that use TUM as a modeling approach as compared to works (eg, work in [9]) that use timed automata, is in the model exploration. Whereas the former use either random or guided walks of the model to generate test cases, the later use evolutionary algorithms to explore the model and generate test cases.

5.2 Markov Decision Process

One of the key assumptions, which were made while designing TUMs (as described in the preceding section), was that the probability distributions for transitions were known *a priori*. This is usually true for deterministic systems. However, as argued by the work in [10], such transition probabilities are often unavailable for non-deterministic systems. Therefore, when testing non-deterministic systems for non-functional properties, such as reliability, TUMs do not present a suitable approach. For such systems, the work of [10] proposes an approach based on Markov-Decision Process (MDP). In particular, the system-level modeling is performed via MDPs. Since MDPs can support non-determinism, it is a suitable platform for capturing the non-determinism in a system. Once an MDP model is created for the system, the work in [10] uses a combination of hypothesis testing and probabilistic model checking to check reliability constraints. Hypothesis testing is a statistical mechanism, in which, one of many competing hypothesis are chosen based on the observed data. In particular, [10] uses hypothesis testing to obtain the reliability distribution of the deterministic components in the system. Such reliability distribution are computed within the specific error bounds that the user needs to provide. Subsequently, probabilistic model checking is used on MDPs to compute the overall reliability of the system.

The work of [11] uses a similar technique to obtain reliability distribution for a real life, healthcare system. The system tested in [11] is an ambient-assisted-living-system for elderly people with dementia. Such embedded systems must function reliably under all operating scenarios. Failure to do so may cause serious injuries to the respective patients. For such systems, the non-determinism in the environmental factors (eg, the input from the sensors and human behavior) makes the system complex and make it challenging to produce the required reliability assurances. However, the work of [11] has shown that an MDP-based approach can be effectively used to test complex, real life systems in a scalable and efficient manner.

5.3 Unified Modeling Language

A different line of work [12–14] uses Unified Modeling Language (UML) to model and test real-time systems for timing-related and safety-related properties. UML provides a well known (and well accepted) standard for software modeling and it is used in different dimensions of software testing. In UML, the structure of a system under test can easily be represented via the utilities provided by UML, such as object diagrams and components diagrams. Additionally, the behavior of the modeled system can be represented by use cases, state charts or message-sequence charts. However, for modeling embedded, real-time systems, UML needs to be extended with additional packages, such as packages for non-functional properties and scheduling or management of resources. These packages can be availed through Modeling and Analysis of Real time Embedded Systems Extension (MARTE) of UML. In particular, constraints (such as timing-related constraints) on real-time system can be captured through a standard language known as Object Constraint Language (OCL). Once the system is modeled with appropriate constraints, failure-inducing test cases can be generated by exploring the model. For instance, the search techniques in [12, 13] compares the effectiveness of their test-generation process for random test-ing, adaptive random testing and evolutionary algorithms, while other works [14] experiment with the effectiveness of genetic algorithms as a sea-rch strategy. These works observe that, at least for the evaluated case studies, none of the search strategies (for test generation) were definitively superior than others. However, subsequent works [13] have claimed better effi-ciency, when searching for failure-inducing test cases, through hybrid search strategies.

5.4 Event Flow Graph

Systematic testing of event-driven applications for non-functional proper-ties, such as energy consumption, is a challenging task. This is primarily because of the fact that like any other non-functional property, information related to energy consumption is seldom present in the source code. Addi-tionally, such information may differ across different devices. Therefore, generating energy-consumption annotation, for each application and device, is definitely time consuming and error-prone. A real-life scenario of such event-driven systems is mobile applications. Mobile applications are usually executed on battery-constrained systems, such as smartphones. Smartphones, in turn, are equipped with energy-hungry components, such as GPS, WiFi and display. This necessitates the development of efficient and automated testing technique to stress energy consumption. One such tech-nique has been presented in [15]. It automatically generates the Event Flow Graph (EFG) [16] of the application under test. An EFG can be described as a directed graph, where the nodes of the graph represent events and the edges capture the *happens-after* relationship between any two events. It is possible (and often the case) that EFGs of mobile applications have cycles (such as the example shown in Fig. 8). Such cycles typically do not have an explicit iter-ation bounds. Therefore, although an EFG has a finite number of events, an unbounded number of event sequences can be generated from the same. This further complicates the process of test generation, as any effective test-ing technique should not only be able to generate all failure-revealing test cases, but also do so in a reasonable amount of time.

The framework presented in [15] has two key innovations that helps it to tackle the challenges described in the preceding paragraph. The first of those two innovations being the definition of a metric that captures the energy inefficiency of the system, for a given input. To design such a metric, it is important to understand what exactly qualifies as energy-inefficient

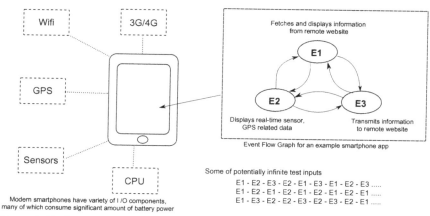

Figure 8 Modern smartphones have a wide variety of I/O and power management utilities, improper use of which in the application code can lead to suboptimal energy-consumption behavior. Smartphone application are usually nonlinear pieces code, systematic testing of which requires addressing a number of challenges.

behavior. In other words, let us consider the following question: *Does high-energy consumption always imply higher energy-inefficiency?* As it turns out [15], the answer to this question is not trivial. For instance, consider a scenario where two systems have similar energy-consumption behavior but one is doing more work (has a higher utilization of its hardware components) than the other. In such a scenario, it is quite intuitive that the system with higher utilization is the more energy-efficient one. Taking inspiration from this observation, the work in [15] defines the metric of *E/U ratio* (energy consumption vs utilization) to measure the energy inefficiency of a system. For a given input, the framework executes the application on a real hardware device and analyses the *E/U ratio* of the device at runtime. An anomalously high *E/U ratio*, during the execution of the application, indicates the presence of an energy hotspot. Additionally, a consistently high E/U ratio, after the application has completed execution, indicates the presence of an energy bug. In general, energy bugs can cause more wastage of battery power than energy hotspots and can drastically reduce the operational time of the smartphone. With the metric of *E/U ratio*, it is possible to find energy-inefficient behavior in the SUT, for a given input. However, another challenge is to generate inputs to stress energy behavior of a given application, in a reasonable amount of time. Interestingly, for smartphone applications, a number of previous studies (primarily based on Android operating system) have observed that most of the energy-hungry components can only be accessed through a predefined set of system calls. The work in [15] uses this information to prioritize the generation of test inputs. In particular, [15] uses a heuristic-based approach. This approach tries to explore all event traces that may invoke system calls to energy-hungry components. Besides, the work also prioritizes inputs that might invoke a similar sequence of system calls compared to an already discovered, energy-inefficient execution.

6. WHITE-BOX ABSTRACTION

In this section, we shall discuss software testing methodologies that are carried out directly on the implementation of an application. Such an implementation may capture the source code, the intermediate code (after various stages of compilation) or the compiled binary of an embedded software. Whereas we only specialize the testing procedures at the level of abstractions they are carried out, we shall observe in the following discussion that several methodologies (eg, evolutionary testing and symbolic execution) can be used to test the implementation of embedded software. The idea of directly testing the implementation is promising in the context of testing embedded software. In particular, if the designer is interested in accurately evaluating the non-functional behaviors (eg, energy and timing) of different software components, such non-functional behaviors are best observed at the level of implementation. On the flip side, if a serious bug was discovered in the implementation, it may lead to a complete redesigning of the respective application. In general, it is important to figure out an appropriate level of abstraction to run the testing procedure. We shall now discuss several works to test the implementation of embedded software and reason about their implications. In particular, we discuss testing methodologies for timing-related properties in Section 6.1 and for functionality-related behaviors in Section 6.2. Finally, in Section 6.3, we discuss challenges to build an appropriate framework to observe and control test executions of embedded software and we also describe some recent efforts in the software engineering community to address such challenges.

6.1 Testing Timing-related Properties

The work in [17] shows the effectiveness of evolutionary search for testing embedded software. In particular, this work targets to discover the maximum delay caused due to *interrupts*. In embedded software, interrupts are common phenomenon. For instance, the incoming signals from sensors or network events (eg, arrival of a packet) might be captured via interrupts.

Besides, embedded systems often consist of multiple tasks, which share resources (eg, CPU and memory). As a result, switching the CPU from a task t to a task t' will clearly induce additional delay to the task t. Such switching of resources are also triggered via interrupts. Therefore, the delay caused due to interrupts might substantially affect the overall timing behavior. For instance, in the fall detection application, each sensor might be processed by a different task and another task might be used to compute a potential fall of the patient. If all these tasks share a common CPU, a particular task might be delayed due to the switching of CPU between tasks.

Fig. 9 illustrates scenarios where the task to compute a fall is delayed by interrupts generated from the accelerometer and the gyroscope. In particular, Fig. 9A demonstrates the occurrence of a single interrupt. On the contrary, Fig. 9B illustrates nested interrupts, which prolonged the execution time of the computation task. In general, arrival of an interrupt is highly non-deterministic in nature. Moreover, it is potentially infeasible to test an embedded software for all possible occurrences of interrupts.

The work in [17] discusses a genetic algorithm to find the maximum interrupt latency. In particular, this work shows that a testing method based on genetic algorithm is substantially more effective compared to random testing. This means that the interrupt latency discovered via the genetic algorithm is substantially larger than the one discovered using random testing. An earlier work [18] also uses genetic algorithm to find the WCET of a program. In contrast to [17], the work in [18] focuses on the uninterrupted execution of a single program. More specifically, the testing method, as proposed in [18], aims to search the input space and more importantly, direct the search toward WCET revealing inputs.

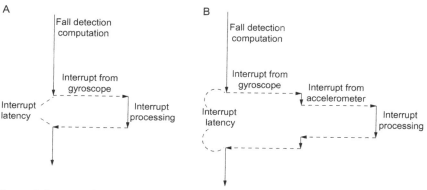

Figure 9 Interrupt latency, (A) single interrupt and (B) Nested interrupts.

It is well known that the processing power of CPUs have increased dramatically in the last few decades. In contrast, memory subsystems are several order of magnitudes slower than the CPU. Such a performance gap between the CPU and memory subsystems might be critical for embedded software, when such software are restricted via timing-related constraints. More specifically, if the software is spending a substantial amount of time in accessing memory, then the performance of an application may have a considerable slowdown. In order to investigate such problems, some recent efforts in software testing [19, 20] have explicitly targeted to discover memory bottlenecks. Such efforts directly test the software binary to accurately determine requests to the memory subsystems. In particular, requests to the memory subsystems might be reduced substantially by employing a cache. Works in [19, 20] aim to exercise test inputs that lead to a poor usage of caches. More specifically, the work in [19] aims to discover *cache thrashing scenarios*. A cache thrashing scenario occurs when several memory blocks replace each other from the cache, hence, generating a substantial number of requests to the memory subsystems. For instance, the code fragment in Fig. 10 may exhibit a cache thrashing when the cache can hold exactly one memory block. In the code fragment, m1 and m2 replace each other from the cache, leading to a *cache thrashing*. This behavior is manifested only for the program input 't'.

The work in [19] shows that the absence of such cache thrashing scenarios can be formulated by systematically transforming the program with assertions. Subsequently, a search procedure on the software input space can be invoked to find violation of such assertions. Any violation of an assertion, thus, will produce a cache thrashing scenario. The methodology proposed in [19] uses a combination of static analysis and symbolic execution to search the input space and discover inputs that violate the formulated assertions.

```
int n = 100;

while (n-- >= 0) {
    if (input == 't') {
        //access memory block m1
        //access memory block m2
    } else {
        //access memory block m1
    }
```

Figure 10 Input dependent cache thrashing.

The work in [20] lifts the software testing of embedded software for massively parallel applications, with a specific focus on general-purpose graphics processing units (GPGPU). It is well known that future technology will be dominated by parallel architectures (eg, multicores and GPGPUs). For such architectures, software testing should take into account the input space of the application, as well as the non-deterministic nature of scheduling multiple threads. The work in [20] formally defines a set of scenarios that capture memory bottlenecks in parallel architectures. Subsequently, a search procedure is invoked to systematically traverse the input space and the space consisting of all possible scheduling decisions among threads. Like the approach in [19], the work in [20] also uses a combination of static analysis and symbolic execution for the search. In summary, both the works [19, 20] revolve around detecting fine-grained events such as memory requests. In general, such fine-grained events are appropriate to test only at the implementation level (eg, software binary). This is because the occurrence of such events would be significantly difficult to predict at intermediate stages of the development.

6.2 Testing Functionality-related Properties

In the preceding Section, we have discussed software testing methodologies that focus on validating timing-related constraints of embedded software. In contrast to such methodologies, the work in [21] primarily targets functional properties of embedded software. In particular, authors of [21] discuss some unique challenges that might appear only in the context of testing embedded software and systems. The key observation is that embedded systems often contain different layers of hardware and software. Besides, an embedded application may contain multiple tasks (eg, programs) and such tasks might be active simultaneously. For instance, in our fall-detection application, the access to hardware components (eg, gyroscope and accelerometers) might be controlled by a supervisory software, such as operating systems (OS). Similarly, sampling signals from sensors and computation of a potential fall might be accomplished by different tasks that run simultaneously in the system. The work in [21] argues the importance of testing interactions between different hardware/software layers and different tasks. Fig. 11 conceptually captures such interactions in a typical embedded system.

In order to exercise interactions between tasks and different software layers, authors of [21] have described a suitable coverage criteria for testing embedded systems. For instance, the interaction between application layer

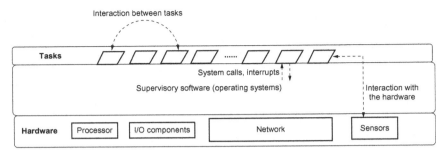

Figure 11 Interaction among different tasks and hardware/software layers.

```
f = 0;
if (input = 'x') {
    g := g + 1;
    f := f + 1;
}
if (f != 0)
    syscall(g);
else
    syscall(0);
```

Figure 12 Interaction between application layer variable and operating system.

and OS layer can happen via system calls. Similarly, the application might directly access some hardware components via a predefined set of application programmer interfaces (APIs). The work in [21] initially performs a static analysis to infer data dependencies across different layers of the embedded system. Besides, if different tasks of the system use shared resources, such an analysis also tracks the data dependencies across tasks. For instance, consider the piece of code fragment in Fig. 12, where syscall captures a system call implemented in the kernel mode. In the code shown in Fig. 12, there exists a data dependency between application layer variable g and the system call syscall. As a result, it is important to exercise this data dependency to test the interaction between application layer and OS layer. Therefore, the work in [21] suggests to select test cases that can manifest the data dependency between variable g and syscall. To illustrate the dependency between multiple tasks, let us consider the code fragment in Fig. 13.

The keyword __shared__ captures shared variables. In Fig. 13, there is a potential data dependency between Task 1 and Task 2. However, to exercise this data dependency, the designer must be able to select an input that satisfies the condition input == 'x'. The work in [21] performs static analysis to discover the data dependencies across tasks, as shown in this example. Once

```
__shared__ int s = 0;

Task 1:                          Task 2:
int y;
y := y + 2;                      if (s > 0)
if (input = 'x')                     //do something
  s = y;
else
  y = y - 1;
```

Figure 13 Interaction between tasks via shared resources (shared variable s).

all data dependencies are determined via static analysis, the chosen test inputs aim to cover these data dependencies.

6.3 Building Systematic Test-execution Framework

So far in this section, we have discussed test input generation to validate either functional or non-functional properties of embedded software. However, as discussed in [22, 23], there exists numerous other challenges for testing embedded software, such as *observability* of faulty execution. *Test oracles* are usually required to observe faulty execution. Designing appropriate oracles is difficult even for traditional software testing. In the context of embedded software, designing oracles may face additional challenges. In particular, as embedded systems consist of many tasks and exhibit interactions across different hardware and software layers, they may often have non-deterministic output. As a result, oracles, which are purely based on output, are insufficient to observe faults in embedded systems. Moreover, it is cumbersome to build output-based oracles for each test case. In order to address these challenges, authors in [22] propose to design property-based oracles for embedded systems. Property-based oracles are designed for each execution platform. Therefore, any application targeting such execution platform might reuse the oracles and thereby, it can avoid substantial manual efforts to design oracles for each test case. The work in [22] specifically targets concurrency and synchronization properties. For instance, test oracles are designed to specify proper usage of binary semaphores and message queues, which are used for synchronization and interprocess communication, respectively. Such synchronization and interprocess communication APIs are provided by the operating system. Once test oracles are designed, a test case can be executed, while instrumenting the application, OS and hardware interfaces simultaneously. Each execution can subsequently be checked for violation of properties captured by an oracle. Thus property-based test oracles can provide a clean interface to observe faulty executions. Apart from test oracles, authors in [23] discuss the importance of giving the designer appropriate tools that control the execution of embedded systems. Since the execution of an embedded system is often non-deterministic, it is, in general difficult to reproduce faulty executions. For instance, consider the fall detection application where a task reads sensor data from a single queue. If new data arrives, an interrupt is raised to update the queue. It is worthwhile to see the presence of a potential data race between the routine that services the interrupt and the task which reads the queue. Unfortunately, the arrival of interrupts is highly non-deterministic in nature. As a result, even after multiple test executions, the testing may not reveal a faulty execution that capture a potential data race. In order to solve this, authors in [23] design appropriate utilities that gives designer the power to raise interrupts explicitly. For instance, the designer might choose a set of locations where she suspects the presence of data races due to interrupts. Subsequently, a test execution can be carried out that raise interrupts exactly at the locations specified by the designer.

Summary
To summarize, in this section, we have seen efforts to generate test inputs and test oracles to validate both functional and non-functional aspects of embedded software. A common aspect of all these techniques is that the testing process is carried out directly on the implementation. This might be appealing in certain scenarios, for instance, when the designer is interested in events that are highly sensitive to the execution platform. Such events include interrupts, memory requests and cache misses, among others.

7. FUTURE DIRECTIONS
As discussed in this chapter, analysis of non-functional properties is crucial to ensure that embedded systems behave as per its specification. However, there exists an orthogonal direction of work, where analysis of non-functional properties, such as power consumption, memory accesses and computational latencies, have been used for security-related exploits. Such exploits are commonly referred to as side-channel attacks and are designed to extract private keys[2] from cryptographic algorithms, such as

---

[2] Cryptographic algorithms such as AES and DES are used to encrypt a message in a manner such that only the person having the private key is capable of decrypting the message.

algorithms used in smart cards and smart tokens. The intention of the attacker is not to discover the theoretical weaknesses of the algorithm. Instead, the attacker aims to break the *implementation* of the algorithms through side channels, such as measuring execution time or energy consumption. In particular, the attacker tries to relate such measurements with the secret key. For instance, if different secret keys lead to different execution time, the attacker can perform statistical analysis to map the measured execution time with the respective key. In general, any non-functional behavior that has a correlation with cryptographic computation, is capable of leaking information, if not managed appropriately. For example, the differential power attack, as proposed in [24], uses a simple, yet effective statistical analysis technique to correlate the observed power-consumption behavior to the private key. Since then, a number of subsequent works have proposed counter-measures (eg, [25]) against side-channel vulnerabilities and bypasses to those counter-measures (eg, [26]). Similarly, researchers have also studied side-channel attacks (and their counter-measures) based on other non-functional behaviors, such as computational latency [27, 28] and memory footprint [29]. Even though works on side-channel attacks have a very different objective compared to those on non-functional testing, there exists a number of commonalities. In essence, both lines of work are looking for test inputs that lead to *undesirable non-functional behavior*. The definition of the phrase *undesirable non-functional behavior* is based on the system under test (SUT). For instance, in an embedded system that has hard timing-related constraints, an undesirable input would be the violation of such constraints. On the contrary, for a cryptographic algorithm, such as implemented in a smart card, an undesirable input may lead to information leaks via side channels. Undesirable non-functional behavior in one scenario may lead to performance loss, sometimes costing human lives (such as in an anti-lock braking system), whereas, in the other scenario undesirable non-functional behavior may cause information leaks, which, in turn may often lead to financial losses. It is needless to motivate the fact that testing embedded cryptographic systems for such undesirable non-functional behaviors is crucial. More importantly, testing methodologies for detecting side-channel attacks need to be automated. However, as of this writing, this line of research is far from being solved. New works on this topic could draw inspiration from earlier works on non-functional testing, such as works described in Section 3.

Another more generic direction is related to the detection of root cause and automatic repair of non-functional properties in embedded systems. In general, the purpose of software testing is to expose suboptimal or unwanted behavior in the SUT. Such suboptimal behaviors, once identified, should be rectified by modifying the system. More specifically, the rectification process can be subdivided into two parts: fault-localization[3] and root-cause detection, followed by debugging and repair. Fault-localization is, in general, the more time-consuming (and expensive) phase of this modification process and therefore, there is a huge demand for effective, automated techniques for fault-localization. Over the past years, several works have proposed methodologies for fault-localization. However, most of these works have focused on the functionality of software. As of this writing, there exists a lack of efforts in fault-localization techniques for non-functional properties. One plausible explanation can be that designing such a framework, for non-functional properties, is significantly more challenging. This is because the non-functional behavior of system depends not only on the source code, but also on the underlying execution platform. Some of the well known techniques [30] for fault-localization include comparing a set of failed execution to a set of passing executions and subsequently, deriving the root cause for the fault. Such works narrow down the search space for the root cause by assigning suspiciousness values to specific regions of source code. As is the case with fault-localization, considerable research needs to be performed on automated debugging and repair of non-functional software properties. As a matter of fact, automated program repair, even in the context of software functionality, is far from being matured, not to mention the lack of research for non-functional software properties. As for embedded software and systems, both functional and non-functional behaviors play crucial roles in validating the respective system. We hope that future works in software testing will resolve these validation challenges faced by embedded system designers.

8. CONCLUSION

Embedded systems are ubiquitous in the modern world. Such systems are used in a wide variety of applications, ranging from common consumer electronic devices to automotive and avionic applications. A property common to all embedded systems is that they interact with the physical environment, often deriving their inputs from the surrounding environment. Due to the application domains such systems are used in, their behavior is often constrained by functional (such as the input–output relationship) as well as

---

[3] In this context, the word "fault" implies all type of suboptimal, non-functional behavior.

non-functional properties (such as execution time or energy consumption). This makes the testing and validation of such systems a challenging task. In this chapter, we discussed a few challenges and their solutions in the context of testing embedded systems. In particular, we take a closer look into existing works on testing non-functional properties, such as timing, energy consumption, reliability, for embedded software. To put the existing works in perspective, we classify them in three distinct categories, based on the level of system abstraction used for testing. These categories include, *black-box*, *grey-box* and *white-box abstraction* based testing approaches. In general, *black-box abstraction* based testing methods use sampling based techniques to generate failure-revealing test cases for the system under test. Such methods consider the system as a black-box and hence are equally applicable to simple and complex systems alike. However, such ease of use usually comes at the cost of effectiveness. In particular, these methods often cannot provide completeness guarantees (ie, by the time the test-generation process completes, all failure revealing test inputs must have been uncovered). The *grey-box abstraction* based approaches are usually more effective than the *black-box abstraction* based approaches. This is because such methods often employ an abstract model of the system under test to generate failure-revealing test cases. Effectiveness of these test-generation methodologies is often dictated by the level of system abstraction being used. *White-box abstraction* based testing approaches use the actual system implementation to generate failure revealing test cases and hence are capable of providing maximum level of guarantee to discover failure revealing inputs. We observe that existing techniques vary hugely in terms of complexity and effectiveness. Finally, we have discussed future research directions related to embedded software testing. One of which was automated fault-localization and repairing of bugs related to non-functional properties. Another direction was related to the development of secure embedded systems. In particular, we explored the possibility of testing techniques to exploit the vulnerability toward side-channel attacks. Over the recent years, there have been a number of works, which analyze non-functional behavior to perform side-channel (security related) attacks. It would be appealing to see how existing testing methodologies can be adapted to test and build secure embedded software.

ACKNOWLEDGMENT

The work was partially supported by a Singapore MoE Tier 2 grant MOE2013-T2-1-115 entitled "Energy aware programming" and the Swedish National Graduate School on Computer Science (CUGS).

REFERENCES

[1] A wearable miniaturized fall detection system for the elderly. http://www.fallwatch-project.eu/press_release.php.

[2] T. Nghiem, S. Sankaranarayanan, G. Fainekos, F. Ivancić, A. Gupta, G.J. Pappas, Monte-carlo techniques for falsification of temporal properties of non-linear hybrid systems, in: Proceedings of the 13th ACM International Conference on Hybrid Systems: Computation and Control, HSCC '10, 2010.

[3] S. Sankaranarayanan, G. Fainekos, Falsification of temporal properties of hybrid systems using the cross-entropy method, in: Proceedings of the 15th ACM International Conference on Hybrid Systems: Computation and Control, HSCC '12, 2012.

[4] Y.S.R. Annapureddy, G.E. Fainekos, Ant colonies for temporal logic falsification of hybrid systems, in: IECON 2010–36th Annual Conference on IEEE Industrial Electronics Society, 2010.

[5] S. Siegl, K. Hielscher, R. German, Introduction of time dependencies in usage model based testing of complex systems, in: Systems Conference, 2010 4th Annual IEEE, 2010, pp. 622–627.

[6] S. Siegl, K. Hielscher, R. German, C. Berger, Formal specification and systematic model-driven testing of embedded automotive systems, in: 4th Annual IEEE Systems Conference, 2010, 2011.

[7] S. Siegl, P. Caliebe, Improving model-based verification of embedded systems by analyzing component dependences, in: 2011 6th IEEE International Symposium on Industrial Embedded Systems (SIES), 2011, pp. 51–54.

[8] P. Luchscheider, S. Siegl, Test profiling for usage models by deriving metrics from component-dependency-models, in: 2013 8th IEEE International Symposium on Industrial Embedded Systems (SIES), 2013, pp. 196–204.

[9] J. Hansel, D. Rose, P. Herber, S. Glesner, An Evolutionary algorithm for the generation of timed test traces for embedded real-time systems, in: 2011 IEEE Fourth International Conference on Software Testing, Verification and Validation (ICST), 2011.

[10] L. Gui, J. Sun, Y. Liu, Y.J. Si, J.S. Dong, X.Y. Wang, Combining model checking and testing with an application to reliability prediction and distribution, in: Proceedings of the 2013 International Symposium on Software Testing and Analysis, ISSTA 2013, 2013.

[11] Y. Liu, L. Gui, Y. Liu, MDP-based reliability analysis of an ambient assisted living system, in: FM 2014: Formal Methods, Lecture Notes in Computer Science, vol. 8442, Springer International Publishing, 2014.

[12] A. Arcuri, M.Z. Iqbal, L. Briand, Black-box system testing of real-time embedded systems using random and search-based testing, in: Proceedings of the 22Nd IFIP WG 6.1 International Conference on Testing Software and Systems, ICTSS'10, 2010, pp. 95–110.

[13] M.Z. Iqbal, A. Arcuri, L. Briand, Combining search-based and adaptive random testing strategies for environment model-based testing of real-time embedded systems, in: Proceedings of the 4th International Conference on Search Based Software Engineering, SSBSE'12, 2012.

[14] M.Z. Iqbal, A. Arcuri, L. Briand, Empirical investigation of search algorithms for environment model-based testing of real-time embedded software, in: Proceedings of the 2012 International Symposium on Software Testing and Analysis, ISSTA 2012, 2012.

[15] A. Banerjee, L.K. Chong, S. Chattopadhyay, A. Roychoudhury, Detecting energy bugs and hotspots in mobile apps, in: Proceedings of the 22Nd ACM SIGSOFT International Symposium on Foundations of Software Engineering, 2014.

[16] A.M. Memon, I. Banerjee, A. Nagarajan, GUI ripping: reverse engineering of graphical user interfaces for testing, in: Working Conference on Reverse Engineering, 2003, pp. 260–269.

[17] S. Weissleder, H. Schlingloff, An evaluation of model-based testing in embedded applications, in: 2014 IEEE Seventh International Conference on Software Testing, Verification and Validation (ICST), 2014, pp. 223–232.

[18] P.P. Puschner, R. Nossal, Testing the results of static worst-case execution-time analysis, in: IEEE Real-Time Systems Symposium, 1998, pp. 134–143.

[19] A. Banerjee, S. Chattopadhyay, A. Roychoudhury, Static analysis driven cache performance testing, in: Real-Time Systems Symposium (RTSS), 2013 IEEE 34th, 2013, pp. 319–329.

[20] S. Chattopadhyay, P. Eles, Z. Peng, Automated software testing of memory performance in embedded GPUs, in: 2014 International Conference on Embedded Software (EMSOFT), 2014, pp. 1–10.

[21] T. Yu, A. Sung, W. Srisa-An, G. Rothermel, An approach to testing commercial embedded systems, J. Syst. Softw. 88 (2014).

[22] T. Yu, A. Sung, W. Srisa-an, G. Rothermel, Using property-based oracles when testing embedded system applications, in: 2011 IEEE Fourth International Conference on Software Testing, Verification and Validation (ICST), 2011, pp. 100–109.

[23] T. Yu, W. Srisa-an, G. Rothermel, SimTester: a controllable and observable testing framework for embedded systems, in: Proceedings of the 8th ACM SIGPLAN/ SIGOPS Conference on Virtual Execution Environments, VEE '12, London, England, UK, ISBN 978-1-4503-1176-2, 2012.

[24] P. Kocher, J. Jaffe, B. Jun, Differential power analysis, 1998. http://www.cryptography. com/public/pdf/DPA.pdf.

[25] M.-L. Akkar, C. Giraud, An implementation of DES and AES, secure against some attacks, in: Proceedings of the Third International Workshop on Cryptographic Hardware and Embedded Systems, CHES '01, 2001.

[26] S. Mangard, N. Pramstaller, E. Oswald, Successfully attacking masked AES hardware implementations, in: Cryptographic Hardware and Embedded Systems, CHES 2005, Lecture Notes in Computer Science, 2005.

[27] P. Kocher, Timing attacks on implementations of diffe-hellman, RSA, DSS, and other systems. http://www.cryptography.com/public/pdf/TimingAttacks.pdf.

[28] B. Köpf, L. Mauborgne, M. Ochoa, Automatic quantification of cache side-channels, in: Proceedings of the 24th International Conference on Computer Aided Verification, CAV'12, Berkeley, CA, Springer-Verlag, Berlin, ISBN 978-3-642-31423-0, 2012, pp. 564–580, http://dx.doi.org/10.1007/978-3-642-31424-7_40.

[29] S. Jana, V. Shmatikov, Memento: learning secrets from process footprints, in: Proceedings of the 2012 IEEE Symposium on Security and Privacy, SP '12, IEEE Computer Society, Washington, DC, ISBN 978-0-7695-4681-0, 2012, pp. 143–157, http://dx.doi.org/10.1109/SP.2012.19.

[30] J.A. Jones, M.J. Harrold, Empirical evaluation of the tarantula automatic fault-localization technique, in: Proceedings of the 20th IEEE/ACM International Conference on Automated Software Engineering, ASE '05, Long Beach, CA, USA, ACM, New York, NY, ISBN 1-58113-993-4, 2005, pp. 273–282, http://dx.doi.org/ 10.1145/1101908.1101949.

ABOUT THE AUTHORS

Abhijeet Banerjee is a Ph.D. scholar at the School of Computing, National University of Singapore. He received his B.E. in Information Technology from Indian Institute of Engineering Science and Technology, Shibpur, India in 2011. His research interests include automated software testing, debugging, and re-factoring with specific emphasis on testing and verification of non-functional properties of software.

Sudipta Chattopadhyay is a Post-doctoral Research Fellow in the Center for IT-Security, Privacy, and Accountability (CISPA) in Saarbrücken, Germany. He received his Ph.D. in computer science from National University of Singapore (NUS) in 2013. His research interests include software analysis and testing, with a specific focus on designing efficient and secure software systems.

Abhik Roychoudhury is a Professor of Computer Science at School of Computing, National University of Singapore. He received his Ph.D. in Computer Science from the State University of New York at Stony Brook in 2000. Since 2001, he has been employed at the National University of Singapore. His research has focused on software testing and analysis, software security, and trust-worthy software construction. His research has received various awards and honors, including his appointment as ACM

Distinguished Speaker in 2013. He is currently leading the TSUNAMi center, a large 5-year long targeted research effort funded by National Research Foundation in the domain of software security. His research has been funded by various agencies and companies, including the National Research Foundation (NRF), Ministry of Education (MoE), A*STAR, Defense Research and Technology Office (DRTech), DSO National Laboratories, Microsoft, and IBM. He has authored a book on "Embedded Systems and Software Validation" published by Elsevier (Morgan Kaufmann) Systems-on-Silicon series in 2009, which has also been officially translated to Chinese by Tsinghua University Press. He has served in various capacities in the program committees and organizing committees of various conferences on software engineering including ICSE, ISSTA, FSE, and ASE. He is currently serving as an Editorial Board member of IEEE Transactions on Software Engineering (TSE).

CHAPTER FOUR

Advances in Web Application Testing, 2010–2014

Sreedevi Sampath*, Sara Sprenkle[†]
*University of Maryland, Baltimore County, Baltimore, MD, USA
†Washington and Lee University, Lexington, VA, USA

Contents

Abstract

As web applications increase in popularity, complexity, and size, approaches and tools to automate testing the correctness of web applications must continually evolve. In this chapter, we provide a broad background on web applications and the challenges in testing these distributed, dynamic applications made up of heterogeneous components. We then focus on the recent advances in web application testing that were published between 2010 and 2014, including work on test-case generation, oracles, testing evaluation, and regression testing. Through this targeted survey, we identify trends in web application testing and open problems that still need to be addressed.

1. INTRODUCTION

When you do just about anything on the web through a web browser, you are likely interacting with a web application. Web applications are applications accessible through the web that dynamically generate web pages, often based on user interactions, the application's data, or other information (eg, current time and the user's location). Web applications are one of the most common ways that people use to interact with other people (eg, Wordpress, Facebook, Twitter) or businesses (eg, bank accounts, travel, shopping). Web applications are ideal for such interactions because they are available 24 hours a day to anyone with internet access and a web browser. Maintaining web applications is simpler for both businesses and clients: since the web application code resides on the web application server, changes to the application can be updated in one location and all users see the changes, without needing special software installed on each client's computer.

To maintain the high reliability required of web applications, we must develop effective testing strategies to identify problems in web applications. While there have been advances in web application testing, there are still many open problems in this nontraditional domain [1]. However, the dynamic, distributed nature of web applications makes testing difficult.

While previous survey papers focused on broader time periods [2, 3] or on specific subfields [4–7], we will focus on web application testing approaches for correctness published between 2010 and 2014. With the number of publications increasing and researchers' abilities to focus on each publication decreasing [8], such focused surveys are increasingly important.

In this chapter, we describe web application architecture, technologies, and characteristics in Section 2. Section 3 presents the challenges, common research questions, and approaches to testing web applications. In Section 4, we present the state of the art in web application testing, including a distant reading of the papers we covered. We conclude in Section 5 with the open questions in web application testing.

2. WEB APPLICATIONS

Web applications are an example of a distributed system—specifically, a client/server architecture, where the clients are web browsers and the servers are the web application servers. Fig. 1 shows the simplest, three-tiered version of the web application architecture. The web application server could be

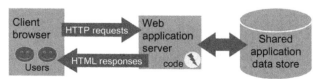

Figure 1 Web application architecture.

Figure 2 Example request to a web application.

implemented as multiple, load-balanced servers handling requests from many clients. Similarly, the data store tier could also be implemented on multiple machines, thus lending to an *n*-tier architecture. The application data store could be maintained in databases, the file system, and external services.

The browsers and servers communicate via the HTTP protocol [9], a stateless protocol, meaning that each request is independent of other requests. Human users make requests using a client browser, eg, Google Chrome, Mozilla Firefox, Microsoft's Internet Explorer, Apple's Safari, and Opera to the server, eg, Apache [10], Apache Tomcat [11], IBM's WebSphere [12], and Google App Engine [13].

A simplified HTTP request is shown in Fig. 2. A request has a request type, typically either GET or POST, a resource (the "R" in URL), and optional parameter name/value pairs. The parameters are the data inputs to the web application. A request may also include cookies [14], which contain data that is passed between the browser and the server to maintain state for the session.

The web application server processes the request, serving up the requested resource, based on the inputs. The server's response—typically an HTML [15] document—is rendered by the browser for the user.

A web application is typically implemented using a variety of programming languages. HTML is the standard markup language used to create web pages. The HTML document often references Cascading Style Sheets (CSS) [16] that define the presentation, style, and layout of the document. Some HTML documents also include scripting—most commonly JavaScript—to allow dynamic user interaction with the web page. Ajax—asynchronous JavaScript and XML [17]—is a set of technologies that allow developers to update parts of the web page through communication with the web application server without updating the whole page. The result of using Ajax is that the user's experience is more like using a desktop application. JavaScript libraries (eg, jQuery[1]) and frameworks (eg, AngularJS[2], Bootstrap[3]) have

---

[1] https://jquery.com/
[2] https://angularjs.org/
[3] http://getbootstrap.com/

been developed to (1) improve the responsiveness of web sites and applications for the variety of devices on which web sites are viewed, (2) provide cross-browser compatibility, and (3) allow faster development of dynamic user experiences on the web.

Many different programming languages can be used to implement the server side of a web application to generate web responses. According to a survey by Web Technology Surveys [18], PHP, ASP.NET, and Java are the most common server-side programming languages for the top 10 million sites where the programming language is known. While the application server used depends on the programming language used to implement the web application, the client browser is independent of the server's programming language choice. More recent development in web applications are to use web services such as RESTful APIs.

Web applications' heterogenous environment in terms of languages, architectures, components, and platforms gives rise to a number of testing challenges, which we discuss in detail in the next section.

3. CHALLENGES TO WEB APPLICATION TESTING

Testers face several challenges to testing web applications:

- **A fast development cycle:** When faults are found or new features are implemented, software updates need to be applied quickly with little downtime.

- **Distributed architecture:** Faults can occur in the server- (including the data tier) or client-side components or in the integration of these components. Thus, it can be difficult for developers to determine the cause of a failure.

- **Multiple languages:** Since web applications are often written in multiple programming languages, developers must employ different techniques to perform program analysis of their application's components based on the language used to implement the component. Furthermore, HTML and CSS are a markup and style sheet language, respectively, that require different validation techniques.

- **Multiple outputs:** The results of executing web application code can be seen in the browser in the form of the presentation of the generated HTML document or changes to the document, in the application data store, in email messages, etc. All of these outputs must be verified for correctness.

- **Dynamic behavior:** Some types of web applications have code generated on the fly, ie, dynamic code generation. Due to this, purely static analysis techniques may not fully be able to test the web application.
- **Cross-browser, cross-platform compatibility:** Since users can use a variety of browsers to access web applications on a variety of platforms, they expect a similar experience. However, despite standards and specifications, browsers may implement functionality slightly differently.
- **Large, complex code base:** The distributed architecture of web applications necessitates a rather large code base that is often difficult for programmers to understand. As Web technology evolves, the code becomes more complex by using multiple coding and development frameworks, making asynchronous calls, creating rich, dynamic user experiences, etc.

To meet these challenges, practitioners and researchers have developed a variety of testing techniques. Fig. 3 depicts a broad overview of the web application testing process. The testing process could be viewed as similar to the testing process of other types of applications, however, the uniqueness of web application testing comes from the definitions, models, and formats that need to be developed for the individual artifacts, such as for a test case's input, expected/actual output, and oracle comparator.

A test case is made up of input to the web application and the expected output from the web application. Sometimes, state information is also included in a test case because web application test cases, in particular, may not be independent of each other and the underlying session/database state. The inputs and expected outputs depend on the part of the web

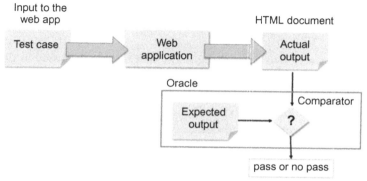

Figure 3 Testing architecture.

application being tested. For example, if server-side code is being tested, the input is likely an HTTP request and the output is likely the HTTP response, typically an HTML document, as well as other relevant outputs.

Academic and industry researchers and commercial tools have proposed and evaluated different forms of these artifacts. For example, the popular web testing tool Selenium IDE [19] uses a test case format of steps that a user performs on a web site, stored in tabular form, written in a domain specific language called Selenese. The Selenium test case also contains the expected output and the oracles are in the form of assertions. Researchers in the domain of capture-replay testing called user-session-based testing have defined a test case as a sequence of user actions stored as text files with HTTP requests or using an XML notation.

To address this open area of web application test case generation, researchers have asked the following research question:

> **Research Question 1:** How should testers define, model, and generate test cases (inputs and expected outputs), such that, when executed, the test cases will cover a large portion of the underlying application code and will expose faults in web applications?
>
> *In Section 4.1, we review the advances in research for test case generation for web application testing that broadly answer the above question.*

Researchers have also defined several oracle comparators based on different formats of expected output, such as the entire HTML page, or only the structure of the HTML page in the form of a sequence of HTML tags, etc. Assertions have also been used as oracles in the literature. Developing oracles is a difficult problem, especially the subareas of automating the fault detection process and defining oracle comparators that are effective at identifying faulty executions. To this end, researchers have studied the following research question:

> **Research Question 2:** Given a test case, how can a tester determine automatically if an application fails?
>
> *In Section 4.2, we review advances in the development of test oracles.*

The notion of when to stop testing is one that is often discussed in the software testing industry. Adequacy criteria are used to determine when to stop testing, as well as to evaluate the thoroughness of the testing conducted so far. This is an area of research that is still growing for web applications, with most researchers using the traditional adequacy criteria of statement, branch, and condition coverage. Researchers are beginning to ask the question:

> **Research Question 3:** What techniques and criteria can be developed and evaluated to determine thoroughness of a web application test suite?

To address this question, in our literature search, we found that research has focused on developing adequacy criteria (Section 4.3.1), operators and techniques for mutation testing (Section 4.3.2), and fault severity classification (Section 4.3.3).

Another aspect of web application testing refers to the testing and maintenance of applications as the application evolves and new versions of the web application are created. Here, additional challenges arise, such as creating new test cases for testing the new and changed parts of the application, repairing, and reusing test cases from previous versions of the system, as well as, managing the size of a regression test suite to maintain high effectiveness. In this subdomain, researchers have addressed the question:

Research Question 4: How can a tester create test cases for changed/new parts of the code as well as maintain an existing large regression test suite?
We elaborate on several different ways in which this question is addressed in the literature in Section 4.4.

4. WEB APPLICATION TESTING, 2010–2014

To develop this survey of recent advances in web application testing, we searched the ACM and IEEE digital libraries for papers published between 2010 and 2014. We used the following search string when searching the libraries

(((((((web) OR website) OR "web application") OR ajax) OR javascript) OR php) AND test)

From that starting point, we looked at papers referenced or cited by the paper we found and looked at the authors' web sites for additional papers.

To keep the survey's scope more manageable, we did not include papers that were focused on static analysis, program repair (eg, [20, 21]), and non-functional properties like security, accessibility, performance, and cross-browser testing. In addition, since Ali Mesbah recently published a survey of advances of testing JavaScript-based applications [6], we do not cover JavaScript testing in this work.

In this section, we present the advances in web application testing published between 2010 and 2014. We end with a textual analysis of the papers to identify trends in the area.

4.1 Test Case Generation

Test case generation is the problem of creating test cases that are effective at covering underlying code and detecting faults. Several approaches are proposed for test case generation, such as model-based, search-based, concolic, etc. We elaborate on each of these approaches to test case generation in the following subsections.

4.1.1 Model-Based Test Case Generation

Model-based test case generation, as its name suggests, has focused on developing a model of the application and then traversing the model to create test sequences, and eventually, executable test cases. Models can be developed in several ways, eg, by capturing navigation behavior of the application or by static analysis.

Tung et al. [22] build a page navigation graph and generate test paths from the graph. Then, they extract data and control dependencies from the source code to assist with test case generation. Data dependence is observed when one page transfers data to another page. When one page can be reached only after following links (link dependence) or as a result of a conditional statement in another page, control dependence is observed. They perform maximal graph walk to generate test paths which are augmented with dependencies. They implement their approach in a prototype tool and evaluate with a small case study.

Offutt and Wu [23] propose a new approach to modeling web applications that models the atomic sections of a web application, specifically the user interface screens. The authors argue that their Atomic Section Model (ASM) is implementation technology independent while also allowing analyses that enable better testing by statically representing dynamic pages. The ASM is made up of two components: (1) the "unit-level" model, the component interaction model (CIM) and (2) the "system-level" model, the application transition graph (ATG). Thummala and Offutt [24] implemented the ASM in a tool called WASP (Web Atomic Section Project) and evaluated the effectiveness of the model.

Chen et al. [25] propose modeling a user's navigation of a web application, specifically the browser interactions and so-called Advanced Navigations, ie, requested navigations whose responses depend on the user's or application's state or history. The authors model the page navigations with an augmented finite state machine (FSM). To generate test cases, the authors suggest traversing the model with modifications to handle cycles in the navigations and generating finite sequences.

Torsel [26] model the web application as a directed graph. In addition, they propose to capture variables of basic types, such as String, in two scopes, permanent and session, and also a variable type to hold data from external sources, like a database. For test case generation, they conduct a breadth-first search to explore the directed graph to identify logical dependencies between navigation paths and build a dependency graph. From the dependency graph, paths are selected for execution as test cases. They also provide some annotation in their model that can serve as test oracles.

Song *et al.* [27] propose the use of a finite state automaton to model the server-side interactions and user interactions in a web application. They use the notion of synchronous product of client and server-side FSM models to build the model incrementally. Depth-first traversal of the FSM is used to generate test cases.

Enderlin *et al.* [28] extend contract-based testing using grammars to generate test cases, test data, and oracles for testing PHP applications. In prior work [29], the authors developed the notion of contracts with realistic domains, which are used to represent all kinds of data and to assign domains to test data for testing PHP applications. In prior work, they developed the *regular expression* domain to describe simple textual data and in this work, they develop the *grammar* domain to describe complex textual data. To generate test cases, they first compute test data from contracts using three algorithms for the grammar domain (a) uniform random, (b) bounded exhaustive, and (c) rule coverage based, then they run the test cases, and use runtime assertion checking of the contract as oracles.

WEBMATE is a tool built on top of Selenium [19] by Dallmeier *et al.* [30]. The tool considers the server side of the web application as a black box, focusing on the browser (HTML/CSS/JavaScript) interface. By exploring the application's interface, WEBMATE creates a usage model, essentially a finite state automaton. To explore forms, the tool applies heuristics to find values for input fields. The authors performed an experimental study to show how the tool improves coverage over a traditional web crawler and present cross-browser compatibility testing as an application of the tool. The tool was an academic prototype but has been further developed into a commercially available tool [31, 32].

Schur *et al.* [33, 34] present an approach implemented in a tool, ProCrawl, to crawl the user interface of a web application and observe behavior of the application to create a behavior model, and then generate and execute test cases to cover the unobserved behavior. The behavior model is a finite state automaton (FSA) where the nodes represent states and the transitions represent actions that user performed to change the state. Their tool can handle multiple simultaneous users accessing the web system.

By using a graph walk algorithm for path generation, they generate test cases as Selenium scripts to test the web system.

4.1.2 Statistical Test Case Generation

Another approach to generating test cases is to create statistical models of user accesses that represent actual user behavior at a lower cost than directly using the user sessions as test cases [35] and without limiting test cases to what users actually did. The most recent work in this area explores (1) configuring models of users' navigation and the resulting test cases from these models [36, 37] and (2) creating privileged role-specific models [38].

To better understand how to model users' behavior and, thus, develop test cases that represent usage, Sprenkle et al. [36, 37] proposed various configurations for representing user behavior and empirically examining the tradeoffs and implications of those choices on the resulting test cases. Sprenkle et al. build on Sant et al.'s [39] work on creating statistical models of user sessions to generate test cases, focusing on the navigation model. The authors found that a relatively small number of user accesses are needed to create navigation models that generate highly representative user navigation behavior in test cases, which is important because users do not access a web application randomly. The authors suggest representing user requests by the resource and parameter names to balance scalability and representation requirements. Furthermore, the authors suggest that a tester can tune the amount of history used to predict a user's navigational next step depending on the tester's goals: increasing the amount of history results in more closely modeling the user's navigational behavior at the cost of larger space and time and of yielding fewer test cases that represent what a user is likely to do but not observed in the user access logs. The journal version of their work [37] extended the number of experiments, analyses, and user access logs used in the original paper [36].

Web applications often have different types of users—some of which have privileged access to specialized functionality. Sprenkle et al. [38] proposed refining their statistical models by partitioning the user sessions by their access privilege and feeding the partitioned user sessions into their model and test case generators. Their empirical study showed that the resulting test cases are often smaller than the aggregate models and represent the specific user type while also allowing new, likely navigations. Since partitioning user sessions by their user privilege may not benefit all applications, the authors suggest analyzing the overlap between the models in terms of the common nodes and the relative frequency that the common nodes are accessed in the user accesses to determine if the common access is sufficiently low to warrant generating user-type-specific test cases.

4.1.3 Concolic Test Case Generation

Artzi *et al.* [40] expand on their previous work [41] and propose generating test suites using a combination of static and dynamic analysis. Specifically, the authors propose combining concrete and symbolic (concolic) and constraint solving to automatically and dynamically discover input values for test cases. The authors focus on two types of web application failures: (1) runtime crashes or warnings and (2) invalid/malformed HTML documents. Thus, their approach includes an HTML validator to detect failures. Their technique involves generating a control-flow predicate based on a given input (perhaps empty), modifying the predicate to yield a different control-flow path, and determining the input that will yield this new path, thus creating a new test case. In addition, the approach maintains shared session state. The authors implement their approach for PHP applications—the most common server-side scripting language—in a tool called *Apollo*.

Statistical fault localization is an approach to finding the cause of faults in code by executing test cases and then determining which executed code elements correlate with the most failed test cases. A limitation to using statistical testing is that a large test suite must be available. Artzi *et al.* [42] address this limitation by proposing concolic techniques to generate test suites designed for fault localization. The techniques include six variations on the *Tarantula* [43, 44] algorithm, which is used to predict statements that are most likely to cause failures based on failed test cases, combined with the authors' proposed enhanced domains and output mapping. The *enhanced domain* for conditional statements allows more accurate localization of errors caused by missing branches. The *output mapping* maps program statements to output fragments they generate, which can then be used to help localize the fault. The authors implemented their techniques in Apollo, a tool for PHP applications, that automatically finds and localizes malformed HTML errors [41].

The same authors [45] explore the tradeoffs between generated test suites' size and localization effectiveness. The authors propose techniques to direct generation of new test cases that are similar to failed test cases using various similarity criteria. Their hypothesis is that similar, failed test cases will be better able to localize failure-causing statements. The approach was implemented in Apollo [41]. The authors found that using path-constraint similarity generated a smaller test suite size with the best fault localization.

In addition, the authors combined and expanded on their fault localization in a 2012 journal paper [46]. Beyond their previous variations on Tarantula [42], the authors also enhanced the fault localization techniques of Ochiai [47] and Jaccard [48] using the enhanced domain for conditional statements and a *source mapping*—the renamed output mapping. The authors implemented the new techniques in Apollo [41] and evaluated the techniques in a large experimental study. An enhanced version of Ochiai and the path-constraint similarity-based generation yielded the best results for fault localization effectiveness.

4.1.4 Requirements-Based Test Case Generation

Requirements, whether formal or natural language based, are often used during manual and automatic test case generation. In this subsection, we present research that investigates using requirements for automatic test case generation.

Matos and Sousa [49] propose using use cases and formal requirements to create Selenium functional test cases and web pages which are user interface prototypes. The inputs to their tool are use cases, system glossary and user interface specifications writing in a controlled natural language that the tool can interpret. Their tool is implemented as an Eclipse plugin.

Thummalapenta *et al.* [50] present a new technique to automatically generate test cases by focusing only on interesting behaviors as defined by business rules, which are a form of functional specification used in the industry. Formally, a business rule is triple consisting of an antecedent, a consequent and a set of invariant conditions. In their technique, they first build an abstract state-transition diagram (STD), where the nodes represent equivalent states, as they crawl the application's GUI. In the next step of their technique, for each business rule, they identify abstract paths relevant to the business rule and refine the paths using a stricter notion of state equivalence until a traversable path is found. This final set of paths are the test cases that are executed to test the application, which also cover all the initially identified business rules. Assertion checking on the consequent condition of the business rule serves as an oracle as well. They implemented their approach in a tool called *WATEG*, Web Application Test Case Generator.

4.1.5 Search-Based Test Case Generation

Alshahwan and Harman [51] explore the notion of using search-based algorithms for test case generation. The search-based approach to test generation they propose has the underlying goal of maximizing branch coverage in the resultant test suite. They start with performing static analysis of the source code and then use the information gathered during the search-based phase. For the search-based phase, they use an algorithm derived from Korel's Alternating Variable Method [52], into which they incorporate constant seeding and the idea of using values mined dynamically as the application executes into the search space for specific branching statements. They implemented their approach in a tool called *SWAT*, Search-based Web Application Tester and evaluated its effectiveness.

In contrast to other research in this area, Tappenden and Miller [53] take a different approach in that they leverage *cookies* for testing. The authors argue that cookies are the common state representatives for all web applications and thus should be leveraged in testing. They propose using the genetic search algorithm Evolutionary Adaptive Random (EAP) for test generation to create tests where cookies are either present or absent in requests. The authors also propose several oracles, discussed in Section 4.2.

4.1.6 Regenerating Test Cases

Alshahwan and Harman [54] suggest that regenerating test suites from existing test suites—for example, by reordering test sequences—can increase the testing value of the test suite. The authors propose using a novel, value-aware data flow analysis on the server-side code to determine which reorderings will be most effective in exercising the server-side state. Since the HTTP protocol is stateless, leveraging the data flow of session variables, cookies, and the application data store in test suite regeneration results in a state-aware test suite. The authors implemented their approach for PHP applications in a tool called SART (State Aware Regeneration Tool).

4.1.7 Test Input Generation

While not specific to web applications, the approach that Shahbaz *et al.* [55] propose to generate valid and invalid test strings as inputs to string validation methods—a common type of method in web applications—can be applied to web application testing. For example, their subject string validation methods used in the experiments include methods from web applications. The authors propose using text analysis of identifiers, web searches, regular expression queries, and mutation to generate the test strings. The web query approach—defined using text analysis of identifiers—was first proposed by the same authors in their 2012 paper [56].

Fujiwara *et al.* [57] propose generating test data using a specification of the application's basic design that is written in UML and Object Constraint

Language (OCL). Given the database tables structures, user interface elements, triggerable events, the approach focuses on the behaviors. Rather than manually generating test data, the authors propose solving constraints using a Satisfiability Modulo Theories solver, which can handle highly structured data types, like string and table. While the approach seems promising, it requires well-trained people to specify the model.

4.2 Oracles

Determining whether a test case passes or fails is a difficult problem, especially for web applications that have a variety of outputs (eg, web pages, data stores, email messages) that are sometimes dynamically generated or nondeterministic. Recent advances have focused on the web page outputs— not simply malformed HTML but more nuanced failures manifested in the pages.

Dobloyi et al. [58] present techniques to automatically compare test case outputs, ie, XML/HTML documents, during regression testing. Their approach—implemented in the tool SMART—is based on a model that exploits similarities in how web applications fail. The authors first inspect a small portion of regression testing output manually and identify structural and syntactic features in the tree structures of XML documents that indicate differences that humans should investigate for failure. The features are then used to train a comparator to apply a threshold to identify which output and test cases require human inspection. Since the approach focuses on the tree-structured output, the approach misses faults involving images and the presentation of HTML elements.

de Castro et al. [59] present an extension to Selenium RC, called SeleniumDB, that allows for testing web applications that interact with databases, such as MySQL and PostGreSQL. Specifically, their tool allows establishing database connections and comparing test data with data stored in the database. They augmented Selenium RC's core with six new assert functions that allow for comparing data outputted during testing with data that exists in the database of the application. For example, an assert statement that was added to the Selenium RC code checks for the last record inserted in the database.

Mahajan and Halfond developed techniques for finding HTML presentation failures using image comparison techniques [60] combined with searching techniques to identify the failure's root cause [61]. Mahajan and Halfond's first take on finding HTML presentation failures [60] leverages image comparison techniques—comparing an image of the expected web page and a screenshot of the actual webpage, finding the pixel-level differences between the two images, and mapping the pixel-level differences to which HTML elements are likely to be the cause of the failure. Mahajan and Halfond's follow up work [60] improved finding a failure's root cause automatically using a search-based technique, where possible faulty elements are permuted to a possibly correct value and the resulting page is compared with the expected image. If the resulting page matches the expected image, then the permuted faulty element is the likely root cause. Both papers contain an experimental evaluation of their approach on web pages in wide use and indicate promising results.

The authors suggest that future work includes customizing the search space based on the root cause, handling multiple failures within one page, and handling when the fault does not visually appear within the faulty HTML element. The authors have two follow-up papers to appear in 2015 [62, 63], out of the scope of this paper and after our submission deadline.

Tappenden and Miller [53] also proposed oracles that do not depend on their cookie-based testing methodology. The authors assert that their proposed structural DOM similarity metrics (similar to Dobolyi and Weimer's [58]), HTML content similarity metrics, and a hybrid of the two metrics was critical to complete their cookie-based automated testing.

4.3 Evaluating Testing Effectiveness

After developing a testing technique, a researcher must then evaluate the technique's effectiveness.

4.3.1 Test Adequacy Criteria

Test adequacy criteria have multiple uses, such as to assess thoroughness of a test suite and also to determine when to stop testing.

Alafi *et al.* [64] propose new criteria for web application testing based on page access, server environment variable use, and database interactions. The criteria are defined as covering all server pages at least once, covering all server environment variables at least once, and covering all SQL statements (including dynamically constructed statements) at least once. They further describe how to instrument an application to capture the information relevant for these criteria, such as server variables, database interactions and page access information and how to record the coverage.

Alshahwan and Harman [65] suggest a new adequacy criterion, *output uniqueness*, and propose four definitions for this criterion with varying levels of strictness. The basic idea of this criterion is to classify the different ways in which the output of HTML web pages can be unique, either unique in entire content, or unique in tags structure, or unique in content, or unique in tags and attributes. Then, they derive new test cases by mutating each test case in an original test suite, executing the new mutated test case, and determining if the new test case produces a unique output as per one of the earlier four definitions.

Sakamoto *et al.* [66] address the integration testing problem for web applications. Their contributions include proposing a new coverage criterion, template variable coverage criterion, and presenting a technique to generate skeleton test code to improve the template variable coverage criterion. Templates refer to a templating system used on the client or server-side that helps the development of reusable HTML elements[4]. Template engines replace these template variables with actual values to create HTML pages. The template variable coverage criterion measures coverage of variables and expressions that are embedded in HTML templates. Their work is implemented in a tool called *POGen*. The tool consists of the following components: HTML template analyzer, HTML template transformer, and a test code generator.

4.3.2 Mutation Testing

Mutation testing is an approach to evaluate the fault-revealing effectiveness of testing techniques. In mutation testing, code is mutated using mutation operators to create a faulty version of the code; the mutation process happens multiple times to create multiple faulty versions of the code. If the testing technique reveals the fault, the technique is said to "kill" the mutant.

Praphamontripong and Offutt [67] developed web-specific mutation operators and implemented these operators in a tool called webMuJava that is built on muJava [68], a framework for automatically generating mutants in Java programs. The mutation operators focus on how web application components communicate, eg, through URLs and forms. While most of the operators are applied to HTML—which is general to all applications, three are specific to JSP but could be translated to similar functionality in other server-side programming languages. The authors evaluated their mutation operators and tool on one small application that showed promising results but also the need for a mutation operator that modifies a variable's scope, eg, from page to session or application scope. With this mutation tool,

---

[4] https://developers.google.com/closure/templates/

researchers can evaluate the ability of their testing approaches to detect faults in web applications.

4.3.3 Fault Severity

Dobolyi and Weimer [69] propose a model of consumer-perceived fault severity, which they argue is the most appropriate way to model fault severity because web applications are user centric. Given a user–centric fault severity model, developers can prioritize the most severe faults. The authors propose two models—one of which is fully automated—based on features in HTML documents that likely indicate a failure. Both models outperformed humans in determining consumer-perceived severity. Based on a fault severity study of 17 subject applications, the authors conclude that traditional fault seeding, which is often used to evaluate the effectiveness of testing techniques, does not generate uniformly severe faults in terms of consumer perception and is therefore not necessarily a good technique for evaluating testing techniques.

4.4 Regression Testing

Regression testing takes place during the maintenance phase of the software development life cycle. Common challenges that are encountered during regression testing are (a) managing the size and quality of an evolving test suite and (b) creating new test cases or reusing old test cases for testing new/changed parts. To address the first challenge, researchers have proposed test case selection strategies, such as reduction and prioritization. For the latter challenge, identifying the changed parts of the code for test case generation and test case repair of older test cases are often the strategies that are used. This section describes the advances in regression testing for the domain of web application testing.

4.4.1 Prioritization Approaches

Bryce *et al.* [70] develop a uniform representation to model both GUI and web software (both are event-driven software that have traditionally been studied independently) and develop a set of prioritization criteria based on this new model that can be used to test both GUI and web software. First, they develop a uniform representation for the building blocks of testing event-driven software, specifically, unified terminology for a window, an action, a parameter, a value and a test case. A test case is modeled as a sequence of windows and associated parameter values. Then, they present eight prioritization criteria, that are based on test case properties, such as the number of two-way interactions between parameters that are covered in a test case (Interaction-based criteria), the length of the test case (Count-based criteria) as measured by total number of actions, total number of parameter-values, unique number of actions in a test case, and the number of frequently occurring sequences of actions (measured in three different ways) in a test case (Frequency-based criteria). They conduct an empirical study with four GUI and three web applications and apply the proposed prioritization criteria. They find that two criteria are always among the top three in effectiveness for all the subject applications. One of the two criteria orders test cases in decreasing order of number of two-way interactions between parameters, and the other criterion orders in decreasing order of length in terms of number of parameter values. These two criteria are recommended by the authors as effective prioritization criteria for testing event-driven software. The authors also explore the effectiveness of hybrid prioritization criteria, where they prioritize test cases based on a frequency criteria until 10% to 20% of the test suite is covered without an increase in APFD [71] and then switch to one of the interaction-based criteria. In their experimental study, they find that hybrid criteria improve effectiveness when compared to the individual criteria used in creating the hybrid.

Sampath et al. [72] present a tool, CPUT, to prioritize and reduce user-session-based test cases of web applications. The tool, developed in Java, consists of two main components. The first component is a logging module that they developed for Apache web server that collects all pertinent usage information that is needed to create user-session-based test cases. The second component is the main CPUT tool that allows import of Apache web server logs, which can then be converted into user-session-based test cases in XML format. CPUT stores the imported log file and the test cases in a PostgreSQL database. CPUT allows for importing new log files, appending to an existing log file that has previously been imported, and an overwrite previously imported log file capability. The test cases can then be prioritized or reduced by several experimentally verified criteria, such as combinatorial, length-based, and frequency-based criteria [70]. CPUT also displays some statistics about each user-session-based test case, such as the number of requests in the test case, the number of parameter values. The tool writes the prioritized/reduced test suite to a text file which can be used by testers to identify tests cases to execute during their maintenance testing cycles.

Garg et al. [73] present a two-level approach to prioritize web application test cases. They build a functional dependence graph (FDG), generated from a UML diagram of the application, to model functional dependencies between modules in a web application. The authors also create an inter-procedural control graph (ICG) from the source code for each functional module in the FDG. The test suite for the application is partitioned into different test sets that can be tied to a functional module/node in the FDG. Test cases within a test set are tied to submodules modeled in the ICG. The two-level approach to prioritization proposed in this paper is based on criteria that rely on first assigning priorities to modules in the FDG and then to sub-modules in the ICG. Modules in the FDG are prioritized based on new and modified functionalities that are added or modified in the FDG, eg, a newly introduced node in the FDG represents newly added functionality and thus gets highest priority, modified FDG nodes get next higher priority, etc. Modules within the ICG are prioritized based on the *degree of modification* of the node in the ICG which is determined by the change in number of lines of code, eg, a new ICG node gets the highest priority, remaining nodes are assigned priorities in decreasing order of *degree of modification*. Finally, test cases are prioritized using criteria in increasing and decreasing order of (a) distance of modified nodes from the root FDG node, (b) number of functional modules executed, and (c) number of changes (as identified in ICG nodes) executed. A small experimental study reveals that prioritizing tests based on the shortest path of modified nodes from the root FDG node has the highest APFD [71] in the first 10% of the test suite. In another work [74], the same authors propose distributing the test sets on multiple machines and executing them in parallel to reduce test execution time. Each machine is approximately allocated an equal number of functional modules and also equal priorities of functional modules.

Garg *et al.* [75] also proposed a new automated test case prioritization technique that automatically identifies changes in the database and prioritizes test cases such that database faults may be detected early. They use a functional dependence graph and a schema diagram which models the relationship between the database tables and fields in their prioritization approach. Using log files that capture details of the database, they identify the FDG modules that are modified as a result of database changes (as captured in the log files) and assign priorities to the modules, eg, assigning higher priority to FDG modules whose modifications are due to new tables in the schema diagram. A small experimental evaluation showed that their approach is able to detect 70% of the seeded database faults by executing 10% of the test suite.

Sampath *et al.* [76] propose *ordering* reduced suites to further increase the effectiveness of test suite reduction strategies. Test suite reduction is a regression testing strategy to reduce the size of the test suite that is executed by using several criteria that will allow the selection of a smaller set of test cases that are comparable in effectiveness to the entire original suite. Test case prioritization, on the other hand, strives to keep all the test cases in the original suite, but proposes that they be ordered based on some criteria such that the ordered test suite can find faults early in the test execution cycle. In their work, Sampath *et al.* [76] first reduce test suites using reduction criteria [77] that select a smaller test set based on characteristics like the actual base requests covered in a test case, the actual parameter names that are covered in a test case, etc., with the goal of creating a reduced set of test cases that cover all base requests of the web application, and all parameter names in the web application, respectively. They, then prioritize the reduced suites by then applying prioritization criteria (specifically, count-, interaction-, and frequency-based criteria) that are shown to be effective in related work [70]. This approach led to the creation of 40 criteria that order reduced suites which are empirically evaluated by Sampath *et al.* using three web applications, seeded faults and user-session-based test cases. Another contribution in this work is the development of a new metric that can be used to compare test suites of unequal lengths. The common metrics used to evaluate the effectiveness of prioritized test suites, APFD [71] and APFD_C [78] require that the compared test suites be of the same size. However, the reduced suites compared in Sampath *et al.*'s work were of varying sizes and thus could not be compared using the traditional effectiveness metrics. Therefore, they developed a new effectiveness metric *Mod_APFD_C* that allows the effectiveness evaluation of prioritization effectiveness of test suites of unequal lengths. The new metric takes into account the number of unique faults detected, the time to generate the ordered reduced suite, and the time to execute the ordered reduced suite. Through their empirical study, they find that in several cases, the ordered reduced suites are more effective than a pure reduced suite and a pure prioritized suite, thus lending evidence to the creation of a promising new approach to regression testing.

Dobuneh [79] *et al.* propose and evaluate a hybrid prioritization criterion for testing web applications. Their hybrid criterion first orders test cases by number of common HTTP requests in the test case, then, orders test cases based on the length of HTTP request chains, and finally, by the dependency of HTTP requests. In their experimental study with one subject application, they find that the hybrid criterion finds all the seeded faults sooner than the first and second criteria used in the hybrid, but is comparable to the third criterion on dependency of HTTP requests. Similar results are observed when evaluating the time taken by the hybrid and the individual criteria to generate the prioritized test suites.

4.4.2 Test Suite Reduction Approaches

Test suite reduction is a regression testing strategy where the goal is to create a smaller test suite that is as effective as the original test suite.

Huang and Lu [80] propose a test suite reduction approach that uses user sessions and service profiles of the application that describe functions of the application, and apply concept analysis [81], a mathematical clustering technique, to perform the reduction. The service profile is essentially a sequence of URLs that is derived from either functional specifications or by reverse engineering from the source code. In a service profile, data dependence between URLs and control dependence between URLs is captured. A matrix that maps user sessions to the service profiles they cover is created and fed as input to concept analysis which then clusters the user sessions such that all the user sessions in a cluster cover the set of service profiles in the cluster. The heuristic to select user sessions from the clusters created by concept analysis selects user sessions that cover all service profiles of the application. The authors also illustrate how concept analysis may be used in the case of evolving services, where services are added/modified or dropped. A small experimental study with a PetShop web application is presented and their approach is evaluated.

Liu *et al.* [82] also propose a clustering approach to reduce the size of a user-session-based test set. Clustering requires a similarity measure based on which similar user sessions are grouped together. Liu *et al.* measure similarity between user sessions based on the number of same URLs and the number of same parameter types contain. After computing the similarity in this manner, they apply agglutinate hierarchy clustering algorithm to cluster the user sessions. They propose an algorithm to select from these clusters to avoid selection of redundant user-session-based test cases. They find that the reduced suite generated in this manner is as effective as the original test suite within a margin of 1–2% in block, function coverage and seeded fault detection.

4.4.3 Creating Test Cases for Changed Parts of Code

Marback *et al.* [83] present an approach that focuses on identifying areas of code that have changed using impact analysis and generating new test cases for the areas impacted by the change using program slicing. They first construct Program Dependence Graphs for two consecutive versions of the application using the Abstract Syntax Trees generated by a PHP Compiler. Then, they use a program differencing tool to identify areas of code that have changed and a program slicer to calculate areas of code that are affected by the change. Finally, they use the slices to generate test paths (or test cases), but first they gather constraints on string and numeric values in the slices and resolve them using constraint solvers. A test execution engine takes the test paths and the resolved input values and uses them as input to the web application. They build upon this work in [84] with more subject applications and experiments.

One of the shortcomings observed in the earlier work was that resolving constraints on inputs required a lot of effort. Hossain *et al.* [85] present a technique to identify constraint values from previous versions of the programs that can be reused when executing regression test paths in the new version. Through an experimental study, they find that a large number of variable constraints can be reused from previous versions. The central idea in their approach is to compare the definitions and uses of variables between previous and current versions of the application to determine if the same constraints on variables can be used.

4.4.4 Maintaining/Repairing a Regression Test Suite

Choudhary *et al.* [86] propose a technique to automatically repair web application test scripts. Specifically, they are able to repair test cases that fail due to a change in values of page elements that causes a mismatch between expected and actual results and test cases that fault due to moved or modified web page elements. In their approach, they take as input the execution of the test case on the old version of the application (where the test case works) and the new version of the application (where the test case fails) and compare several DOM properties in the two executions to locate failing points and repair the test cases.

Kumar and Goel [87] explore the use of modeling the original and modified web application as event-dependency graphs that are then converted into event trees to remove cyclic dependencies, and finally compare the trees to identify changed nodes and nodes that are affected by the changed nodes. Identifying the affected nodes in the application is then used to guide regression test selection. Three types of dependencies are modeled in the event-dependency graph, specifically, link dependencies, invisible effect and visible effect dependencies. Chopra and Madan [88] explore the possibility of using test paths obtained from a page flow diagram of a web application to test the application.

Leotta *et al.* [89] use the concept of *page object pattern* which is an abstraction of a web application's page to improve maintainability of Selenium WebDriver test cases and conduct a case study in an industry environment to evaluate the effectiveness of the approach. They found that when Selenium WebDriver test cases are written without using any patterns, the code in the test methods is highly coupled with the implementation in the web page. This leads to problems during maintenance, ie, when the web page code is updated, all the test cases need to undergo updating as well. The central idea in using page object patterns is that each page is abstracted into a page object and the functionality offered by the web page becomes methods offered by the page object, which can then be called in a test case. This allows for creating test cases that can be changed relatively easily when the web page undergoes changes.

Leotta *et al.* [90] also address the problem constantly fixing broken web page element locators (ie, XPATH locators) when the application is undergoing changes. They develop an algorithm that automatically generates robust XPATH-based locators that could work in a newer version of the application as well, thus reducing the aging of test cases. They define four transformations that are designed to make the XPATH expressions in the web application more specific and iteratively apply one of these transformations starting from the most general XPATH expression.

Andrews and Do [91] use a FSM-based model of the web application, FSMWeb, developed in prior work to create test cases. As the application undergoes changes and the model changes, they classify test cases as reusable, obsolete, and re-testable test cases. Then, they evaluate the cost-benefit tradeoffs of applying brute force regression testing and selective regression testing by quantifying the costs involved in each case. Further, they propose two assumptions, first, that the cost of executing and validating a test case is proportional to the length of the test case or the number of inputs on each edge, and second, the cost of classification (as obsolete, reusable, or re-testable) is proportional to the size of the test suite. They conduct a case study comparing the two regression testing approaches and discuss a decision making process for practitioners.

Hirzel *et al.* [92] adapt an existing selective regression testing technique developed for Java applications to work in the context of Google Web Kit compiler, which converts Java code into JavaScript. The idea is to select test cases that execute changed parts of the code. Web test cases execute JavaScript code but the code that is changed is the Java code. Therefore, when the Java code undergoes changes, the changes need to be traced back to JavaScript which is difficult to accomplish because of code obfuscation. Also, additional code originating from libraries and dynamic typing make the trackback to Java difficult. They first build control flow graphs of the two Java application versions and compare them. Since the test cases are executed on the JavaScript code and not the Java code, they need a mapping between the test cases and the Java code. To establish a mapping, they instrument the test cases by introducing a code identifier (CID) for methods, statements or expressions which can be traced from the JavaScript to the Java code for that code entity. After comparing the old and new versions of the application, test cases are selected for reexecution if they touch at least one changed Java code entity as identified by the CID. Their technique is implemented as an Eclipse plugin and they empirically evaluate their approach.

4.4.5 Empirical Studies

Christophe et al. [93] conduct an empirical study to determine how widely Selenium's test cases are used in open source software and how long these test cases are maintained over time as the application evolves. As a result of these investigations, they are able to identify the parts of a functional test case that are most prone to change. They studied 287 GitHub repositories and classified the applications as web service providers, frameworks for building web applications, Selenium extensions, web application examples for learning, and a miscellaneous category. They found that 25% of the applications from the web services category use Selenium to a large extent for testing. They also found that Selenium test cases are modified as the project evolves. And finally, they found that the constants and assert statements are the most frequently changed statements as the Selenium test cases evolve.

4.5 Distant Reading of Surveyed Papers

We used the Paper Machines[5] extension for Zotero[6] to perform textual analyses of the 60 papers we survey in this chapter. In addition to the standard English stop words, we added words specific to this corpus, alphabetically: acm, application, applications, case, cases, conference, fig, figure, googletag, ieee, international, paper, proceedings, pubad, public, section, software, standard, table, target, test, testing, tests, and web. These text analyses are

---

[5] http://papermachines.org/
[6] https://www.zotero.org/

not perfect in that they rely on extracting the text from the PDF files. Our spot checking of the text extraction showed that most text extraction was performed correctly; however, there are some issues with special characters, such as dashes, quotes, and ligatures, like "ff." The analyses also do not weight words differently, for example, words found in titles and footnotes are counted the same. Despite these limitations, we believe these distant readings allow us to see trends in the research.

The word cloud in Fig. 4 shows the proportional prevalence of words in the corpus (in our case, the surveyed papers), where the most common words are in the largest font. As expected, the most common words are related to web applications, eg, user, HTML, pages, request/s, sessions, server, database, browser, form, http, parameter; code, eg, code, program, source, expressions, statements, line/s, variable/s; and testing, eg, values, suite/s, fault/s, failure/s, coverage.

Distinct characteristic of web applications are reflected in the word cloud, such as navigation (sequence/s, transition/s, control) and user interaction (users, GUI, interactions). In addition, we see words like PHP and Java, which are the languages used to implement the web application. In our survey, we did not find work that developed techniques specific to other language/frameworks, such as ASP or Ruby on Rails. Of the words that imply a common web application functionality (eg, search and order), login is distinct because it is unlikely to have meanings other than the web application functionality (as opposed to search-based testing or "in order to" statements). Login's prominence seems to imply that it is important functionality that researchers must address.

Figure 4 A word cloud of the most common words in the papers studied.

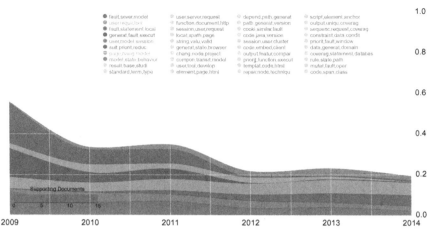

Figure 5 A topic model of the most common groupings of words in the papers studied.

Words like model/s, technique/s, approach/es, and algorithm as well as result/s and, to a lesser extent, evaluation words (eg, study, percentage, and average) are all prominent in the cloud, implying that researchers developed novel approaches and evaluated those approaches. The prominence of tool/s and automate implies that researchers implemented their approaches in automated tools. Our survey supports both of these observations.

With respect to words related to the testing research focus, generation, regression, prioritization, reduction, and localization are all prominent in the word cloud. On the other hand, the word oracle is much smaller. Again, our survey reflects the relative weights of these topics.

While the word cloud presents individual words, Fig. 5 presents the proportional prevalence of 40 *topics* in the papers (*y*-axis) by their publication date (*x*-axis).[7] Despite imperfections in the analysis (eg, two papers published in 2010 are represented in 2009), the visualization helps to show the research trends. The figure highlights eight of the most common topics. We chose not to highlight topics that represent the documents' metadata or topics that represent components of web applications (eg, {user, server, request} or {function, document, http}). Despite being more prevalent, these topics are listed after the highlighted topics.

In general, the visualization supports our claim that the papers emphasize approaches and techniques (eg, {fault, sever, model}, {user, model, session},

---

[7] We cannot get a more readable figure, eg, a larger font for the legend or grayscale patterns, from the Paper Machines tool. Also, the order of the bars is not the same as the order of the legend.

{user, requir, tool}, {page, navig, model}) over empirical studies. User tools (fourth from bottom) and user modeling (third bar from the bottom) have remained fairly constant in prevalence over the time period perhaps an indication of how important users are, with respect to testing and use of web applications.

While fault localization (bottom bar) has remained relatively constant in prevalence throughout the time period, other fault-related topics are on the decline. Work on fault severity models (second bar from top) is sharply declining in prevalence, yet is still an open problem and could be a direction for future work. The fourth bar from the top {generat, fault, execut} is also surprisingly on the decline in prevalence; perhaps the recent increase in prevalence of static analysis techniques (eg, the slight increase in {model, state, behavior}, top bar, despite not including many papers on static analysis techniques in our survey) explains the decline.

The topic of test suite selection (represented by {suit, priorit, reduc}, third from bottom) is on an upwards trend. As application sizes—and therefore their test suites—continue to grow, it is crucial that testers can test in more cost-effective ways, and thus it is important that research addresses this important problem.

While most of the topics (eg, fault localization) seem to have constant prevalence throughout the time period, {user, session, model} and {fault, sever, model} are less prevalent more recently. Research on traditional user session-based testing—{user, model, session) in the bottom bar—seems to be on the decline, while {session, user, request} is not. In our search for relevant papers, we found work on JavaScript-based capture-replay, which is also user session based. We do not include this work in our survey or in this analysis because it was out of scope and, therefore, is not reflected in the figure. Work on severity models is lacking and could be a direction for future work.

5. CONCLUSION

As web applications continue to grow in complexity and in popularity, testing their correctness will continue to deserve the attention of researchers. In this chapter, we studied and reported on the advances in web application testing literature between the years of 2010 and 2014. We found that research in this period broadly could be categorized in the areas of test case generation, oracle development, criteria, and approaches to evaluate effectiveness of a test suite, and regression testing approaches.

In this section, we summarize some open areas of research that we see trending in the next few years based on our analysis of the past 4 years of research.

- We found that several tools and techniques developed in the literature are built on top of Selenium [19], either as an extension to Selenium RC, or built on top of WebDriver. The end goal of incorporating with Selenium is to create test cases that Selenium can execute. The research community recognizes the prevalent use of Selenium in the industry and thus has focused on developing add-ons to attract the target audience that already uses Selenium in their testing process. This leads us to believe that Selenium is a web testing tool that will become increasingly popular in academia and industry in the future.

- Another trend, or lack thereof, that we observed is the limited research in the area of developing adequacy criteria for web applications. Several researchers focused on fault detection as an evaluation measure or on using traditional coverage criteria of statement, method, and branch coverage. With the different types of web languages used today, the development and use of frameworks such as Rails and the popularity of JavaScript in all aspects of web development, there might be scope for development of new coverage criteria that target unique character-istics of web applications. In companies where systematic testing is followed, adequacy criteria tend to be the most common method to determine when to stop testing. Thus, advancements in this domain and practical applicability of proposed criteria could find widespread acceptance.

- In terms of evaluating effectiveness of testing techniques, we found very limited research in the area of developing fault severity classi-fications. Fault severity is a commonly used metric in the industry to prioritize testing and development efforts. Advances in developing solid, empirically evaluated fault severity criteria for web application testing, that addresses fault severity from the point of view of multiple stake holders could be of significant importance in both academic and industry circles.

- In the domain of test case generation for traditional applications, we find an increasing use of search-based algorithms. Applying search-based algorithms to test case generation web domain is only recently gaining importance. This could be an area of research that could see growth in the near future, as scalable test case generation continues to be a chal-lenge in the web application testing domain.

- Another trend that we observed from our analysis is that researchers tend to focus on developing new approaches and techniques to test web applications, whether in the area of test generation or oracle development, etc. Though most researchers include a strong empirical component that evaluates the effectiveness of their approach, there is a lack of empirical studies that compare and contrast the various approaches to web testing, lack of studies that replicate existing studies and results, and a lack of surveys and qualitative studies designed to understand testing practices in small/large companies, etc. Empirical research can serve as a strong foundation for identifying new research problems that the community can address in the future. We believe more empirical research is an area the web testing community can focus on and benefit from in the near future.

- Much of the work surveyed is focused on individual components on the server-side or the client-side to great results. Several authors mention that future work involves combining their work with others' work. We can envision many possible fruitful collaborations. For example, the concolic test case generation work in Section 4.1.3 may be able to be combined with the oracle work that finds differences in HTML from Section 4.2 to yield even better fault localization.

- Finally, as a whole genre of applications and services are moving to the cloud, we believe that testing techniques that can scale to the cloud [94] and the notion of offering web testing as a service in the cloud are areas of research that could gain prominence in the coming years.

REFERENCES

[1] A. Orso, G. Rothermel, Software testing: a research travelogue (2000-2014), in: Proceedings of the Future of Software Engineering, FOSE 2014, New York, NY, USA, ACM, ISBN 978-1-4503-2865-4, 2014, pp. 117–132. http://dx.doi.org/10.1145/2593882.2593885, 00005.

[2] V. Garousi, A. Mesbah, A. Betin-Can, S. Mirshokraie, A systematic mapping study of web application testing, Inf. Softw. Technol. 55 (8) (2013) 1374–1396, ISSN 0950-5849. http://dx.doi.org/10.1016/j.infsof.2013.02.006, 00015, http://www.sciencedirect.com/science/article/pii/S0950584913000396.

[3] Y.-F. Li, P.K. Das, D.L. Dowe, Two decades of web application testing–a survey of recent advances, Inf. Syst. 43 (2014) 20–54, ISSN 0306-4379, http://dx.doi.org/10.1016/j.is.2014.02.001, 00003, http://www.sciencedirect.com/science/article/pii/S0306437914000271.

[4] M.H. Alalfi, J.R. Cordy, T.R. Dean, Modelling methods for web application verification and testing: state of the art, Softw. Test. Verif. Reliab. 19 (4) (2009) 265–296, ISSN 1099-1689, http://dx.doi.org/10.1002/stvr.401, 00064, http://onlinelibrary.wiley.com/doi/10.1002/stvr.401/abstract.

[5] X. Li, Y. Xue, A survey on server-side approaches to securing web applications, ACM Comput. Surv. 46 (4) (2014) 54:1–54:29, ISSN 0360-0300, http://dx.doi.org/10.1145/2541315, 00006.

[6] A. Mesbah, Chapter five–advances in testing JavaScript-based web applications, in: A.M. Memon (Ed.), Advances in Computers, vol. 97, Elsevier, 2015, pp. 201–235, 00000, http://www.sciencedirect.com/science/article/pii/S0065245814000114.

[7] S. Sampath, Chapter 3–advances in user-session-based testing of web applications, in: A. Hurson, A. Memon (Eds.), Advances in Computers, vol. 86, Elsevier, 2012, pp. 87–108, 00000, http://www.sciencedirect.com/science/article/pii/B978012396535600003X.

[8] P.D.B. Parolo, R.K. Pan, R. Ghosh, B.A. Huberman, K. Kaski, S. Fortunato, Attention decay in science, arXiv:1503.01881 [physics] (2015) arXiv: 1503.01881, http://arxiv.org/abs/1503.01881.

[9] W3C, HTTP–HyperText Transfer Protocol Overview, 2015, http://www.w3.org/Protocols/.

[10] Apache, Apache HTTP server project 2015, http://httpd.apache.org/.

[11] Apache, Apache Tomcat 2015, http://tomcat.apache.org/.

[12] IBM, WebSphere application server 2015, http://www-03.ibm.com/software/products/en/appserv-was.

[13] Google, App engine–run your applications on a fully-managed Platform-as-a-Service (PaaS) using built-in services–Google Cloud Platform, 2015, https://cloud.google.com/appengine/.

[14] W3C, HTTP state management mechanism 2015, http://www.w3.org/Protocols/rfc2109/rfc2109.

[15] W3C, HTML, the web's core language 2015, http://www.w3.org/html/.

[16] W3C, Cascading style sheets 2015, http://www.w3.org/Style/CSS/Overview.en.html.

[17] W3C, JavaScript Web APIs 2015, http://www.w3.org/standards/webdesign/script.html.

[18] Web Technology Surveys, Usage statistics and market share of server-side programming languages for websites, April 2015, 2015, http://w3techs.com/technologies/overview/programming_language/all.

[19] Selenium, SeleniumHQ browser automation 2015, http://www.seleniumhq.org/.

[20] H.V. Nguyen, H.A. Nguyen, T.T. Nguyen, T.N. Nguyen, Auto-locating and fix-propagating for HTML validation errors to PHP server-side code, in: 2011 26th IEEE/ACM International Conference on Automated Software Engineering (ASE), 2011, pp. 13–22, http://dx.doi.org/10.1109/ASE.2011.6100047, 00016.

[21] H. Samimi, M. Schfer, S. Artzi, T. Millstein, F. Tip, L. Hendren, Automated repair of HTML generation errors in PHP applications using string constraint solving, in: Proceedings of the 34th International Conference on Software Engineering, ICSE '12, Piscataway, NJ, USA, IEEE Press, ISBN 978-1-4673-1067-3, 2012, pp. 277–287, 00039, http://dl.acm.org/citation.cfm?id=2337223.2337257.

[22] Y.-H. Tung, S.-S. Tseng, T.-J. Lee, J.-F. Weng, A novel approach to automatic test case generation for web applications, in: 2010 10th International Conference on Quality Software (QSIC), IEEE, ISBN 978-1-4244-8078-4, 2010, pp. 399–404, http://dx.doi.org/10.1109/QSIC.2010.33, 00015, http://ieeexplore.ieee.org/lpdocs/epic03/wrapper.htm?arnumber=5562993.

[23] J. Offutt, Y. Wu, Modeling presentation layers of web applications for testing, Softw. Syst. Model. 9 (2) (2010) 257–280, ISSN 1619-1366, 1619-1374, http://dx,doi.org/10.1007/s10270-009-0125-4.

[24] S. Thummala, J. Offutt, An evaluation of the effectiveness of the atomic section model, in: J. Dingel, W. Schulte, I. Ramos, S. Abraho, E. Insfran (Eds.), Model-Driven Engineering Languages and Systems, no. 8767 in Lecture Notes in Computer Science, Springer International Publishing, ISBN 978-3-319-11652-5, 978-3-319-11653-2, 2014, pp. 35–49. http://link.springer.com/chapter/10.1007/978-3-319-11653-2_3.

[25] S. Chen, H. Miao, B. Song, Y. Chen, Towards practical modeling of web applications and generating tests, in: 2010 4th IEEE International Symposium on Theoretical Aspects of Software Engineering (TASE), 2010, pp. 209–217, http://dx.doi.org/10.1109/TASE.2010.25, 00003.

[26] A. Torsel, Automated test case generation for web applications from a domain specific model, in: 2011 IEEE 35th Annual Computer Software and Applications Conference Workshops (COMPSACW), 2011, pp. 137–142, http://dx.doi.org/10.1109/COMPSACW.2011.32.

[27] B. Song, S. Gong, S. Chen, Model composition and generating tests for web applications, in: 2011 Seventh International Conference on Computational Intelligence and Security (CIS), 2011, pp. 568–572, http://dx.doi.org/10.1109/CIS.2011.131, 00001.

[28] I. Enderlin, F. Dadeau, A. Giorgetti, F. Bouquet, Grammar-based testing using realistic domains in PHP, in: 2012 IEEE Fifth International Conference on Software Testing, Verification and Validation (ICST), 2012, pp. 509–518, http://dx.doi.org/10.1109/ICST.2012.136, 00003.

[29] I. Enderlin, F. Dadeau, A. Giorgetti, A.B. Othman, Praspel: a specification language for contract-based testing in PHP, in: B. Wolff, F. Zadi (Eds.), Testing Software and Systems, no. 7019 in Lecture Notes in Computer Science, Springer, Berlin, ISBN 978-3-642-24579-4, 978-3-642-24580-0, 2011, pp. 64–79. http://link.springer.com/chapter/10.1007/978-3-642-24580-0_6.

[30] V. Dallmeier, M. Burger, T. Orth, A. Zeller, WebMate: generating test cases for Web 2.0, in: D. Winkler, S. Biffl, J. Bergsmann (Eds.), Software Quality. Increasing Value in Software and Systems Development, no. 133 in Lecture Notes in Business Information Processing, Springer, Berlin, ISBN 978-3-642-35701-5, 978-3-642-35702-2, 2013, pp. 55–69. http://link.springer.com/chapter/10.1007/978-3-642-35702-2_5.

[31] A. Zeller, We are creating a start-up in web testing, 2013, http://andreas-zeller.blogspot.com/2013/03/we-are-creating-start-up-in-web-testing.html.

[32] Testfabrik Consulting + Solutions AG, webmate, 2015, https://app.webmate.io/.

[33] M. Schur, A. Roth, A. Zeller, ProCrawl: mining test models from multi-user web applications, in: Proceedings of the 2014 International Symposium on Software Testing and Analysis, ISSTA 2014, New York, NY, USA, ACM, ISBN 978-1-4503-2645-2, 2014, pp. 413–416, http://dx.doi.org/10.1145/2610384.2628051, 00000.

[34] M. Schur, A. Roth, A. Zeller, Mining behavior models from enterprise web applications, in: Proceedings of the 2013 9th Joint Meeting on Foundations of Software Engineering, ESEC/FSE 2013, New York, NY, USA, ACM, ISBN 978-1-4503-2237-9, 2013, pp. 422–432, http://dx.doi.org/10.1145/2491411.2491426.

[35] S. Elbaum, G. Rothermel, S. Karre, M. Fisher, Leveraging user-session data to support Web application testing, IEEE Trans. Softw. Eng. 31 (3) (2005) 187–202, ISSN 0098-5589, http://dx.doi.org/10.1109/TSE.2005.36.

[36] S. Sprenkle, L. Pollock, L. Simko, A study of usage-based navigation models and generated abstract test cases for web applications, in: Proceedings of the 2011 Fourth IEEE International Conference on Software Testing, Verification and Validation, ICST '11, Washington, DC, USA, IEEE Computer Society, ISBN 978-0-7695-4342-0, 2011, pp. 230–239, http://dx.doi.org/10.1109/ICST.2011.34.

[37] S.E. Sprenkle, L.L. Pollock, L.M. Simko, Configuring effective navigation models and abstract test cases for web applications by analysing user behaviour, Softw. Test. Verif.

Reliab. 23 (6) (2013) 439–464, ISSN 1099-1689, http://dx.doi.org/10.1002/stvr.1496, 00003, http://onlinelibrary.wiley.com/doi/10.1002/stvr.1496/abstract.

[38] S. Sprenkle, C. Cobb, L. Pollock, Leveraging user-privilege classification to customize usage-based statistical models of web applications, in: Proceedings of the 2012 IEEE Fifth International Conference on Software Testing, Verification and Validation, ICST '12, Washington, DC, USA, IEEE Computer Society, ISBN 978-0-7695-4670-4, 2012, pp. 161–170, http://dx.doi.org/10.1109/ICST.2012.96, 00005.

[39] J. Sant, A. Souter, L. Greenwald, An exploration of statistical models for automated test case generation, in: ACM SIGSOFT Software Engineering Notes, vol. 30, ACM, 2005, pp. 1–7, http://dl.acm.org/citation.cfm?id=1083256.

[40] S. Artzi, A. Kiezun, J. Dolby, F. Tip, D. Dig, A. Paradkar, M.D. Ernst, Finding bugs in web applications using dynamic test generation and explicit-state model checking, IEEE Trans. Softw. Eng. 36 (4) (2010) 474–494, ISSN 0098-5589, http://dx.doi.org/10.1109/TSE.2010.31, 00075.

[41] S. Artzi, A. Kiezun, J. Dolby, F. Tip, D. Dig, A. Paradkar, M.D. Ernst, Finding bugs in dynamic web applications, in: Proceedings of the 2008 International Symposium on Software Testing and Analysis, ISSTA '08, New York, NY, USA, ACM, ISBN 978-1-60558-050-0, 2008, pp. 261–272, http://dx.doi.org/10.1145/1390630.1390662, 00158.

[42] S. Artzi, J. Dolby, F. Tip, M. Pistoia, Practical fault localization for dynamic web applications, in: 2010 ACM/IEEE 32nd International Conference on Software Engineering, vol. 1, 2010, pp. 265–274, http://dx.doi.org/10.1145/1806799.1806840.

[43] J.A. Jones, M.J. Harrold, Empirical evaluation of the tarantula automatic fault-localization technique, in: Proceedings of the 20th IEEE/ACM International Conference on Automated Software Engineering, ASE '05, New York, NY, USA, ACM, ISBN 1-58113-993-4, 2005, pp 273–282, http://dx.doi.org/10.1145/1101908.1101949, 00601.

[44] J.A. Jones, M.J. Harrold, J. Stasko, Visualization of test information to assist fault localization, in: Proceedings of the 24th International Conference on Software Engineering, ICSE '02, New York, NY, USA, ACM, ISBN 1-58113-472-X, 2002, pp. 467–477, http://dx.doi.org/10.1145/581339.581397, 00680.

[45] S. Artzi, J. Dolby, F. Tip, M. Pistoia, Directed test generation for effective fault localization, in: Proceedings of the 19th International Symposium on Software Testing and Analysis, ISSTA '10, New York, NY, USA, ACM, ISBN 978-1-60558-823-0, 2010, pp. 49–60, http://dx.doi.org/10.1145/1831708.1831715.

[46] S. Artzi, J. Dolby, F. Tip, M. Pistoia, Fault localization for dynamic web applications, IEEE Trans. Softw. Eng. 38 (2) (2012) 314–335, ISSN 0098-5589, http://dx.doi.org/10.1109/TSE.2011.76, 00018.

[47] R. Abreu, P. Zoeteweij, A.J.C. van Gemund, An evaluation of similarity coefficients for software fault localization, in: Proceedings of the 12th Pacific Rim International Symposium on Dependable Computing, PRDC '06, Washington, DC, USA, IEEE Computer Society, ISBN 0-7695-2724-8, 2006, pp. 39–46, http://dx.doi.org/10.1109/PRDC.2006.18.

[48] M.Y. Chen, E. Kiciman, E. Fratkin, A. Fox, E. Brewer, Pinpoint: problem determination in large, dynamic Internet services. in: Proceedings of the International Conference on Dependable Systems and Networks, 2002, DSN 2002, 2002, pp. 595–604, http://dx.doi.org/10.1109/DSN.2002.1029005.

[49] E.C.B. de Matos, T.C. Sousa, From formal requirements to automated web testing and prototyping, Innov. Syst. Softw. Eng. 6 (1-2) (2010) 163–169, ISSN 1614-5046, 1614-5054, http://dx,doi.org/10.1007/s11334-009-0112-5.

[50] S. Thummalapenta, K.V. Lakshmi, S. Sinha, N. Sinha, S. Chandra, Guided test generation for web applications, in: Proceedings of the 2013 International Conference on Software

Engineering, ICSE '13, Piscataway, NJ, USA, IEEE Press, ISBN 978-1-4673-3076-3, 2013, pp. 162–171. http://dl.acm.org/citation.cfm?id=2486788.2486810.

[51] N. Alshahwan, M. Harman, Automated web application testing using search based software engineering, in: 2011 26th IEEE/ACM International Conference on Automated Software Engineering (ASE), 2011, pp. 3–12, http://dx.doi.org/10.1109/ASE.2011.6100082, 00049.

[52] B. Korel, Automated software test data generation, IEEE Trans. Softw. Eng. 16 (8) (1990) 870–879, ISSN 0098-5589, http://dx.doi.org/10.1109/32.57624.

[53] A.F. Tappenden, J. Miller, Automated cookie collection testing, ACM Trans. Softw. Eng. Methodol. 23 (1) (2014) 3:1–3:40, ISSN 1049-331X, http://dx.doi.org/10.1145/2559936, 00003.

[54] N. Alshahwan, M. Harman, State aware test case regeneration for improving web application test suite coverage and fault detection, in: Proceedings of the 2012 International Symposium on Software Testing and Analysis, ISSTA 2012, New York, NY, USA, ACM, ISBN 978-1-4503-1454-1, 2012, pp. 45–55, http://dx.doi.org/10.1145/2338965.2336759.

[55] M. Shahbaz, P. McMinn, M. Stevenson, Automatic generation of valid and invalid test data for string validation routines using web searches and regular expressions, Sci. Comput. Program. 97, Part 4 (2015) 405–425, ISSN 0167-6423, http://dx.doi.org/10.1016/j.scico.2014.04.008, 00002, http://www.sciencedirect.com/science/article/pii/S0167642314001725.

[56] P. McMinn, M. Shahbaz, M. Stevenson, Search-based test input generation for string data types using the results of web queries, in: 2012 IEEE Fifth International Conference on Software Testing, Verification and Validation (ICST), 2012, pp. 141–150, http://dx.doi.org/10.1109/ICST.2012.94, 00027.

[57] S. Fujiwara, K. Munakata, Y. Maeda, A. Katayama, T. Uehara, Test data generation for web application using a UML class diagram with OCL constraints, Innov. Syst. Softw. Eng. 7 (4) (2011) 275–282, ISSN 1614-5046, 1614-5054, http://dx.doi.org/10.1007/s11334-011-0162-3.

[58] K. Dobolyi, E. Soechting, W. Weimer, Automating regression testing using web-based application similarities, Int. J. Softw. Tools Technol. Transfer 13 (2) (2010) 111–129, ISSN 1433-2779, 1433-2787, http://dx.doi.org/10.1007/s10009-010-0170-x, 00000.

[59] A. de Castro, G.A. Macedo, E.F. Collins, A.C. Dias-Neto, Extension of Selenium RC tool to perform automated testing with databases in web applications, in: 2013 8th International Workshop on Automation of Software Test (AST), 2013, pp. 125–131, http://dx.doi.org/10.1109/IWAST.2013.6595803.

[60] S. Mahajan, W.G.J. Halfond, Finding HTML presentation failures using image comparison techniques, in: Proceedings of the 29th ACM/IEEE International Conference on Automated Software Engineering, ASE '14, New York, NY, USA, ACM, ISBN 978-1-4503-3013-8, 2014, pp. 91–96, http://dx.doi.org/10.1145/2642937.2642966, 00003.

[61] S. Mahajan, B. Li, W.G.J. Halfond, Root cause analysis for HTML presentation failures using search-based techniques, in: Proceedings of the 7th International Workshop on Search-Based Software Testing, SBST 2014, New York, NY, USA, ACM, ISBN 978-1-4503-2852-4, 2014, pp. 15–18, http://dx.doi.org/10.1145/2593833.2593836, 00000.

[62] S. Mahajan, W.G.J. Halfond, Detection and Localization of HTML Presentation Failures Using Computer Vision-Based Techniques, in: Proceedings of the 8th IEEE International Conference on Software Testing, Verification and Validation (ICST), IEEE, 2015.

[63] S. Mahajan, W.G.J. Halfond, WebSee: A Tool for Debugging HTML Presentation Failures, in: Proceedings of the 8th IEEE International Conference on Software Testing, Verification and Validation (ICST) - Tool Track, IEEE, 2015.

[64] M.H. Alalfi, J.R. Cordy, T.R. Dean, Automating coverage metrics for dynamic web applications, in: 2010 14th European Conference on Software Maintenance and Reengineering (CSMR), 2010, pp. 51–60, http://dx.doi.org/10.1109/CSMR.2010.21, 00010.

[65] N. Alshahwan, M. Harman, Augmenting test suites effectiveness by increasing output diversity, in: 2012 34th International Conference on Software Engineering (ICSE), 2012, pp. 1345–1348, http://dx,doi.org/10.1109/ICSE.2012.6227083, 00003.

[66] K. Sakamoto, K. Tomohiro, D. Hamura, H. Washizaki, Y. Fukazawa, POGen: a test code generator based on template variable coverage in gray-box integration testing for web applications, in: V. Cortellessa, D. Varr (Eds.), Fundamental Approaches to Software Engineering, no. 7793 in Lecture Notes in Computer Science, Springer, Berlin, ISBN 978-3-642-37056-4, 978-3-642-37057-1, 2013, pp. 343–358. http://link.springer.com.ezproxy.wlu.edu/chapter/10.1007/978-3-642-37057-1_25.

[67] U. Praphamontripong, J. Offutt, Applying mutation testing to web applications, in: 2010 Third International Conference on Software Testing, Verification, and Validation Workshops (ICSTW), 2010, pp. 132–141, http://dx.doi.org/10.1109/ICSTW.2010.38, 00021.

[68] Y.-S. Ma, J. Offutt, Y.R. Kwon, MuJava: an automated class mutation system, Softw. Test. Verif. Reliab. 15 (2) (2005) 97–133, ISSN 1099-1689, http://dx.doi.org/10.1002/stvr.308. http://onlinelibrary.wiley.com/doi/10.1002/stvr.308/abstract.

[69] K. Dobolyi, W. Weimer, Modeling consumer-perceived web application fault severities for testing, in: Proceedings of the 19th International Symposium on Software Testing and Analysis, ISSTA '10, New York, NY, USA, ACM, ISBN 978-1-60558-823-0, 2010, pp. 97–106, http://dx.doi.org/10.1145/1831708.1831720, 00007.

[70] R.C. Bryce, S. Sampath, A.M. Memon, Developing a single model and test prioritization strategies for event-driven software, IEEE Trans. Softw. Eng. 37 (1) (2011) 48–64, ISSN 0098-5589, http://dx.doi.org/10.1109/TSE.2010.12.

[71] G. Rothermel, R.H. Untch, C. Chu, M.J. Harrold, Prioritizing test cases for regression testing, IEEE Trans. Softw. Eng. 27 (10) (2001) 929–948, ISSN 0098-5589, http://dx.doi.org/10.1109/32.962562.

[72] S. Sampath, R.C. Bryce, S. Jain, S. Manchester, A tool for combination-based prioritization and reduction of user-session-based test suites, in: Proceedings of the 2011 27th IEEE International Conference on Software Maintenance, ICSM '11, Washington, DC, USA, IEEE Computer Society, ISBN 978-1-4577-0663-9, 2011, pp. 574–577, http://dx.doi.org/10.1109/ICSM.2011.6080833, 00007.

[73] D. Garg, A. Datta, T. French, A two-level prioritization approach for regression testing of web applications, in: 2012 19th Asia-Pacific Software Engineering Conference (APSEC), vol. 2, 2012, pp. 150–153, http://dx.doi.org/10.1109/APSEC.2012.34, 00001.

[74] D. Garg, A. Datta, Parallel execution of prioritized test cases for regression testing of web applications, in: Proceedings of the Thirty-Sixth Australasian Computer Science Conference–Volume 135, ACSC '13, Darlinghurst, Australia, Australia, Australian Computer Society, Inc., ISBN 978-1-921770-20-3, 2013, pp. 61–68, 00001. http://dl.acm.org/citation.cfm?id=2525401.2525408.

[75] D. Garg, A. Datta, Test case prioritization due to database changes in web applications, in: 2012 IEEE Fifth International Conference on Software Testing, Verification and Validation (ICST), 2012, pp. 726–730, http://dx.doi.org/10.1109/ICST.2012.163, 00006.

[76] S. Sampath, R.C. Bryce, Improving the effectiveness of test suite reduction for user-session-based testing of web applications, Inf. Softw. Technol. 54 (7) (2012) 724–738, ISSN 0950-5849, http://dx.doi.org/10.1016/j.infsof.2012.01.007, 00010.

[77] S. Sampath, S. Sprenkle, E. Gibson, L. Pollock, A.S. Greenwald, Applying concept analysis to user-session-based testing of web applications, IEEE Trans. Softw. Eng. 33 (10) (2007) 643–658, ISSN 0098-5589, http://dx.doi.org/10.1109/TSE.2007. 70723.

[78] S. Elbaum, A. Malishevsky, G. Rothermel, Incorporating varying test costs and fault severities into test case prioritization, in: Proceedings of the 23rd International Conference on Software Engineering, 2001, ICSE 2001, 2001, pp. 329–338, http://dx.doi. org/10.1109/ICSE.2001.919106.

[79] M.R. Nejad Dobuneh, D.N.A. Jawawi, M. Ghazali, M.V. Malakooti, Development test case prioritization technique in regression testing based on hybrid criteria, in: 2014 8th Malaysian Software Engineering Conference (MySEC), 2014, pp. 301–305, http://dx.doi.org/10.1109/MySec.2014.6986033, 00000.

[80] Y. Huang, L. Lu, A methodology for test suit reduction in user-session-based testing, in: 2010 IEEE Fifth International Conference on Bio-Inspired Computing: Theories and Applications (BIC-TA), 2010, pp. 864–868, http://dx.doi.org/10.1109/ BICTA.2010.5645239, 00005.

[81] G. Birkhoff, Lattice Theory, Volume 5, American Mathematical Soc. Colloquium Publications, 1940.

[82] Y. Liu, K. Wang, W. Wei, B. Zhang, H. Zhong, User-session-based test cases optimization method based on agglutinate hierarchy clustering, in: Internet of Things (iThings/CPSCom), 2011 International Conference on and 4th International Conference on Cyber, Physical and Social Computing, 2011, pp. 413–418, http://dx.doi.org/ 10.1109/iThings/CPSCom.2011.135.

[83] A. Marback, H. Do, N. Ehresmann, An effective regression testing approach for PHP web applications, in: 2012 IEEE Fifth International Conference on Software Testing, Verification and Validation (ICST), 2012, pp. 221–230, http://dx.doi.org/10.1109/ ICST.2012.102, 00006.

[84] H. Do, M. Hossain, An efficient regression testing approach for PHP web applications: a controlled experiment, Softw. Test. Verif. Reliab. 24 (5) (2014) 367–385, ISSN 1099-1689, http://dx.doi.org/10.1002/stvr.1540, 00000, http://onlinelibrary.wiley. com/doi/10.1002/stvr.1540/abstract.

[85] M. Hossain, H. Do, R. Eda, Regression testing for web applications using reusable constraint values, in: Proceedings of the 2014 IEEE International Conference on Software Testing, Verification, and Validation Workshops, ICSTW '14, Washington, DC, USA, IEEE Computer Society, ISBN 978-1-4799-5790-3, 2014, pp. 312–321, http://dx.doi.org/10.1109/ICSTW.2014.35.

[86] S.R. Choudhary, D. Zhao, H. Versee, A. Orso, WATER: Web Application TEst Repair, in: Proceedings of the First International Workshop on End-to-End Test Script Engineering, ETSE '11, New York, NY, USA, ACM, ISBN 978-1-4503-0808-3, 2011, pp. 24–29, http://dx.doi.org/10.1145/2002931.2002935.

[87] A. Kumar, R. Goel, Event driven test case selection for regression testing web applications, in: 2012 International Conference on Advances in Engineering, Science and Management (ICAESM), 2012, pp. 121–127, 00004.

[88] R. Chopra, S. Madan, Reusing black box test paths for white box testing of websites, in: 2013 IEEE 3rd International Advance Computing Conference (IACC), 2013, pp. 1345–1350, http://dx.doi.org/10.1109/IAdCC.2013.6514424, 00000.

[89] M. Leotta, D. Clerissi, F. Ricca, C. Spadaro, Improving test suites maintainability with the page object pattern: an industrial case study, in: 2013 IEEE Sixth International Conference on Software Testing, Verification and Validation Workshops (ICSTW), 2013, pp. 108–113, http://dx.doi.org/10.1109/ICSTW.2013.19.

[90] M. Leotta, A. Stocco, F. Ricca, P. Tonella, Reducing web test cases aging by means of robust XPath locators, in: 2014 IEEE International Symposium on Software Reliability Engineering Workshops (ISSREW), 2014, pp. 449–454, http://dx.doi.org/10.1109/ISSREW.2014.17, 00000.

[91] A. Andrews, H. Do, Trade-off analysis for selective versus brute-force regression testing in FSMWeb, in: Proceedings of the 2014 IEEE 15th International Symposium on High-Assurance Systems Engineering, HASE '14, Washington, DC, USA, IEEE Computer Society, ISBN 978-1-4799-3466-9, 2014, pp. 184–192, http://dx.doi.org/10.1109/HASE.2014.33, 00002.

[92] M. Hirzel, Selective regression testing for web applications created with Google web toolkit, in: Proceedings of the 2014 International Conference on Principles and Practices of Programming on the Java Platform: Virtual Machines, Languages, and Tools, PPPJ '14, New York, NY, USA, ACM, ISBN 978-1-4503-2926-2, 2014, pp. 110–121, http://dx.doi.org/10.1145/2647508.2647527.

[93] L. Christophe, R. Stevens, C. De Roover, W. De Meuter, Prevalence and maintenance of automated functional tests for web applications, in: 2014 IEEE International Conference on Software Maintenance and Evolution (ICSME), 2014, pp. 141–150, http://dx.doi.org/10.1109/ICSME.2014.36.

[94] J. Cai, Q. Hu, Analysis for cloud testing of web application, in: 2014 2nd International Conference on Systems and Informatics (ICSAI), 2014, pp. 293–297, http://dx.doi.org/10.1109/ICSAI.2014.7009302.

ABOUT THE AUTHORS

 **Sreedevi Sampath** is an Associate Professor in the Department of Information Systems at the University of Maryland, Baltimore County. She earned her Ph.D. and M.S. in Computer and Information Sciences from the University of Delaware in 2006 and 2002, respectively, and her B.E. degree from Osmania University in Computer Science and Engineering in 2000. Her research interests are in the areas of software testing and quality assurance, web applications, software maintenance and software security. She has served on the program committees of international conferences, such as the International Conference on Software Testing Verification and Validation (ICST), International Symposium on Software Reliability Engineering (ISSRE), and the International Conference on Empirical Software Engineering and Measurement (ESEM). She is a member of the IEEE Computer Society.

Sara Sprenkle is an Associate Professor of Computer Science at Washington and Lee University. She received her Ph.D. in Computer and Information Sciences from the University of Delaware in 2007. She earned her M.S. in Computer Science from Duke University in 2004, and her B.S. from Gettysburg College in 1999. Her current research focuses on automatically testing web applications and web services, including cost-effective approaches to generating test cases and determining that the application is behaving appropriately. She is also exploring the challenges in developing and testing web applications for digital humanities projects. She has served on the program committees of international conferences, such as the International Conference on Software Testing Verification and Validation (ICST) and International Symposium on Software Reliability Engineering (ISSRE). She is a member of the ACM and the IEEE Computer Society.

CHAPTER FIVE

Approaches and Tools for Automated End-to-End Web Testing

Maurizio Leotta*, Diego Clerissi*, Filippo Ricca*, Paolo Tonella†
*DIBRIS, Università di Genova, Genova, Italy
†Fondazione Bruno Kessler, Trento, Italy

Contents

Abstract

The importance of test automation in web engineering comes from the widespread use of web applications and the associated demand for code quality. Test automation is

Advances in Computers, Volume 101
ISSN 0065-2458
http://dx.doi.org/10.1016/bs.adcom.2015.11.007

considered crucial for delivering the quality levels expected by users, since it can save a lot of time in testing and it helps developers to release web applications with fewer defects. The main advantage of test automation comes from fast, unattended execution of a set of tests after some changes have been made to a web application. Moreover, modern web applications adopt a multitier architecture where the implementation is scattered across different layers and run on different machines. For this reason, end-to-end testing techniques are required to test the overall behavior of web applications.

In the last years, several approaches have been proposed for automated end-to-end web testing and the choice among them depends on a number of factors, including the tools used for web testing and the costs associated with their adoption. They can be classified using two main criteria: the first concerns how test cases are developed (ie, Capture-Replay and Programmable approaches), while, the second concerns how test cases localize the web elements to interact with (ie, Coordinates-based, DOM-based, and Visual approaches), that is what kind of *locators* are used for selecting the target GUI components.

For developers and project managers it is not easy to select the most suitable automated end-to-end web testing approach for their needs among the existing ones. This chapter provides a comprehensive overview of the automated end-to-end web testing approaches and summarizes the findings of a long term research project aimed at empirically investigating their strengths and weaknesses.

1. INTRODUCTION

Web applications are key assets of our society. A considerable slice of modern software consists of web applications executed in the user's web browser, running on computers or smartphones. The web has a significant impact on all aspects of our society and in the last years has changed the life of billions of people. Associations, enterprizes, governmental organizations, companies, scientific groups use the web as a powerful and convenient way to promote activities/products and carry out their core business. People daily use online services as source of information, means of communication, source of entertainment, and venue for commerce. In a sentence, *web applications pervade our life, being crucial for a multitude of economic, social and educational activities.*

The importance of the web in our lives stresses the quality with which these applications are developed and maintained [1]. End-to-end web testing is one of the main approaches for assuring the quality of web application [2]. The goal of end-to-end web testing is exercising the web application under test as a whole to detect as many failures as possible, where a *failure* can be considered as a deviation from the expected behavior. In many software projects, end-to-end web testing is neglected because of time or cost constraints. However, the impact of failures in a web application may be very serious, ranging from simple inconvenience (eg, malfunction and so users' dissatisfaction), economic problems (eg, interruption of business), up to catastrophic impacts.

The simplest solution is to manually interact with the web application under development to see if it behaves as expected. Unfortunately, this practice is error prone, time consuming, and ultimately not very effective. For this reason, most teams automate manual web testing by means of automated testing tools. The process contains a first manual step: producing the test code able to instrument the web application. Test code provides input data, operates on GUI components, and retrieves information to be compared with oracles (eg, using assertions). The main benefit of test automation comes from the fast and unattended execution of a test suite after some changes have been made to the web application under test (ie, for regression purposes).

1.1 Approaches to Automated End-to-End Web Testing

End-to-end testing of web applications is a type of black box testing based on the concept of test scenario, that is a sequence of steps/actions performed on the web application (eg, insert username, insert password, click the login button). One or more test cases can be derived from a single test scenario by specifying the actual data to use in each step (eg, *username=John.Doe*) and the expected results (ie, defining the assertions). The execution of each test case can be automated by implementing a test script following any of the existing approaches (eg, Programmable and DOM-based localization). The choice among the various approaches depends on a number of factors, including the technology used by the web applications and the tools (if any) used for web testing.

Broadly speaking, there are two main orthogonal criteria [3] to classify the approaches to end-to-end web testing that are related to: (1) test scripts implementation and (2) web page elements localization. Fig. 1 shows a classification grid based on these two criteria that can be applied to existing tools. For what concerns the first criterion, we can find two main approaches [4]:

			How develop test cases	
			Capture - Replay	Programmable
How localize web elements	Generation	3rd	Visual	Sikuli IDE	Sikuli API
		2nd	DOM - based	Selenium IDE	Selenium WebDriver
		1st	Coordinates - based		

Figure 1 Orthogonal classification of end-to-end web testing approaches and tools.

Capture-Replay (C&R) Web Testing consists of recording the actions performed by the tester on the web application GUI and generating a test script that repeats such actions for automated, unattended reexecution. *Programmable Web Testing* aims at unifying web testing with traditional testing, where test scripts are themselves software artifacts that developers write, with the help of specific testing frameworks. Such frameworks allow developers to program the interactions with a web page and its elements, so that test scripts can, for instance, automatically fill-in and submit forms or click on hyper-links.

An automated end-to-end test case interacts with several web page elements such as links, buttons, and input fields, and different methods can be used to locate them. Thus, concerning the second criterion, we can find three different cases [3]:

Coordinate-based localization: the tools implementing this approach just record the screen coordinates of the web page elements and then use this information to locate the elements during test case replay. This approach is nowadays considered obsolete, because it produces test scripts that are extremely fragile. Hence, it is not considered any further in this work.

DOM-based localization: the tools implementing this approach (eg, Selenium IDE[1] and Selenium WebDriver[2]) locate the web page elements using the information contained in the Document Object Model (DOM) and, usually, provide several ways to locate web page elements. For instance, Selenium WebDriver is able to locate a web page element using: (1) the values of attributes id, name, and class; (2) the tag name of the element; (3) the text string shown in the hyperlink, for anchor elements; (4) CSS and (5) XPath expressions. Not all these locators are applicable to any arbitrary web element; eg, locator (1) can be used only if the target element has a unique value of attribute id, name, or class in the entire web page; locator (2) can be used if there is only one element with the chosen tag name in the whole page; and, locator (3) can be used only for links uniquely identified by their text string. On the other hand, XPath/CSS expressions can always be used. In fact, as a baseline, the unique path from root to target element in the DOM tree can always be turned into an XPath/CSS locator that uniquely identifies the element.

Visual localization: the tools implementing this approach have emerged recently. They make use of image recognition techniques to identify

---

[1] http://seleniumhq.org/projects/ide/
[2] http://seleniumhq.org/projects/webdriver/

and control GUI components. The tool Sikuli IDE[3] and Sikuli API[4] belong to this category.

1.2 Chapter Contributions

For test developers and project managers it is not easy to select the most suitable automated end-to-end web testing approach for their needs among the existing ones. This chapter gives a comprehensive overview of the automated end-to-end web testing approaches and summarizes the findings of a long term research project [3–6] aimed at empirically investigating their strengths and weaknesses.

The main contribution of this chapter is twofold:

- Providing the reader with a complete overview of the most relevant approaches in the context of the automated end-to-end web testing.
- Analyzing such approaches in order to point out their strengths and weaknesses.

The considered approaches have been analyzed by means of a series of empirical studies [3–4] in which we developed and compared several test suites for six open source web applications. In particular:

(1) Concerning *test case development and maintenance*, we empirically investigated the trade-off between capture-replay (C&R) and programmable web testing [4]. In addition to validating our initial hypothesis, that C&R test cases are cheaper to write from scratch than programmable test cases, but are also more expensive to maintain during software evolution, we have determined the number of software releases after which the savings of programmable test cases overcome the costs initially paid for their development (see Fig. 2).

We have instantiated our empirical analysis for two state-of-the-practice tools, Selenium IDE (ie, C&R), and Selenium WebDriver (ie, programmable).

(2) Concerning *how test cases localize the web element to interact with*, we have evaluated and compared the visual and DOM-based approaches [3] considering: the robustness of *locators*, the initial test suite development effort, the test suite evolution cost, and the test suite execution time. Our empirical assessment of the robustness of locators is quite general and tool independent, while the developers' effort for initial test suite development and the effort for test suite evolution were measured with

---

[3] http://www.sikuli.org/
[4] https://code.google.com/p/sikuli-api/

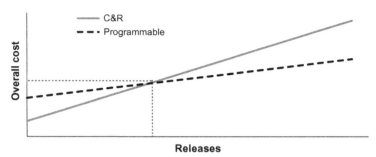

Figure 2 Evolution costs for C&R and programmable test cases.

reference to specific implementations of the two approaches. We have instantiated such analysis for two tools, Sikuli API and Selenium WebDriver, both adopting the programmable approach but differing in the way they localize the web elements to interact with during the execution of the test cases. Indeed, Sikuli API adopts the visual approach, thus using images representing portions of the web pages, while Selenium WebDriver employs the DOM-based approach, thus relying on the HTML structure. Since visual tools are known to be computational demanding, we also measured and compared the test suite execution time.

The findings reported in this chapter provide practical guidelines for developers who want to make an informed decision among the available approaches and who want to understand which of them could fit more or less well for a specific web development context.

The chapter is organized as follows: Sections 2 and 3 provide an overview on the main classical approaches to automated end-to-end web testing and report several examples of tools instantiating such approaches. Specifically, these sections describes how the test cases development approaches (ie, capture-replay and programmable) can be combined with the DOM-based and the visual localization approaches. Section 4 describes how the evolution of the web application impacts on the test cases created by following each approach. Section 5 summarizes and discusses the results of the empirical studies we conducted to analyze the strengths and the weaknesses of various approaches for automated end-to-end web testing. Section 6 analyses some tools and techniques that have been recently proposed, overcoming the limitations of the classical approaches to automated end-to-end web testing. In particular Section 6.1 provides some example of tools/techniques that go beyond the simple adoption of one approach, ie, solutions that are able to combine more approaches at the same time (eg, Visual + DOM based or C&R + Programmable). Then, Section 6.2 analyses a set of techniques that have been proposed in the literature in order to solve specific problems in the context of automated end-to-end web testing (robustness, test case repair upon software evolution, page object creation, and migration between approaches). Section 7 concludes the chapter.

2. CAPTURE-REPLAY WEB TESTING

Capture-Replay web testing is based on the usage of capture/replay automated tools. These tools have been developed to validate interactive applications (GUI or web applications). Using a capture/replay tool, a software tester can run a web application and record the entire interaction session. The tool (semi-) automatically records all the user's events in the navigated web pages, such as the key presses and mouse clicks, in a script, allowing a session to be rerun automatically without further human interaction. Finally, the test script is completed by adding one or more assertions to the recorded actions. Capture/replay tools support automatic regression testing by replaying a given test script on a new version of the Web Application Under Test (WAUT).

Implementing test cases using this approach is a relatively simple task. Even a person without programming expertise can easily build a complete test suite for a complex web application. However, this approach has a few drawbacks [4]: (1) test scripts generated using the C&R approach often contain hard-coded values (eg, test inputs and assertion values), that have to be changed if anything varies during the evolution of the WAUT or if the same test case has to be executed using different input values (eg, to exercise various corner cases); (2) test scripts are strongly coupled with web pages, with the consequence that even a small change in the WAUT (eg, in the layout of the page) leads to one or more broken test cases (eg, test scripts fail to locate a link, an input field or a submission button because of the layout change) and, hence, (3) often different test scripts composing a test suite contain a lot of duplicated code. Indeed, when the same functionality is invoked within multiple test cases (eg, login), the same code fragments are repeated across all such test scripts. We will elaborate more on these aspects in the second part of the chapter.

2.1 DOM-Based Capture-Replay Web Testing

As seen before, DOM-based tools locate the web page elements using the information contained in the Document Object Model. Selenium IDE is

```
<form name="loginform" action="home.asp" method="post">
 Username: <input type="text" id="UID" name="username"><br>
 Password: <input type="text" id="PW" name="password"><br>
 <a href="javascript:loginform.submit()" id="login">Login</a>
</form>
```

Figure 3 Fragment of home.asp—Page and source.

the tool for web application testing adopting the DOM-based Capture-Replay approach that we considered in our empirical evaluation. Selenium IDE is a complete IDE (Integrated Development Environment), as suggested by its name, for the development and execution of end-to-end web tests. It is implemented as a Firefox extension. It provides several smart features such as: (1) testers can record, edit, and debug test cases written in the Selenese language[5] ; (2) testers can use smart field selection (eg, using IDs, names, or XPath locators, as needed) and can invoke a *locator assistance* function; (3) testers can save test cases as HTML, or export them as Java code (useful, as first step, for the migration toward the programmable approach); and (4) assertions on the various web page elements are automatically suggested by the tool to testers.

Let us assume that we have to test a portion of a web application used to authenticate users. In a very simplified case, we have a portion of the home page (eg, called home.asp) that allows users to enter their credentials, ie, *username* and *password* (see Fig. 3). When the user has inserted the credentials and has clicked on the "Login" button, the application evaluates the credentials correctness. If credentials are correct, the username (eg, *John.Doe*), contained in a HTML tag with the attribute ID="LoggedUser," and the logout button are reported in the upper right corner of the home page. Otherwise, the login form is still shown in the home.asp page.

As an example, we report a test case for this simple functionality implemented using the capture/replay facility of Selenium IDE (see Fig. 4). The test script produced by Selenium IDE performs a valid login, using correct credentials (ie, *username=John.Doe* and *password=123456*) and verifies that in the home page the user results to be correctly authenticated (assertText, id=LoggedUser, John.Doe). It can be noticed that all web

---

[5] Each Selenese line is a triple: (command, target, value). See: http://release.seleniumhq.org/selenium-core/1.0.1/reference.html

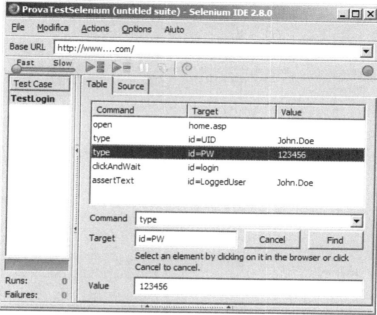

Figure 4 TestLogin test case in Selenium IDE.

elements are located using the values of the id attributes that can be found in
the DOM. Specifically, during the test script recording phase, Selenium IDE
is able to detect the actions performed on the web page elements and to
automatically generate the locators for such web elements. Selenium IDE
contains a locator generation algorithm that produces locators using different
strategies (implemented by the so-called locator builders) and it ranks them
depending on an internal robustness heuristic.

2.2 Visual Capture-Replay Web Testing

Several Capture–Replay tools are available to implement test cases adopting
visual locators. An example is Sikuli IDE, a stand-alone open source tool that
allows to automate every action that can be performed on a computer GUI
(ie, it is not dedicated only to web applications). Sikuli IDE assists the tester
in test case implementation and allows the tester to automatically reexecute
the various test case steps. Fig. 5 reports a Sikuli IDE test script for the login
functionality described before. The Sikuli IDE test script performs a valid
login, using correct credentials (ie, inserts the username, *John.Doe*, and
the password, *123456*, in the input fields matching the respective visual

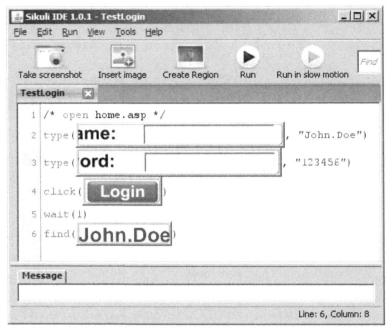

Figure 5 TestLogin test case in Sikuli IDE.

locators, and then clicks the login button) and verifies that in the home page the user results to be correctly authenticated (ie, it verifies that the name of the user, John.Doe, is shown in the home page). In Sikuli IDE, test case recording is semiautomatic: the tester has to specify what action she wants to perform on the user interface; creation of the visual locators is assisted by the tool (testers must indicate the portion of page on which the action has to be performed).

3. PROGRAMMABLE WEB TESTING

Programmable web testing is based on manual creation of a test script. Web test scripts can be written using ad-hoc languages and frameworks or general purpose programming languages (such as Java and Ruby) with the aid of specific libraries able to play the role of the browser. Usually, these libraries extend the programming language with user friendly APIs, providing commands to, eg, click a button, fill a field, and submit a form. Test scripts are completed with assertions (eg, JUnit assertions if the language chosen is Java).

Test scripts built in this way are more flexible than the ones built using capture/replay tools [4]. For example, programmable testing allows developers to take advantage of conditional statements, used when multiple test cases have different, condition-dependent behaviors. They also support the creation of *data-driven test cases*, ie, test cases that are executed multiple times, each time with different arguments (ie, different inputs and expected values). Thus, in general, programmable web testing techniques can handle the complexity of web software better than C&R web testing techniques. On the other hand, they require nontrivial programming skills and they demand for substantial initial development time.

3.1 The Page Object and Factory Patterns

The *Page Object*[6,7] pattern is a quite popular web test design pattern, which aims at improving the test case maintainability and at reducing the duplication of code. A Page Object is a class that represents the web page elements as a series of objects and that encapsulates the features of the web page into methods. Adopting the page object pattern in test script implementation allows testers to follow the *Separation of Concerns* design principle, since the test scenario is decoupled from the implementation. Indeed, all the implementation details are moved into the page objects, a bridge between web pages and test cases, with the latter only containing the test logics. Thus, all the functionalities to interact with or to make assertions about a web page are offered in a single place, the Page Object, and can be easily called and reused within any test case. Usually page objects are initialized by a Page Factory,[8] a factory class that checks the correct mapping and initialization of the web elements. Usage of *Page Object* and *Page Factory* patterns reduces the coupling between web pages and test cases, promoting reusability, readability, and maintainability of the test suites [4, 5].

3.2 DOM-Based Programmable Web Testing

In this work, we consider Selenium WebDriver as a representative tool for implementing DOM-based programmable web test suites (for short, WebDriver). WebDriver is a state-of-the-art tool, widely used for web application testing [7]. It provides a comprehensive programming interface used to control the browser. WebDriver test cases are written in the Java

---

[6] http://martinfowler.com/bliki/PageObject.html
[7] https://code.google.com/p/selenium/wiki/PageObjects
[8] https://code.google.com/p/selenium/wiki/PageFactory

programming language, by integrating WebDriver commands with JUnit or TestNG assertions. We chose WebDriver as representative of DOM-based programmable tools, because: (1) it is a quite mature tool, (2) it is open-source, (3) it is one of the most widely-used open-source solutions for web test automation, (4) during our previous industrial collaborations, we gained a considerable experience in its usage [5, 6].

In Fig. 6, we show an example of a simple WebDriver test case for our running example application, corresponding to a successful authentication. This automated test case submits a valid login, using correct credentials (ie, *username=John.Doe* and *password=123456*) and verifies that in the home page the user appears as correctly authenticated (the string "John.Doe" is displayed in the top-right corner of the home page, as verified by method checkLoggedUser).

The first step for building this test case is creating the HomePage.java page object (see Fig. 7), corresponding to the home.asp web page. The page object

```
public void testLogin() { //WebDriver
  WebDriver driver = new FirefoxDriver();
  driver.get("http://www.....com/home.asp");
  HomePage HP = new HomePage(driver);
  HP.login("John.Doe","123456");
  assertTrue(HP.checkLoggedUser("John.Doe"));
}
```

Figure 6 TestLogin test case in Selenium WebDriver.

```
                public class HomePage {
                  private final WebDriver driver;
                  @FindBy(id="UID")
Locators          private WebElement username;
Declarations      @FindBy(xpath="./form/input[2]")
                  private WebElement password;
                  @FindBy(linkText="Login")
                  private WebElement login;
                  @FindBy(id="LoggedUser")
                  private WebElement loggedUser;
                  public HomePage(WebDriver driver)
                  {this.driver = driver;}
                  public void login(String UID, String PW){
                    username.sendKeys(UID);
PO Methods          password.sendKeys(PW);
                    login.click();
                  }
                  public Boolean checkLoggedUser(String name){
                    return loggedUser.getText().equals(name);
                  }
                }
```

Figure 7 HomePage page object in Selenium WebDriver.

HomePage.java offers a method to log into the application. It takes in input username and password, inserts them in the corresponding input fields and clicks the Login button. Moreover, HomePage.java contains also a method that verifies the authenticated username in the application. As shown in Fig. 7, web page elements can be located using different kinds of DOM-based locators (eg, ID, LinkText, XPath).

The second step requires to develop the test case making use of the page object methods (see Fig. 6). In the test case, first, a WebDriver object of type FirefoxDriver is created to control the Firefox browser as a real user does; second, WebDriver (ie, the browser) opens the specified URL and creates a page object that instantiates HomePage.java; third, using method login(...) , the test tries to login in the application; finally, the test case assertion is checked.

3.3 Visual Programmable Web Testing

The testing tool belonging to the Visual Programmable category that we considered in this work is Sikuli API. Sikuli API is an open-source visual tool able to automate and test graphical user interfaces using screenshot images. It provides image-based GUI automation functionalities to Java programmers.

As an example, the Sikuli API version of the testLogin test case is shown in Fig. 8, while the related page object is given in Fig. 9. The test case developed in Sikuli API performs the same conceptual steps as the WebDriver test case. The first operation, CommonPage.open(...), aims at opening the browser at a specified URL. In a purely visual test case, this involves locating and clicking on the Firefox icon on the desktop, inserting the URL into the address bar, and then clicking on the "go" arrow (these operations are encapsulated in the class CommonPage).

The following steps are basically the same in Sikuli API and Selenium WebDriver, the only differences being that in Sikuli API driver is not a parameter of the HomePage constructor and the assertion checking method

```
public void testLogin() { //Sikuli
    CommonPage.open("http://www.....com/home.asp");
    //WebDriver driver = new FirefoxDriver();
    //driver.get("http://www.....com/home.asp");
    HomePage HP = new HomePage();
    HP.login("John.Doe","123456");
    assertTrue(HP.checkLoggedUser());
}
```

Figure 8 TestLogin test case in Sikuli API.

```
        public class HomePage {
          private String path = "locators/HomePage/";
          private Target username
              = new ImageTarget(new File(path+"username.png"));
          private Target password                      ⮡ ne: [          ]
              = new ImageTarget(new File(path+"password.png"));
          private Target login                          ⮡ rd: [          ]
              = new ImageTarget(new File(path+"login.png"));
          private Target loggedUser                     ⮡ [ Login ]
              = new ImageTarget(new File(path+"loggedUser.png"));
                                                        ⮡ John.Doe
        public HomePage(){}
        public void login(String UID, String PW){
          type(username, UID);
          type(password, PW);
          click(login);
        }
        public Boolean checkLoggedUser(){
          ScreenRegion ris = locate(loggedUser);
          if (ris == null) return false; else return true;
        }
        public ScreenRegion locate(Target element){
          ScreenRegion screen = new DesktopScreenRegion();
          ScreenRegion ris = screen.find(element);
          Mouse mouse = new DesktopMouse();
          while (ris == null){ //web element could be not visible
            mouse.wheel(1,2);   //scroll down the page to find it
            ris = screen.find(element);
            if (page.endOfPageReached()) return null;
          }
          return ris;
        }
        public void click(Target element) throws ElementNotFound{
          Mouse mouse = new DesktopMouse();
          ScreenRegion ris = locate(element);
          if (ris == null) throw new ElementNotFound();
          mouse.click(ris.getCenter());
        }
        public void type(Target element, String value)
                                        throws ElementNotFound{
          click(element);
          Keyboard keyboard = new DesktopKeyboard();
          keyboard.type(value);
        }
      }
```

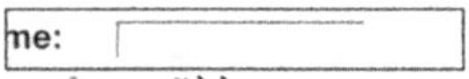

Locators Declarations · PO Methods · Auxiliary Visual Methods

Figure 9 HomePage page object in Sikuli API.

does not need any string parameter. On the contrary, Sikuli API's page object is quite different from Selenium WebDriver's. As shown in Fig. 9, the command locate is invoked to search for the portion of a web page that looks like the image representing the rendering of the web element to be located. The image must have been previously saved in the file system as a file or must be available online. Once the web element has been located, a ScreenRegion is returned by method locate, which can be used to perform operations such as clicking and typing into it (see, eg, method type in Fig. 9).

Thus, in Sikuli API *locators are images*. While using DOM-based tools it is possible to verify whether an HTML element contains textual information (see the last line in Fig. 7), with visual tools it is necessary to check that the page contains an image displaying such text (see Fig. 9, method checkLoggedUser). Moreover, some useful and quite general Selenium WebDriver methods are not natively available in Sikuli API (eg, click() and sendKeys()). Thus, when using Sikuli API, they must be implemented explicitly in the page object class as auxiliary methods (eg, methods click() and type()).

4. TEST CASE EVOLUTION

The main benefits of adopting test automation are the possibility of: (1) executing the test cases more often, (2) finding bugs in the early stage of development, and (3) reusing test code across successive releases of the web application under test (ie, for regression testing). The main cost associated with test automation is related to the fragility of test cases: a fragile test is a test that is broken when the web application under test is slightly modified. Specifically, when a web application evolves to accommodate requirement changes, bug fixes, or functionality extensions, test cases may become broken (eg, test cases may be unable to locate some links, input fields, and submission buttons), and software testers have to repair them. This is a tedious and expensive task since it has to be performed manually by software testers (automatic evolution of test suites is a research topic under active investigation [8]).

Depending on the kind of maintenance task that has been performed on the target web application, a software tester has to execute a series of test case repair activities that can be categorized into two types: *logical* and *structural*.

Logical Changes involve the modification of the web application functionality. To repair the test cases, the tester has to modify one or more steps of the broken test cases and, when adopting the programmable approach, the corresponding page objects may also need to be modified or new ones need to be created accordingly. An example of a change request (CR1) that needs a logical repair activity is enforcing the security by means of stronger authentication and thus adding a new web page, containing an additional question that is displayed to the user when she clicks on the login button of page home.asp, shown in Fig. 3.

Structural Changes involve the modification of the web page layout/structure only. For instance, in the web page of Fig. 3 the string of the login button may be changed to Submit (CR2) or the id="UID" may be changed to id="UserID" (CR3). Usually, the impact of a structural change is smaller than a logical change. To repair the test cases after a structural change, it is often enough to modify one or more localization lines, ie, lines containing locators.

The strategy used by a software tester to repair a test case depends mainly on two factors: (1) the tool used to build the test cases (C&R, like Selenium IDE, or programmable, like Selenium WebDriver) and (2) the kind of change (logical or structural).

C&R Approach + logical change. The tester keeps the portion of script up to the command that precedes the broken action command, deletes the rest, and captures the new execution scenario by starting from the last working command. For instance, in the case of a Selenium IDE test script, if (CR1) is implemented, the assertion shown in Fig. 4 will fail and the tester will have to delete it. Then, the tester has to complete the test script starting from the command clickAndWait, id=login and capturing the new scenario, which includes the new web page providing the additional authentication question. Similar changes have to be implemented in the case of the Sikuli IDE test script shown in Fig. 5, in particular by removing line 6 and recording the new additional steps.

C&R Approach + structural change. The tester modifies the locators or the assertion values used in the test script. In the case of Selenium IDE, she runs the test script and finds the first broken command (ie, the Selenese command that is highlighted in red after test case execution), which can be an action command (eg, type or click) or an assertion. At this point, the tester repairs the broken command and then reexecutes the test script, possibly finding the next broken command (if any). For example, if (CR3) is implemented then the test script shown in Fig. 4 needs to be repaired. The tester has to replace UID with UserID in the command used to insert the username in the input field. The repair process is similar in the case of Sikuli IDE. It is interesting to note that a structural change can affect differently DOM-based and visual test scripts. Indeed, in case (CR3) is implemented, no modifications are required to the Sikuli IDE test script shown in Fig. 5, while (CR2) requires to modify both Selenium IDE and Sikuli IDE test scripts.

Programmable Approach + logical change. Depending on the magnitude of the executed maintenance task, the tester has to modify the broken test cases and/or the corresponding page objects. In some cases, new page objects have to be created. For example, if (CR1) is implemented then the tester has to create a new page object for the web page providing the additional authentication question. Moreover, she has to repair the testLogin test case in Fig. 6 (and similarly the one shown in Fig. 8), adding a new Java statement that calls the method offered by the new page object.

Programmable Approach + structural change. The tester modifies one or more page objects that the broken test case links to. For example, in the case of Selenium WebDriver, if (CR2) is implemented, the tester has to repair the line: @FindBy(linkText="Login") in the HomePage.java page object (see Fig. 7). Similarly, in the case of Sikuli API, the tester has to update the image login.png in the HomePage.java page object (see Fig. 9).

5. ANALYSIS OF THE APPROACHES

This section summarizes a series of empirical studies [3–5] we conducted to analyze the strengths and the weaknesses of various approaches to automated end-to-end web testing. We analyzed the four main approaches currently adopted in the context of automated functional web testing. In particular, for what concerns the test scripts implementation, we compared C&R and Programmable approaches, while concerning the web page elements localization we compared Visual and DOM-based approaches.

The results of these studies are interpreted according to two *perspectives*: (1) *project managers*, interested in understanding which approach could lead to potentially lower costs and could maximize the return of the investment; (2) *researchers*, interested in empirical data about the impact of different approaches on web testing.

The experiments have been conducted on a sample of six open-source web applications from *SourceForge.net* (see Table 1). More details on the employed web applications can be found in our ICWE paper [3]. We considered only applications that: (1) are quite recent, so that they can work without problems on the latest releases of Apache, PHP, and MySQL, technologies we are familiar with (since the analyzed/used techniques and tools operate on the HTML code processed by the client browser, the server side technologies do not affect the results of the various studies); (2) are well known and used (some of them have been downloaded more than 100,000 times last year); (3) have at least two major releases (we have excluded minor releases because with small differences between releases the majority of the locators—and, thus, of the corresponding test cases—are expected to work without problems); (4) belong to different application domains.

Table 1 Web Applications from *SourceForge.net*

	Description	web Site
MantisBT	Bug tracking system	sourceforge.net/projects/mantisbt/
PPMA	Password manager	sourceforge.net/projects/ppma/
Claroline	Collaborative learning environment	sourceforge.net/projects/claroline/
Address Book	Address/phone book, contact manager	sourceforge.net/projects/php-addressbook/
MRBS	Meeting rooms multisite booking system	sourceforge.net/projects/mrbs/
Collabtive	Collaboration software	sourceforge.net/projects/collabtive/

5.1 Experimental Procedure

Overall, the empirical evaluation has been performed as follows (further details on each experiment can be found in our previous works [3, 4]):

(1) Six open-source web applications have been selected from *SourceForge. net* as explained before.

(2) For each selected application, four equivalent test suites have been built. We implemented them choosing a tool instantiating each combination of the considered approaches: Sikuli API (ie, Programmable + Visual), Selenium WebDriver (ie, Programmable + DOM based), Selenium IDE (C&R + DOM based) and Sikuli IDE (C&R + Visual). The DOM-based test suites were developed for our first work [4], the Sikuli API test suites for the following work [3], while the Sikuli IDE test suites have been specifically built for this work.

All the test suites have been developed following well-known best practices. For instance, regarding the Selenium WebDriver and Sikuli API test suites (programmable approach) the page object pattern was used and, concerning the Selenium IDE and WebDriver test suites (DOM-based localization) ID locators were preferred whenever possible (ie, when HTML tags are provided with IDs), otherwise Name, LinkText, CSS, and XPath locators were used.

For each test suite, we measured the number of locators produced and the development effort for the implementation as clock time. Each test suite is equivalent to the others because the included test cases test exactly the same functionalities, using the same sequences of actions (eg, locating the same web page elements) with the same input data and oracle.

(3) Each test suite has been executed against the second release of the web application. First, we recorded the failed test cases. We also checked that no real regression bugs were found and that all the failures were due to broken locators or to modifications to the test case logics. Then, in a second phase, we repaired the broken test cases. We measured the number of broken locators and the repair effort as clock time. Finally, for comparing the efficiency of the various localization techniques, we executed 10 times (to average over any random fluctuation of the execution time) each Sikuli API and Selenium WebDriver test suite and recorded the execution times.

5.2 Test Suite Development Costs

We have analyzed the development effort associated with the various approaches. Regarding *how test cases are developed* we found that C&R test suites (ie, Selenium IDE and Sikuli IDE) required consistently less development time than programmable test suites (ie, Selenium WebDriver and Sikuli API), see Fig. 10. Focusing for instance on the two Selenium tools, we noticed that in all six cases, the development of the Selenium WebDriver test suites required more time than the Selenium IDE test suites.

Varying the *localization approach* also influences the test suite development time. Fig. 10 clearly shows that DOM-based test suites require less time for their development. Focusing on the two tools adopting the programmable approach (ie, Selenium WebDriver and Sikuli API), we found that in all six

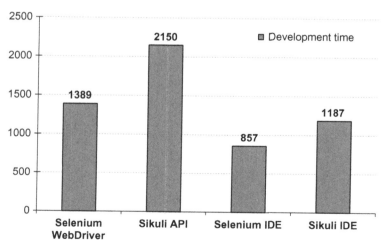

Figure 10 Overall test suites development time (minutes).

cases, development of the WebDriver test suites required less time than the Sikuli test suites (with a reduction between 22% and 57%).

Summary: Employing C&R tools and adopting DOM-based locators contribute to reduce the overall development time.

5.3 Test Suites Evolution Costs

Then, we analyzed the evolution effort associated with the various approaches. For what concerns the tool classification criterion *"how test cases are developed"*, we found that C&R test suites (ie, Selenium IDE and Sikuli IDE) required consistently more evolution time than programmable test suites, as shown in Fig. 11. Focusing for instance on the two tools part of the Selenium framework, we noticed that for all the applications: (1) the repair time of the Selenium IDE test suites was longer than the repair time of the Selenium WebDriver test suites; and, (2) the number of repaired Selenium IDE test cases is greater or equal to the number of repaired Selenium WebDriver test cases. The evolution of the Selenium IDE test suites required from 19% more time to 104% more time.

Adopting a different *localization approach* also influences the test suite evolution. Fig. 11 shows that DOM-based test suites require less time for their evolution. Focusing on the two tools implementing the programmable

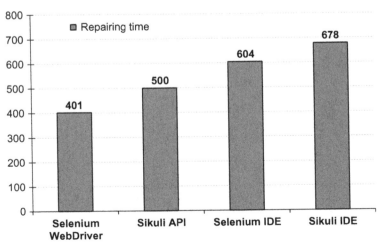

Figure 11 Overall test suites evolution time (minutes).

approach we found that results depend on the respective robustness of the two kinds of locators (DOM based vs Visual) employed by the two tools and thus follow the same trend: in four cases out of six, repairing the Selenium WebDriver test suites required less time (from 33% to 57% less) than repairing Sikuli API test suites, in one case slightly more. In just one case (ie, Collabtive) Selenium WebDriver required substantially (10×) more effort than Sikuli API.

Summary: Employing a programmable tool contributes to reduce the evolution costs for repairing automated end-to-end test suites. Concerning the web element localization approach, the DOM-based approach contributed to reduce the evolution costs in most cases.

5.4 Overall Development and Evolution Costs

In the previous sections, we have analyzed the costs for (1) developing and (2) maintaining automated end-to-end test suites separately. Concerning the web element localization approach, the DOM-based approach guarantees, in most of the cases, lower costs during both test suites development and evolution. On the other hand, concerning how test suites are developed and evolved, we found that adopting the C&R approach is preferable during initial test suites development, while the programmable one is preferable during test suites evolution.

Thus an interesting question for the practitioner is: "When do programmable test suites become convenient with respect to the C&R ones?".

By comparing the two tools part of the Selenium framework, we can notice that in most of the cases the cumulative cost of initial development and evolution of programmable test cases (ie, Selenium WebDriver test suites) is lower than that of C&R test cases (ie, Selenium IDE test suites) after a small number of releases (more precisely, between 1 and 3 releases).

We estimated that programmable test cases are more expensive to write from scratch than C&R test cases, with a median ratio between the two costs equal to 1.58. During software evolution, test suite repair is substantially cheaper for programmable test cases than for C&R test cases, with a median ratio equal to 0.65. Such cost/benefit trade-off becomes favorable to the programmable test suites after a small number of releases the median of which is 1.94. The most important practical implication of these results is that for any software project which is expected to deliver two or more releases over time, programmable test cases offer an advantageous return of the initial investment. In fact, after two or more releases, the evolution of the test suites will be easier and will require less effort if a programmable approach (such as WebDriver) is adopted. However, specific features of a given web application might make the trade-off more or less favorable to programmable tests. In particular, the possibility to capture reusable abstractions in page objects plays a major role in reducing the test evolution effort for programmable test cases. In the following, we analyze each factor that might affect the trade-off between C&R and programmable test cases.

Summary: According to our estimate, after two major releases, programmable test cases become more convenient than C&R ones. Of course, the actual benefits may depend on specific features of the web application under test.

5.5 Capture & Replay vs Programmable Approaches

In the following, we report the reasons and implications of the results reported in the previous sections, in particular focusing on the comparison between C&R and programmable approaches, considering respectively the two tools that are part of the Selenium framework (Selenium IDE and Selenium WebDriver).

5.5.1 Number of Page Objects Per Test Case

We observed that the number of page objects per test case varies considerably among the considered applications (from 0.20 to 0.73 page objects per test case). This number gives an indication of the degree of reuse that page objects have across test cases. A higher reuse is associated with a lower maintenance effort, since reused page objects will be maintained only once for all their clients (see the example—on the right—in Fig. 12). The variability observed for the objects used in our study is due to different characteristics of these applications.

The degree of reuse may amplify or reduce the benefits of adopting the *page object* pattern and then the programmable approach.

For instance, in the case of MantisBT (number of page objects per test cases equal to 0.73) we have that 14 page objects (among 17) are used by only one or two test cases that have been repaired. In this case, we have few advantages in terms of maintenance effort reduction from adopting the *page object* pattern, since each repair activity on a page object, done just

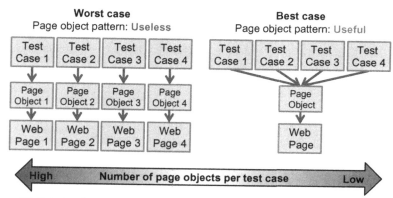

Figure 12 Relation between test cases and page objects.

once, affects only one or at most two test cases. On the other hand, in our study we found three applications out of six that have a number of page objects per test cases about 0.25 or lower. Thus, in these cases, the potential advantages of adopting the PO pattern are higher.

It is interesting to note that, at the beginning of the test suite development, a lot of page objects have to be created. For instance, the first test case could require to create even four or five page objects. But usually, as new test cases are added to the existing test suite, the number of new page objects that the tester has to create decreases. Indeed, the tester has to create a page object for each logical page of the web application (eg, login, home, user details), while he could potentially develop a test for each path that could be followed to reach a specific page. Thus, probably, comprehensive test suites (ie, testing the web application in depth) benefit more of the page object pattern since the level of page objects reuse is higher.

Summary: The web page modularity of the web application under test affects the benefits of programmable test cases. Web applications with well modularized functionalities, implemented through reusable web pages, are associated with reusable pages objects that are maintained just once during software evolution.

5.5.2 Number of Test Cases Repaired

In five cases out of six, the number of repaired test cases is lower when Selenium WebDriver is used instead of Selenium IDE. At first sight, this result could appear strange since each pair of test suites (IDE and WebDriver) has

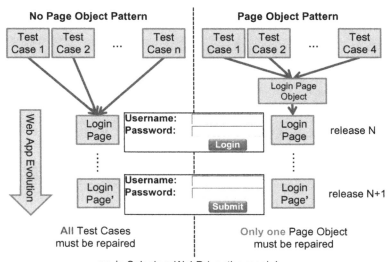

Figure 13 Page object adoption and repair effort.

been developed equivalently, using the same locators. Actually, the number of broken test cases is the same for each pair of test suites, but the number of repaired test cases is lower with Selenium WebDriver because of the adoption of the *page object* pattern. With the page object pattern each offered method can be reused more times in a test suite. Thus, *a change at the level of the page object can repair more than one test case at once* (see the example in Fig. 13). Clearly, the reduction of the number of repaired test cases is related with the number of times a method in a page object is (re-)used.

Let us consider a specific example. In Claroline, between the two considered releases a modification of the part of the application managing the login process occurred. Since this modification involved also the attribute used to locate the user credentials submission button, all the test cases were impacted (since all of them start with the authentication). In the Selenium WebDriver test suite we repaired only the page object offering method `DesktopPage login(String user, String pass)`. In this way, we automatically resolved the problem for the entire test suite. On the contrary, in the Selenium IDE test suite, we had to modify all the test cases (ie, 40 test cases).

Summary: Page objects reuse reduces dramatically the test cases repair effort.

5.5.3 Number of Locators

Globally, in the six test suites, we have approximately the same number of modifications made to address logical changes (ie, 108 and 122, respectively, in Selenium IDE and WebDriver), but we can observe a huge difference in terms of modified locators to repair the broken test cases due to structural changes (respectively 727 out of 2735 locators changed with IDE vs 162 out of 487 locators changed with WebDriver).

Summary: Adopting the *page object* pattern avoids the duplication of locators as well as the need for their repeated, consistent evolution.

Note that for each target web element, the locators used by Selenium IDE and WebDriver are exactly the same as well as their robustness. Thus the problem of the C&R approach is only due to the locators duplication.

5.5.4 Other Advantages of the Programmable Approach

As already mentioned, a programmable tool like Selenium WebDriver usually offers a comprehensive programming interface and so a higher flexibility as compared to a standard C&R as Selenium IDE. For example, Selenium WebDriver allows developers to create test cases enriched with functionalities that natively Selenium IDE does not provide, such as: conditional statements, loops, logging, exception handling, and parameterized test cases. In our test suites we have not used these features to keep as much as possible fair the comparison between the two approaches and to obtain equivalent test suites, but a project manager should definitely consider also these features when selecting between the two testing approaches. In a previous work [5], we found that these features are indeed quite useful in industrial projects.

Summary: Additional benefits of programmable test cases (eg, parametric test cases) should be taken into account when choosing between programmable and C&R web testing.

5.6 Visual vs DOM-Based Approaches

In the following we report the reasons and implications of the results reported in the previous sections, in particular focusing on the comparison between visual and DOM-based approaches, considering respectively the two tools Sikuli API and Selenium WebDriver.

5.6.1 Number of Locators

The adoption of different localization approaches can potentially influence the number of locators that have to be created. In our experiments, the number of locators required to build the six test suites varies from 81 to 158 when adopting the visual approach and from 42 to 126 when adopting the DOM-based one. For all six applications the visual approach has always required a higher number of locators. Considering the data in aggregate form, we created 45% more Visual locators than DOM locators (706 visual vs 487 DOM-based locators). The visual approach requires more locators in the following situations: (1) web elements changing their state, (2) elements with complex interaction, and (3) data-driven test cases.

Web Elements Changing their State. When a web element changes its state (eg, a check box is checked or unchecked, see the example in Fig. 14), a visual locator must be created for each state, while with the DOM-based approach only one locator is required. This occurred during the development of all the visual test suites (eg, Sikuli API) and it is one of the reasons why, in all of them, we have more locators than in the DOM-based test suites (eg, Selenium WebDriver). As a consequence, more effort both during the development and maintenance is required to create the visual test suites (quite often more than one locator had to be created and later repaired for each web element).

Web Elements with Complex Interaction. Complex web elements, such as drop-down lists and multilevel drop-down menus, are quite common in modern web applications. For instance, let us consider a form that asks to select the manufacturer of the car (see Fig. 15). Typically, this is implemented using a drop-down list containing a list of manufacturers.

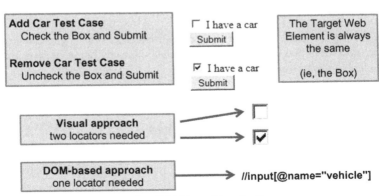

Figure 14 State changes: Visual vs DOM-based localization.

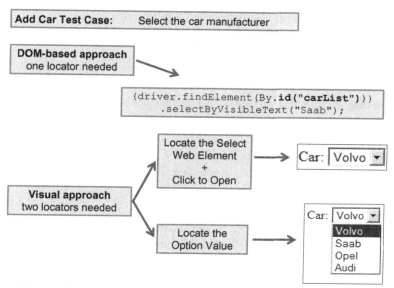

Figure 15 Complex interaction: Visual vs DOM-based localization.

A DOM-based tool like Selenium WebDriver can provide a command to select directly an element from the drop-down list (in the example only one ID-based locator is required). On the contrary, when adopting the visual approach the task is much more complex. One could, for instance: (1) locate the drop-down list (more precisely the arrow that shows the menu) using an image locator; (2) click on it; (3) if the required list element is not shown, locate and move the scrollbar (eg, by clicking the arrow); (4) locate the required element using another image locator; and, finally, (5) click on it. All these steps together require more LOCs in the page objects and locators. Actually, in this case the visual approach performs exactly the same steps that a human tester would do.

Data-driven Test Cases. Often in the industrial practice [5], to improve the coverage reached by a test suite, test cases are reexecuted multiple times using different values. This is very well supported by a programmable testing approach. However, benefits depend on the specific programmable approach that is adopted (eg, visual vs DOM-based). For instance, in Selenium WebDriver it is possible to use data from various sources, such as CSV files or databases, or even to generate them at runtime. In Sikuli it is necessary to have images of the target web elements, so even if we can use various data sources (eg, to fill input fields), when assertions are evaluated, images are still needed to represent the expected data. For this reason, in the visual approach it is not possible to create complete data-driven test cases (ie, including both data driven inputs and assertions). This happens because in the DOM-based approach there is a clear separation between the locator for a web element (eg, an ID value) and the content of that web element (eg, the displayed string), so that we can reuse the same locator with different contents (eg, test assertion values). On the contrary, using a visual tool, the locator for a web element and the displayed content are the same thing, thus if the content changes, the locator must be also modified. Moreover, it is important to highlight that, if necessary, parameterizing the creation of DOM-based locators is usually an easy task (eg, .//*[@id='list']/tr[X]/td[1] with X=1..n), while this is not the case with visual locators.

In our case study, we experienced this limitation of the visual approach, since we had, in each test suite, at least one test case that performs multiple, repeated operations that differ only in the data values being manipulated, such as: insert/remove multiple different users, projects, addresses, or groups (depending on the considered application). In such cases we used: (1) a single parameterized locator in Selenium WebDriver, and (2) several different image locators in Sikuli API (eg, for evaluating the assertions), with the effect that, in the second case, the number of locators required is substantially higher.

Summary: Adopting the Visual approach requires to generate more locators than with the DOM-based approach. This happens in the following situations: (1) web elements changing their state, (2) web elements with complex interaction, and (3) data-driven test cases.

5.6.2 Locators Robustness

The localization method affects the robustness of the locators. In our experiments, we observed that in the majority of the cases (four out of six), DOM-based locators are more robust than visual locators. However, the result is not clear-cut. Generally, DOM-based locators are more robust but in certain cases, depending on the kind of modifications between consecutive releases, visual locators proved to be more robust. When the rendering of the user interface changes across releases, visual locators are more likely to be broken, while in other cases the opposite may happen, that is, visual rendering remains stable while the underlying DOM changes. In the following, we analyze the latter case, which we name "Changes behind the Scene."

Summary: DOM-based locators proved to be in general slightly more robust than Visual locators. However, much depends on the specific characteristics of the web application.

Changes behind the Scene. Sometimes the HTML code is modified without any perceivable impact on how the web application appears. An extreme example is changing the layout of a web application from the "deprecated" table-based structure to a div-based structure, without affecting its visual aspect in any respect. In this case, the vast majority of the DOM-based locators (in particular the navigational ones, eg, XPath) used by DOM-based tools may be broken. On the contrary, this change is almost insignificant for visual test tools. A similar problem occurs when autogenerated ID locators (eg, *id1, id2, id3, ... , idN*) are used in DOM-based locators. In fact, these tend to change across different releases, while leaving completely unaffected the visual appearance of the web page (hence, no maintenance is required on the visual test suites). For example, the addition of a new link in a web page might result in a change of all IDs of the elements following the new link. Such "changes behind the scene" occurred in our empirical study and explain why, in the case of Collabtive, the Sikuli test suite has required by far a lower maintenance effort. In detail, across the two considered releases, a minor change has been applied to almost all the HTML pages of Collabtive: an unused div tag has been removed. This little change impacted quite strongly several of the XPath locators (XPath locators were used because IDs were not present) in the WebDriver test suite. The majority of the 36 locators (all of them are XPaths) was broken and had to be repaired (an example of repair is from .../div[2]/... to .../div[1]/...). No change was necessary on the Sikuli visual test suite for this structural change. Overall, in Sikuli, we had only few locators broken. For this reason, there is a large difference in the maintenance effort between the two test suites. A similar change across releases occurred also in MantisBT, although it had a lower impact in this application.

5.6.3 Execution Time

The execution time required when adopting the Visual approach was always higher than the time required when adopting the DOM-based approach. This is expected, since executing an image recognition algorithm requires more computational resources (and thus, generally, more time) than navigating the DOM. However, surprisingly, the difference in percentage between the two approaches is not high, being only 30–48%. It is not so much, considering that: (1) Sikuli is a quite experimental tool, (2) it is not focused on web application testing and, (3) manual management of the page loading delay (achieved through *sleep* commands) is not optimal. The reason for such a delay is that a browser needs time to open a web page. Thus, before starting to perform any action on the page the test automation tool has to wait. Selenium WebDriver provides specific commands to deal with this problem (ie, waiting for the web page loading). In Sikuli API this is not available and testers have to insert an explicit delay (eg, `Thread.sleep(200)`). However, according to our estimates, the overhead due to the web page loading delay is not a major penalty for Sikuli API (only 20–40 s per test suite) as compared to the total processing time. Indeed, we carefully tuned the delays in order to find the smallest required.

Summary: DOM-based test suites require less time to complete their execution w.r.t. visual test suites. However the difference is not so high.

5.6.4 Repeated Web Elements

When in a web page there are multiple instances of the same kind of web element (eg, an input box), creating a visual locator requires more time than creating a DOM-based locator. Let us consider a common situation, consisting of a form with multiple, repeated input fields to fill (eg, multiple lines, each with *Name, Surname*), all of which have the same size, thus appearing identical. In such cases, it is not possible to create a visual locator using only an image of the web element of interest (eg, the repeated *Name* input field), but we have to: (i) include also some context around it (eg, a label) in order to create an unambiguous locator, (ie, an image that matches only one specific portion of the web page), as in the example in Fig. 16, or, when this is not easily feasible, (ii) locate directly a unique web element close to the input field of interest and then move the mouse of a certain amount of pixels, in order to reach the input field. Both solutions locate the target web element by means of another, easier to locate, element (eg, a label). This is not straightforward and natural for the test developer (ie, it requires more effort and time). Actually, both solutions are not quite convenient. Solution (i) requires to create large image locators, including more than one web element (eg, the label and the corresponding input field). On the other hand, even if it allows to create a small locator image for only one web element (eg, the label), Solution (ii) requires to calculate a

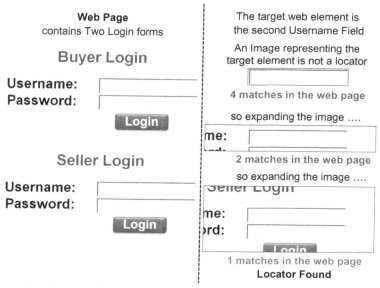

Figure 16 Visual locator creation for repeated web element.

distance in pixels (similarly to first generation tools), which is not so simple to determine. Both solutions have problems in case of variations of the relative positions of the elements in the next releases of the application. Thus, this factor has a negative effect on both the development and maintenance of the visual test suites.

Summary: Creating Visual locators could be difficult when a web page contains multiple instances of the same kind of web element (eg, a list of input boxes in a form).

5.6.5 Invisible Elements

Selenium WebDriver locates the web page elements by using the DOM so it does not care of what is actually displayed by the browser GUI. On the contrary, Sikuli can locate only elements that are visible in the browser GUI. Let us consider a long form to be filled. Using Sikuli, it is necessary to scroll the form in order to make the needed page portion visible. This requires to add some LOCs to the Sikuli test suites. Thus, this factor could have a negative impact on the development (to insert the right scroll) and maintenance (eg, if the element changes positions and the previously inserted scroll leaves it invisible) of the Sikuli test suites. In our case study, all the test suites have at least a test case using mouse scroll. For instance, in Claroline, during the creation of a new course it is necessary to scroll the page to reach some of the web elements in the form. The same happens in MRBS when filling the room reservation form.

Summary: DOM-based test suites can interact with all the DOM-elements regardless of whether they are displayed on the screen or not.

5.6.6 Web Page Loading

Usually, when moving from one web page to another (eg, after having submitted a form or clicked on a link), a little amount of time is required for loading the new web page. If the test case goes ahead without taking into account this, it may not find the next target web element and thus it may return an error. Selenium WebDriver provides specific commands to deal with this problem,[9] ie, explicit and implicit *waits*. In our test suites we used implicit waits, allowing WebDriver to poll the DOM for a certain amount of time (eg, up to 5 s) when trying to find a web element if it is not immediately available. In Sikuli this is not available and testers have to insert an explicit delay (eg, `Thread.sleep(1000)`). This factor could have a negative impact on the development (when the right waiting times have to be inserted) and maintenance (eg, in case the required waiting times change) of the Sikuli test suites.

Summary: Choosing a tool that provides specific commands for managing web page loading is useful for creating test cases easily. If equipped with such commands, test cases are also more robust and faster to execute.

5.6.7 Test Case Comprehensibility

The locators used by the two approaches have often a different degree of comprehensibility. For instance, by comparing a visual and a DOM-based locator (eg, an XPath or CSS expression), it is clear that the visual locator is much easier to understand than the corresponding DOM-based locator (see the examples in Fig. 17). In fact, the visual approach works in a manner

---

[9] http://docs.seleniumhq.org/docs/04_webdriver_advanced.jsp

Examples of Visual Locators

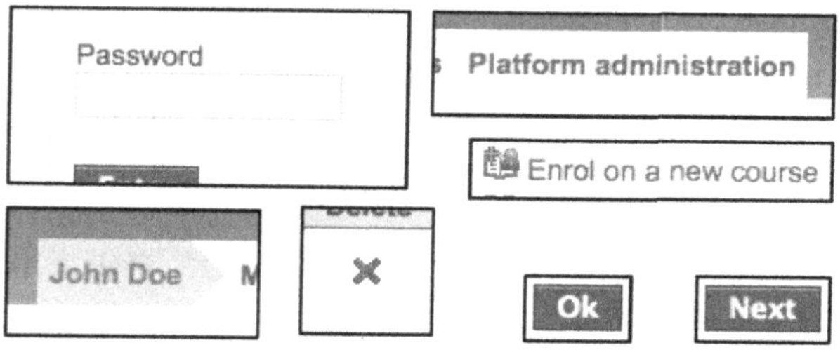

Examples of DOM-based Locators

```
//input[2]
linkText = Platform administration
//td[contains(text(),'John Doe')]
//img[@src="/web/img/edit.png?1232379976"]
//*[@id='body']/table[2]/tbody/tr/td[4]/a/img[4]
```

Figure 17 Examples of visual and DOM-based locators.

that is closer to humans than the DOM-based approach. In our case study, we experienced this several times. For instance, during test suite maintenance, understanding why a locator is broken is generally easier and faster with Sikuli than with WebDriver.

> **Summary:** For the tester, Visual locators are usually simpler to match with the actual web page elements than DOM-based locators.

5.6.8 Test Suites Portability vs Rendering Validation

When a Visual test suite is executed on a different machine, where the screen resolution or the font properties are different, it may happen that test cases do not work properly. We experienced this problem 2 times while executing the Sikuli API test suites on two different computers: in one case because the default font size was different, resulting in broken image locators, and in another case because the screen resolution was lower than expected, thus more mouse scroll operations were required. On the other hand, Visual test suites that behave differently in different platforms may point to web page rendering issues, as for instance the existence of web elements that become unreachable if the screen resolution is too low. So, the two approaches have complementary strengths.

Summary: The DOM-based and the Visual approaches have different strengths: the former creates portable test suites, while the latter can test the correct rendering of web pages across platforms.

6. OVERCOMING THE LIMITATIONS OF THE EXISTING APPROACHES

In the previous sections we provided an overview of the existing, consolidated approaches to automated end-to-end web testing and some examples of tools implementing them. In this section we discuss recent research works and existing commercial tools that try to overcome their main limitations.

6.1 Hybrid Web Testing

In the last few years, researchers and companies have proposed hybrid solutions employing more approaches at the same time that therefore do not fit our classification. In the following we provide three examples of them.

6.1.1 Contextual Clues

Yandrapally *et al.* [9] proposed a capture-replay approach and a corresponding tool called ATA-QV that locates the web elements of interest without relying solely on the underlying DOM or on image recognition. The idea is identifying a web element by means of so-called contextual clues, ie, labels or images in the proximity of the target web element that together uniquely identify it on the web page. In this way ATA-QV generates scripts that are relatively platform and tool agnostic, therefore, highly portable and resilient to changes in internal properties or visual renderings. Specifically, the approach first tries to create a locator by using a combination of labels (ie, strings) that can be found in the page (ie, in the DOM) and checks whether they are able to define a unique sub tree of the DOM containing the target web element.

Let us consider a web page reporting a smartphone catalogue. The target web element, eg, the "View Details" link, could be located using the following locator: "View Details" near "IPhone 6". If in this way it is not possible to find a locator for the web element of interest, the approach tries to compute three other types of locators: negation, proximity-based, and ordinal-based locators. Negation locators add negation predicates in order to obtain expressions able to uniquely identify the web element. Let us assume that we have two identical portions of the catalogue page describing IPhone 6 and IPhone 6 Plus, and that the word "Plus" is reported in a nested tag (eg, under the smartphone name). We want to see the details of the standard IPhone 6 (ie, the test case should click on its "View Details" link). In such case an example of negation locator is "View Details" NOT near "Plus" near "IPhone 6".

Proximity-based locators are based on labels that are visually close to the target web element in the left, bottom, right, and top directions (eg, CheckBox under "IPhone 6"). Finally, if the technique does not find any proximity-based locators, it attempts to generate ordinal-based ones that are more expressive and include both directional and positional clues (eg, second CheckBox under "IPhone 6"). Finally, if all previous techniques fail to find a locator, ATA-QV resorts to an XPath expression.

The advantages of this approach are twofold: (1) locators based on contextual clues proved to be robust [9], and (2) test cases are very simple to read even for a nonexpert, see for instance the example in Fig. 18, showing an ATA-QV test case for our running example.

6.1.2 Ranorex

RANOREX is a GUI test automation framework for testing desktop, web-based and mobile applications. Concerning automated end-to-end web testing, RANOREX is able to record the steps performed by the tester on the web application and to create an executable test case from them. The creation of the assertions is aided and the tester can choose among a set of possible proposals. Thus RANOREX behaves as a C&R tool, but, on the other hand, it provides also some functionalities typical of programmable tool, such as: (1) Code Modularization: once the test cases have been recorded, it is possible to group sequences of steps in order to create reusable procedures (as done with the PO pattern); (2) Data Driven: it is possible to reexecute the same test case using different values stored in internal (simple data tables) or external (Excel or CSV files, SQL Databases) data sets; (3) Module Development: it is possible to develop test code modules using for instance the C# and VB.NET languages and then to integrate them with the recorded test cases.

---

1. Enter "John.Doe" in the text box to the *right* of "Username"
2. Enter "123456" in the text box to the *right* of "Password"
3. Click on "Login"
4. Verify that "John.Doe" exists

Figure 18 TestLogin test case in ATA-QV.

Concerning the localization methods, the tool supports both the DOM-based and the Visual approaches. Indeed, RANOREX employs the RanoreXPath language, an expression language similar to XPath, providing a search mechanism for finding single or multiple web elements within a web page. At the same time, it provides also the capability of defining visual locators both for localizing web elements to interact with and for defining assertions.

6.1.3 JAutomate

JAUTOMATE is a commercial tool able to create test scripts similarly to how they can be produced using Selenium IDE. Indeed, the tester clicks the record button, performs the test case steps and finally completes the test script by inserting assertions. Test script recording is fully automatic, since the tool is able to (1) detect the actions executed on the user interface (eg, click on a button, write in an input form or scroll the web page using the mouse) and (2) generate the locators. JAUTOMATE is based on the visual localization of the target web elements but it is also able to provide functionalities that go beyond the typical visual approach [10], like verifying that a text is displayed in a web page by means of: (a) runtime generation of a visual locator representing such text, and (b) an OCR (Optical Character Recognition) algorithm, both of which are very useful for creating data-driven test cases. In case of several identical images on the screen, it is possible to specify which has to be selected by using an index position, similarly to how this is done in an XPath expression (eg, //input[3]). Moreover, JAUTOMATE employs two complementary image recognition algorithms [11], which, once combined, can identify images with inverted colors or images with transparent backgrounds. JAUTOMATE tries to overcome some limitations typical of existing C&R tools by integrating/combining features of the programmable approach [10], for instance, by providing constructs to (1) implement loops, (2) create parametric test cases (eg, by loading data values from CSV files) and (3) call/include other test scripts. Moreover, it provides an API for developing test scripts directly in Java. A JAUTOMATE test case that has a behavior close to the ones shown in the previous sections is shown in Fig. 19.

6.2 Reducing the Development and Maintenance Effort

In the last years, several researchers investigated the following problems associated with automated end-to-end testing of web application: (1) improving the robustness of the locators used in the test cases, (2) automating test cases

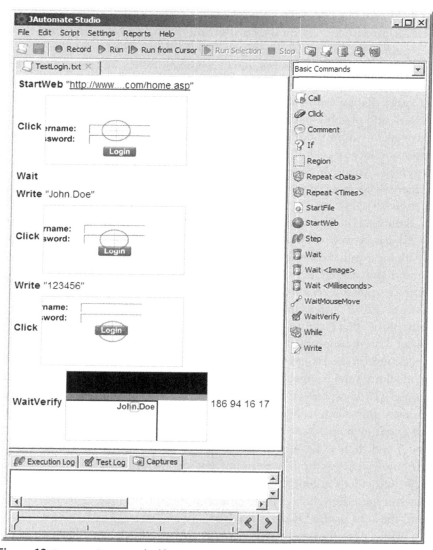

Figure 19 TestLogin test case in JAUTOMATE.

repair during software evolution, (3) automating the generation of page objects, and (4) automating the migration across different approaches. The provided solutions, strongly based on static, dynamic and code transformations [12, 13], can be very useful for reducing the test case development and maintenance effort.

6.2.1 Improving Locators Robustness

Test scripts heavily rely on locators for interacting with the elements on a web page—for instance to identify and fill the input portions of a web page (eg, the form fields), to execute some computations (eg, by locating and clicking on buttons), and to verify the correctness of the output (by locating the web page elements showing the results). Locators need to be checked for correctness and possibly updated at every new release of the software. Sometimes even a slight modification of the application under test has a massive impact on locators. This problem makes the maintenance of web test suites extremely expensive. Several approaches and techniques have been proposed to increase locators robustness such for example, Contextual Clues [9] (see Section 6.1), ROBULA [14, 15], Montoto *et al.* [16], and MULTILOCATOR [17].

ROBULA [14, 15] is an algorithm able to automatically generate robust DOM-based web element locators. The algorithm starts with a generic XPath locator that returns all nodes ("//*"). It then iteratively refines the locator until only the element of interest is selected. In such iterative refinement, ROBULA applies a set of refinement transformations, according to a set of heuristic XPath specialization steps. The empirical evaluation of the algorithm shows that ROBULA generates consistently locators that are much more robust than those produced by existing state of the art tools and algorithms.

Montoto *et al.* [16] proposed an algorithm for identifying the target elements during the navigation of AJAX websites. The algorithm starts from a simple XPath expression that is progressively augmented with textual and attribute information. More precisely, the algorithm first tries to identify the target element according to its associated text (if the element is a leaf node) and then it conjuncts, one after the other, predicates based on the attribute values (without prescribing any specific order of insertion). If this is not sufficient for generating a unique locator for the target element, each ancestor (and the values of its attributes) is subjected to the same procedure, until the root of the DOM is reached.

While algorithms exist that produce robust DOM-based locators to be used in web test scripts, no algorithm is perfect and different algorithms are exposed to different fragilities when the software evolves. Based on such observation, a new type of locator has been proposed, named MULTI-LOCATOR [17], which selects the best locator among a candidate set of locators produced by different algorithms. Such selection is based on a voting procedure that assigns different voting weights to different locator generation algorithms. Experimental results show that the multi-locator is more robust than each single locator (about −30% of broken locators w.r.t. the most robust single locator) and that the execution overhead required by the multiple queries done with different locators is negligible.

6.2.2 Automatic Test Case Repair

Other approaches focus on how to reduce the effort related to the repair of broken test cases. The general problem of repairing broken test cases has been addressed by several researchers (eg, TESTCAREASSISTANT [18] and REASSERT [19]), but only a few techniques are focussed on repairing automated end-to-end web test cases:

WATER [20] is a tool that suggests changes that can be applied to repair test scripts for web applications. This technique is based on differential testing: by comparing the behavior of a test case on two successive versions of the web application and analyzing the difference between the two executions, WATER suggests repairs that can be applied to update the scripts.

Test cases make use of input data while exercising the web application under test. One factor limiting the usage of web application test automation techniques is the cost of finding appropriate input values. To mitigate this problem, Elbaum *et al.* [21] proposed a family of techniques based on user-session data. User session data are collected in previous releases and then reused as input data in the current release. However, user session data also suffer the evolution problem: session data may become invalid due to changes in the application. Techniques repairing the input data have been proposed to alleviate this problem. For instance Harman and Alshahwan [22] investigated an algorithm based on the concept of "session repair." In particular, when a session becomes invalid due to changes in the web application, the algorithm attempts to repair it by constructing a new session that closely resembles the original.

6.2.3 Automatic Page Objects Generation

As we have seen, the adoption of the page object pattern improves the test suite maintainability by reducing the duplication of code across test cases. The implementation of page objects is usually done manually. Some open source frameworks have been proposed to assist the tester during the creation of page objects. These tools mostly wrap the HTML content of the page and offer an aided creation of the source code. The most important ones are: OHMAP,[10] *SWD Page Recorder,*[11] *WTF PageObject Utility Chrome*

---

[10] http://ohmap.virtuetech.de/

[11] https://github.com/dzharii/swd-recorder

Extension.[12] Despite these tools provide useful features, most of the effort is still put on testers. Moreover, they suffer several limitations [23], in particular: *(i)* only one page at a time is taken into account, without considering any notion of dynamism or web application structure, *(ii)* only a subset of web elements that can be used in a test is taken into account, *(iii)* the generated code consists of a basic class skeleton, while the key characteristics of the page objects (ie, exposing the web application functionalities through methods) are lacking. Especially this last important feature is *completely missing* in all these tools. Recently, a step ahead has been made with the proposal of APOGEN.

APOGEN [23] is a tool for the automatic generation of page objects for web applications. The tool automatically derives a testing model by reverse engineering the target web application and uses a combination of dynamic and static analysis to generate Java page objects for the Selenium WebDriver framework. APOGEN consists of three main modules: a Crawler, a Static Analyzer, and a Code Generator. The input of APOGEN is any web application, together with the login credentials if necessary, while the output is a set of Java files, representing a code abstraction of the web application, organized using the Page Object and Page Factory design patterns, as supported by the Selenium WebDriver framework. A preliminary study comparing the generated page objects with the ones created manually by a human tester shows promising results.

6.2.4 Automatic Migration between Approaches

An important point of concern is how to automate the migration of an existing test suite to different approaches. Migrating from the C&R to the programmable approach is relatively a simple task and is already supported by some tools. For instance, Selenium IDE allows to migrate the test cases recorded in Selenese to Selenium WebDriver test cases implemented in Java. In this way, the tester can then refactor the Java code in order to take full advantage of the programmable approach. On the other hand, it is much more complex migrating the test cases to different localization approaches (eg, to the visual approach). A proposal in this direction is PESTO.

PESTO [24] is a tool proposed for automating the migration of a DOM-based web test suite, created using Selenium WebDriver and adopting the page object (PO) pattern, into a visual web test suite based on the Sikuli image recognition capabilities, while still adopting the PO pattern. Even

---

[12] https://github.com/wiredrive/wtframework/wiki/WTF-PageObject-Utility-Chrome-Extension

if PESTO has been developed to transform Selenium WebDriver test suites to Sikuli API, the techniques and architectural solutions adopted for its implementation are quite general and can be easily used within any web test transformation activity involving abstractions similar to the ones provided by the PO. PESTO determines automatically the screen position of a web element located in the DOM by a DOM-based test case. It then determines a rectangle image centered around the web element so as to ensure unique visual matching. Based on such automatically extracted images, the original test suite is rewritten into a visual test suite. Experimental results [24] show that this approach is accurate, hence potentially saving substantial human effort in the creation of visual web tests from DOM-based ones.

7. CONCLUSIONS

In this chapter we have provided an overview of the most relevant approaches and tools to automated end-to-end web testing. First, for each approach we have given a detailed description based on existing implementations; second, we have deeply analyzed their strengths and weaknesses by discussing the results of a series of empirical studies. Third, we have described some recent techniques and tools that try to overcome the limitations of the existing approaches by combining them into hybrid methods. Finally, we have analyzed a set of techniques that have been proposed in the literature in order to solve specific problems in the context of the automated end-to-end web testing.

Concerning the methods used for developing and maintaining web test cases, we found that programmable tests involve higher development effort (between 32% and 112%) but lower maintenance effort (with a saving between 16% and 51%) than C&R tests. We have estimated that, on average, after two major releases, programmable test cases become more convenient than C&R ones. However, the actual benefits depend on specific features of the web application, including its degree of modularity, which maps to reusable page objects that need to be evolved only once, when programmable test cases are used. Moreover, there are useful features of programmable test cases, such as the possibility to define parametric and repeated test scenarios, which might further amplify their advantages.

Concerning the approach used for localizing the web elements to interact with, we found that DOM-based locators are generally more robust than visual locators, and that DOM-based test cases can be developed from scratch at lower cost. Most of the times they are also evolved at lower cost.

However, on specific web applications visual locators were easier to repair, because the visual appearance of such applications remained stable across releases, while their structure changed a lot. DOM-based test cases required a lower execution time than visual test cases, due to the computational demands of image recognition algorithms used by the visual approach, although the difference is not dramatic. Overall, the choice between DOM-based and visual locators is application-specific and depends quite strongly on the expected structural and visual evolution of the application. Other factors may also affect the testers' decision, such as the availability/ unavailability of visual locators for web elements that are important during testing and the presence of advanced, RIA functionalities which cannot be easily tested using DOM-based locators. Moreover, visual test cases are definitely easier to understand, which, depending on the skills of the involved testers, might also play a role in the decision.

REFERENCES

[1] F. Ricca, P. Tonella, Detecting anomaly and failure in web applications, IEEE Multimed. 13 (2) (2006) 44–51, ISSN 1070-986X, http://dx.doi.org/10.1109/MMUL.2006.26.

[2] F. Ricca, P. Tonella, Analysis and testing of web applications, in: Proceedings of the 23rd International Conference on Software Engineering, ICSE 2001, IEEE, 2001, pp. 25–34.

[3] M. Leotta, D. Clerissi, F. Ricca, P. Tonella, Visual vs. DOM-based web locators: an empirical study. in: Proceedings of the 14th International Conference on Web Engineering (ICWE 2014), LNCS, Toulouse, France, vol. 8541, Springer, 2014, pp. 322–340, http://dx.doi.org/10.1007/978-3-319-08245-5_19.

[4] M. Leotta, D. Clerissi, F. Ricca, P. Tonella, Capture-replay vs. programmable web testing: an empirical assessment during test case evolution, in: Proceedings of the 20th Working Conference on Reverse Engineering, WCRE 2013, Koblenz, Germany, IEEE, 2013, pp. 272–281, http://dx.doi.org/10.1109/WCRE.2013.6671302.

[5] M. Leotta, D. Clerissi, F. Ricca, C. Spadaro, Improving test suites maintainability with the Page Object pattern: an industrial case study, in: Proceedings of the 6th IEEE International Conference on Software Testing, Verification and Validation Workshops, ICSTW 2013, IEEE, 2013, pp. 108–113, http://dx.doi.org/10.1109/ICSTW.2013.19.

[6] M. Leotta, D. Clerissi, F. Ricca, C. Spadaro, Comparing the maintainability of Selenium WebDriver test suites employing different locators: a case study. in: Proceedings of the 1st International Workshop on Joining AcadeMiA and Industry Contributions to testing Automation, JAMAICA 2013, ACM, 2013, pp. 53–58, http://dx.doi.org/10.1145/ 2489280.2489284.

[7] A. van Deursen, Beyond page objects: testing web applications with state objects, ACM Queue 13 (6) (2015) 20:20–20:37, ISSN 1542-7730, http://dx.doi.org/ 10.1145/2791301.2793039.

[8] M. Mirzaaghaei, Automatic test suite evolution, in: Proceedings of the 19th ACM SIGSOFT Symposium and the 13th European conference on Foundations of Software Engineering, ESEC/FSE 2011, Szeged, Hungary, ACM, ISBN 978-1-4503-0443-6, 2011, pp. 396–399.

[9] R. Yandrapally, S. Thummalapenta, S. Sinha, S. Chandra, Robust test automation using contextual clues, in: Proceedings of the 2014 International Symposium on Software

Testing and Analysis, ISSTA 2014, San Jose, CA, USA, ACM, ISBN 978-1-4503-2645-2, 2014, pp. 304–314, http://dx.doi.org/10.1145/2610384.2610390.

[10] Swifting AB, JAutomate Manual, 2014.

[11] E. Alegroth, M. Nass, H.H. Olsson, JAutomate: a tool for system- and acceptance-test automation, in: Proceedings of the 6th IEEE International Conference on Software Testing, Verification and Validation, ICST 2013, IEEE, ISBN 978-0-7695-4968-2, 2013, pp. 439–446, http://dx.doi.org/10.1109/ICST.2013.61.

[12] P. Tonella, F. Ricca, A. Marchetto, Recent advances in web testing, Adv. Comput. 93 (2014) 1–51.

[13] F. Ricca, P. Tonella, I.D. Baxter, Web application transformations based on rewrite rules, Inf. Softw. Technol. 44 (13) (2002) 811–825, URL http://dblp.uni-trier.de/db/journals/infsof/infsof44.html#RiccaTB02.

[14] M. Leotta, A. Stocco, F. Ricca, P. Tonella, Reducing web test cases aging by means of robust XPath locators. in: Proceedings of the 25th IEEE International Symposium on Software Reliability Engineering Workshops, ISSREW 2014, IEEE, 2014, pp. 449–454, http://dx.doi.org/10.1109/ISSREW.2014.17.

[15] M. Leotta, A. Stocco, F. Ricca, P. Tonella, ROBULA+: an algorithm for generating robust XPath locators for web testing, J. Softw. Evol. Process (under review)

[16] P. Montoto, A. Pan, J. Raposo, F. Bellas, J. Lopez, Automated browsing in AJAX websites, Data Knowl. Eng. 70 (3) (2011) 269–283, ISSN 0169-023X, http://dx.doi.org/10.1016/j.datak.2010.12.001, URL http://www.sciencedirect.com/science/article/pii/S0169023X10001503.

[17] M. Leotta, A. Stocco, F. Ricca, P. Tonella, Using multi-locators to increase the robustness of web test cases, in: Proceedings of 8th IEEE International Conference on Software Testing, Verification and Validation, ICST 2015, IEEE, 2015, pp. 1–10, http://dx.doi.org/10.1109/ICST.2015.7102611.

[18] M. Mirzaaghaei, F. Pastore, M. Pezze', Automatic test case evolution, Softw. Test. Verif. Reliab. 24 (5) (2014) 386–411, ISSN 1099-1689, http://dx.doi.org/10.1002/stvr.1527.

[19] B. Daniel, D. Dig, T. Gvero, V. Jagannath, J. Jiaa, D. Mitchell, J. Nogiec, S.H. Tan, D. Marinov, ReAssert: a tool for repairing broken unit tests, in: Proceedings of the 33rd International Conference on Software Engineering, ICSE 2011, IEEE, ISSN 0270-5257, 2011, pp. 1010–1012, http://dx.doi.org/10.1145/1985793.1985978.

[20] S.R. Choudhary, D. Zhao, H. Versee, A. Orso, WATER: web application test repair, in: Proceedings of the 1st International Workshop on End-to-End Test Script Engineering, ETSE 2011, Toronto, Ontario, Canada, ACM, ISBN 978-1-4503-0808-3, 2011, pp. 24–29.

[21] S. Elbaum, G. Rothermel, S. Karre, M. Fisher II, Leveraging user-session data to support web application testing, IEEE Trans. Softw. Eng. 31 (3) (2005) 187–202, ISSN 0098-5589, http://dx.doi.org/10.1109/TSE.2005.36.

[22] M. Harman, N. Alshahwan, Automated session data repair for web application regression testing, in: Proceedings of the 1st International Conference on Software Testing, Verification, and Validation, ICST 2008, 2008, pp. 298–307, http://dx.doi.org/10.1109/ICST.2008.56.

[23] A. Stocco, M. Leotta, F. Ricca, P. Tonella, Why creating web page objects manually if it can be done automatically? in: Proceedings of 10th IEEE/ACM International Workshop on Automation of Software Test, AST 2015, Florence, Italy, IEEE, 2015, pp. 70–74, http://dx.doi.org/10.1109/AST.2015.26.

[24] M. Leotta, A. Stocco, F. Ricca, P. Tonella, Automated generation of visual web tests from DOM-based web tests, in: Proceedings of 30th ACM/SIGAPP Symposium on Applied Computing, SAC 2015, Salamanca, Spain, ACM, 2015, pp. 775–782, http://dx.doi.org/10.1145/2695664.2695847.

ABOUT THE AUTHORS

Maurizio Leotta is a research fellow at the University of Genova, Italy. He received his PhD degree in Computer Science from the same University, in 2015, with the thesis "Automated Web Testing: Analysis and Maintenance Effort Reduction." He is author or coauthor of more than 30 research papers published in international conferences and workshops. His current research interests are in Software Engineering, with a particular focus on the following themes: Web Application Testing, Functional Testing Automation, Business Process Modelling, Empirical Software Engineering, Model-Driven Software Engineering.

Diego Clerissi is a PhD student in Computer Science at the University of Genova, Italy. In 2015 he received his master degree from the same University, with the thesis: "Test Cases Generation for Web Applications from Requirements Specification: Preliminary Results." At the time of writing he is coauthor of 10 research papers published in international conferences and workshops. His research interests are in Software Engineering, Model-Based Testing, Software Testing, Web Applications, System Modeling.

Filippo Ricca is an associate professor at the University of Genova, Italy. He received his PhD degree in Computer Science from the same University, in 2003, with the thesis: "Analysis, Testing and Re-structuring of Web Applications." In 2011 he was awarded the ICSE 2001 MIP (Most Influential Paper) award, for his paper: "Analysis and Testing of Web Applications." He is author or coauthor of more than 100 research papers published in international journals and conferences/ workshops. He was Program Chair of CSMR/WCRE 2014, CSMR 2013, ICPC 2011, and WSE 2008. Among the others, he served in the program committees of the following conferences: ICSM, ICST, SCAM, CSMR, WCRE, and ESEM. From 1999 to 2006, he worked with the Software Engineering group at ITC-irst (now FBK-irst), Trento, Italy. During this time he was part of the team that worked on Reverse engineering, Re-engineering, and Software Testing. His current research interests include: Software modeling, Reverse engineering, Empirical studies in Software Engineering, Web applications, and Software Testing. The research is mainly conducted through empirical methods such as case studies, controlled experiments, and surveys.

Paolo Tonella is head of the Software Engineering Research Unit at Fondazione Bruno Kessler (FBK), in Trento, Italy. He received his PhD degree in Software Engineering from the University of Padova, in 1999, with the thesis: "Code Analysis in Support to Software Maintenance." In 2011 he was awarded the ICSE 2001 MIP (Most Influential Paper) award, for his paper: "Analysis and Testing of Web Applications." He is the author of "Reverse Engineering of Object Oriented Code," Springer, 2005. He participated in several industrial and EU projects on software analysis and testing. His current research interests include code analysis, web and object oriented testing, search-based test case generation.

AUTHOR INDEX

SUBJECT INDEX

Note: Page numbers followed by "*f*" indicate figures, and "*t*" indicate tables.

CONTENTS OF VOLUMES IN THIS SERIES

Volume 82

Volume 83

Volume 84

Volume 94

Volume 95

Volume 96

Volume 97

Printed in the United States
By Bookmasters